MORAL AND P
PHILOSO

**This book is to be returned on or before
the last date stamped below.**

MORAL AND POLITICAL PHILOSOPHY

KEY ISSUES, CONCEPTS AND THEORIES

Paul Smith

palgrave
macmillan

First published in 2008 by
PALGRAVE MACMILLAN
Houndmills, Basingstoke, Hampshire RG21 6XS and
175 Fifth Avenue, New York, N.Y. 10010
Companies and representatives throughout the world.

PALGRAVE MACMILLAN is the global academic imprint of the Palgrave Macmillan division of St. Martin's Press, LLC and of Palgrave Macmillan Ltd. Macmillan® is a registered trademark in the United States, United Kingdom and other countries. Palgrave is a registered trademark in the European Union and other countries.

ISBN-13: 978–0–230–55275–3 hardback
ISBN-10: 0–230–55275–7 hardback
ISBN-13: 978–0–230–55276–0 paperback
ISBN-10: 0–230–55276–5 paperback

This book is printed on paper suitable for recycling and made from fully managed and sustained forest sources. Logging, pulping and manufacturing processes are expected to conform to the environmental regulations of the country of origin.

A catalogue record for this book is available from the British Library.

A catalog record for this book is available from the Library of Congress.

10 9 8 7 6 5 4 3 2 1
17 16 15 14 13 12 11 10 09 08

Printed and bound in Great Britain by
CPI Antony Rowe, Chippenham and Eastbourne

CONTENTS

PREFACE

This book is written primarily for undergraduates in philosophy and cognate subjects, such as politics or law. It aims to be accessible, clear and concise. Consequently, it avoids technicalities, complications and details (some of which some people will think should not have been avoided). A book of this length must be highly selective in its topics and their discussion. I have selected some key concepts and theories that are central to moral and political philosophy and some controversial practical moral and political issues. These issues are selected to engage students and to develop their interest in the moral and political concepts and theories. The topic of each chapter has been the subject of whole books that offer comprehensive surveys. However, I have been highly selective, aiming to focus on the essentials of each topic.

The book starts with four chapters on practical moral and political issues that are important, perennially topical, controversial and provocative. As well as engaging with students' interests, these practical issues raise and illustrate general issues in moral and political theory. Arguments about the practical issues appeal to moral and political concepts and principles, particularly to liberty, liberty-limiting principles, rights, equality and social justice. These are explored in chapters 5–8. Discussion of practical moral and political issues and of the concepts and principles continually raises questions about general moral and political theories, which are discussed systematically in chapters 9–12. (The distinctions between issues, concepts and theories are not clear-cut but porous, as they permeate each other.)

The chapters are interconnected and are best read in sequence. However, each chapter is written so that it can be read independently and so they can be read in any order. This necessitates some repetition, but is intended to make the book useful to diverse courses. Each chapter is intended to be thought-provoking and each concludes with questions for discussion, inviting students to think critically about the issues raised and to continue the debate.

ACKNOWLEDGEMENTS

I am grateful to two anonymous readers for their very helpful comments, one on drafts of the first two chapters and one on the whole draft typescript.

Chapter 1 is based on 'Drugs, Morality, and the Law', *Journal of Applied Philosophy*, 19, 3 (2002). I am grateful to Blackwell Publishing for permission to use this material.

Chapter 2 is based on 'Justifications of Punishment', *Dialogue*, 25 (2005). I am grateful to Dr Jeremy Hall, the editor of *Dialogue*, for permission to use this material.

1

DRUG LAWS

In many countries, it is illegal to possess certain drugs, such as cannabis, ecstasy, amphetamine, LSD, cocaine or heroin. (In other countries, alcohol is illegal.) As a result, many drug users are punished. So it is important to know whether laws that prohibit the possession or supply of drugs are justified. Are they an unjust infringement of personal liberty, or is drug use immoral and rightly illegal? Do drug laws reduce or increase the harms associated with drugs? Should illegal drugs be legalized?[1] The justifiability of drug laws is a highly controversial practical issue. Philosophy can clarify the public debate by sorting out the different arguments, analysing them, thus disclosing their underlying principles, and critically assessing them.

Legalization of illegal drugs has been advocated by some philosophers on grounds of liberty rights,[2] by some economists who advocate free markets[3] and by some journalists on consequentialist grounds of harm-minimization.[4] Some senior police officers and judges have supported the idea.[5] However, governments generally refuse to entertain the idea.

This chapter surveys, sorts, analyses and assesses the various arguments that are deployed in debate over drug prohibition. It considers, first, arguments over whether or not adults have a moral right to the freedom to use dangerous drugs and, second, arguments over whether prohibition has, or legalization would have, the better consequences in terms of minimizing drug-related harm for all affected.

Arguments for a right to the freedom to use drugs[6]

In liberal societies, there is a general presumption that adults have a right to 'live as seems good to themselves',[7] provided that they do

1

not violate the rights of others, and, in particular, that they have a right to do what they choose to their own bodies and minds, including unhealthy and dangerous things, if they endanger only themselves. Adults are assumed to have a right to do risky things such as smoke tobacco or engage in dangerous sports (for example, mountaineering, boxing, motor sports, parachuting, skiing). If the law prohibited such activities, it would be widely seen as a violation of individual rights, an intolerable infringement of liberty. So it is claimed that the right to take dangerous drugs, for pleasure or escapism, is just another application of the right to do unhealthy or dangerous things to oneself. John Stuart Mill, for example, argued that the only justification for the law to coerce individuals is to prevent harm to others, not harm to oneself: 'over himself, over his own body and mind, the individual is sovereign'.[8]

The idea of a right to use dangerous drugs is prone to misunderstanding. It does not include a right to harm others (for example, by driving under the influence) or to offend others (for example, by being intoxicated in public). Advocacy of such a right does not mean advocacy of drug use: advocates may believe that use of dangerous drugs is unwise or immature, but hold that adults have a right to make unwise or immature choices. A moral right to use drugs does not imply that drug use is morally right. One can have the moral right to do something that is morally wrong (for example, waste one's time or money, never give to charity). It is not incoherent to say that adults have a moral right to use dangerous drugs, but that it is morally wrong for them to do so.

The argument for a right to the freedom to use drugs might be summarized thus:

1   Adults have a right to live as seems good to themselves, within the limits of others' rights.
2   Drug use does not infringe or violate others' rights.
3   Therefore, adults have a right to use drugs.[9]

One response to this argument is to question its first premise. Although in liberal societies there may be a widespread belief in the moral right to the liberty to live as seems good to oneself – of which drug use is a controversial application – what arguments are there for it? One argument is Mill's utilitarian claim that liberty maximizes happiness. Liberty enables individuality, which is a principal ingredient of human happiness, and humankind benefits from allowing each adult 'to live as seems good to themselves'.[10] Mill's two reasons for this liberty apply to drug use. Freedom allows individuals to satisfy their own wants (provided they are informed about the dangers) and it allows experimentation in ways of living from which everyone can learn.

Another argument for the liberty to live as seems good to oneself (within the limits of others' rights) is contractualist (see chapter 5, second section). Contractualism holds that the most reasonable moral principles are those that rational and reasonable people would agree to for mutual advantage. People reasonably and inevitably disagree over what is a good way to live. Despite that, reasonable people could agree on Mill's principle of liberty to live according to one's own judgement of what is good, and toleration of others' different judgements and different, harmless ways of living. It would be irrational to agree to compulsion to live according to others' judgements or to prohibition of living harmlessly according to one's own, and it would be unreasonable to expect others to do so. For example, no one could rationally agree to being compelled to live according to religious beliefs that are not their own or to their own religion being prohibited, but reasonable people with different religious beliefs could agree on principles of religious liberty and toleration. Similarly, no one could rationally agree to being compelled to live according to sexual preferences that are not their own or to prohibition of their consensual sexual preferences, but reasonable people with different sexual preferences can agree on a principle of sexual freedom and toleration among consenting adults.[11] Similarly, people disagree over whether use of a particular drug is good or bad. Being forced (by prohibition or compulsion) to live according to another's drug preferences is unacceptable, but reasonable people with different drug preferences could agree to a right to the freedom to use drugs. As with sexual preferences, it could be agreed that what consenting adults do in private is no business of the law.

Competing conceptions of the political implications of individual moral rights apply to the right to use dangerous drugs. The libertarian view that individual rights require free markets and a minimal state, applied to drugs, implies free markets in drugs with little or no legal regulation (perhaps laws on a minimum age and on driving under the influence) and no state-provided drugs education, health care or treatment. On this view, adults have the right to take dangerous drugs but, if they choose to do so, must accept the consequences; they have no right to public help. The liberal view, in contrast, that individual rights require government-regulated markets and a welfare state, applied to drugs, implies government-regulated drug markets, like those for alcohol and tobacco (regulating quality, strength, price, labelling and advertising) and state provision of education about drugs and of health care and treatment for drug users.

The great value that most people in liberal societies attach to their personal liberty perhaps implies the presumption of liberty such that the burden of proof falls on prohibitionists – it is prohibition, not liberty, that needs to be justified. So, let's turn to the arguments against a moral right to use drugs and thus for legal prohibition.

Arguments against a right to the freedom to use drugs

Many reasons are given against the idea of a right to use drugs. Joel Feinberg's analysis of liberty-limiting principles (the subject of chapter 6),[12] that is, principles claimed to justify laws that restrict individuals' liberty, enables the sorting, analysis, clarification and assessment of the arguments.

Drug use harms others (appeal to the harm principle)

Everyone (except some anarchists) accepts that it is legitimate for the criminal law to prohibit some serious harm to others. Drug use harms not only the user but, indirectly, others too. By harming their own health and personality, some drug users make themselves less good family members or parents than they might otherwise be, so they harm their families. Some make themselves less productive employees than they might otherwise be, so harm their employers and the economy. Some impose health care costs on, and so harm, society generally. So, in various ways, some drug users indirectly harm others and so the law should prohibit drug use.

The argument might be summarized thus:

1 The law should prohibit harming others (an unqualified harm principle).
2 By harming themselves, drug users indirectly harm others (family, economy, society).
3 Therefore, the law should prohibit drug use.

At first glance, appeal to the harm principle might seem a strong argument for prohibition. However, its major premise needs to be qualified. Not all harm to others is wrong (for example, justified punishment, fair competition), and not all wrongful harm is, or ought to be, criminalized (for example, adultery). As for making oneself less healthy, less productive or a less good parent than one might otherwise be, even if it could be established that these actions are morally wrong, they are not criminal. If the law should prohibit such indirect harm to others, that would include not only illegal drug use but also use of alcohol and tobacco and other unhealthy lifestyles and diets, as well as dangerous sports. People risk indirect harm to their family and others in these ways, but few think such indirect harm should be illegal. The harm principle must be qualified by individual liberty rights.

Violence is another kind of harm that is invoked to justify prohibition. It is claimed that illegal drug use causes violence. However, many illegal drugs (opiates, cannabis, ecstasy) reduce aggression. Cocaine *may* cause or increase aggression, but the drug most strongly linked to violence is alcohol. So, if a link to violence is a reason for prohibition, alcohol should be prohibited. However, even most drug prohibitionists think it right that adults should be free to use alcohol and that only aggression, under its influence or otherwise, should be illegal.

Drug use harms oneself (appeal to
legal paternalism)

The most common justification of prohibition refers to the harm
that drug users do to themselves and thus appeals to legal paternalism. The argument may be stated thus:

1   The law should prohibit voluntarily causing or risking
    self-harm (legal paternalism).
2   Drug use risks self-harm.
3   Therefore, the law should prohibit drug use.

The main reply to this argument is that paternalism is objectionable. While children may be unable to be the best judge of
their own interests and so may justifiably be protected from their
own unwise choices, when the state prohibits adults from voluntarily risking harm to themselves it treats them as children. Anti-
paternalists insist that adults have the right to live according to
their own values, judgements and choices, including those that
risk harm to themselves (through dangerous sports, unhealthy
lifestyles or dangerous drugs). The dangers of a drug are a good
reason for providing information, not for prohibition. Indeed,
prohibition reduces the availability of reliable information for
drug users, because illegal suppliers provide none while licensed
sellers could be required to do so.

A second objection, to the second premise, is that although
illegal drug use is harmful, some illegal drug use is less harmful than legal drug use. Medical and other experts judge alcohol
and tobacco to be more harmful than cannabis, LSD and ecstasy
(despite the researchers' perversely counting intensity of pleasure as a harm).[13] The paternalist should consider the comparative
harms of prohibited and legal drugs (see Table 1.1).

Table 1.1   Number of drug-related deaths
per annum in the UK[14]

All illegal drugs	1,388
Alcohol	6,000
Tobacco	100,000

For the USA, Douglas Husak notes that annually 25,000 deaths are attributed to all illegal drugs (many of which are due to their illegality rather than to the drug), whereas at least 100,000 are attributed to alcohol and 430,000 to tobacco.[15] Certainly, the number of deaths from illegal drugs constitutes a great deal of harm to those individuals and their families, but, on these figures, legal drugs account for almost 99 per cent of UK drug-related deaths and over 95 per cent in the USA. However, the fact that legal drugs are more widely used must be taken into account (see Table 1.2).

Table 1.2 suggests that some legal drugs are more dangerous than some illegal drugs. This needs to be qualified by the fact that illegal drugs often kill young people while tobacco takes many years to kill many of its users (although a slow and painful death from the effects of tobacco is a greater self-harm in that respect than a sudden death from a heroin overdose).

Risk of death is not the only self-harm of drug use. The risk of addiction must also be considered. The proportion of cocaine, heroin or alcohol users in the USA who are addicted is approximately 10 per cent, while for nicotine it is approximately 90 per cent.[17]

The principle of legal paternalism, if applied consistently, would criminalize tobacco use. If those who advocate drug prohibition on paternalist grounds find this implication oppressive, this should cause them to question their paternalism and its application to those who choose other dangerous drugs.

Peter de Marneffe offers a paternalistic defence of prohibition that, unusually, acknowledges the relative harms of legal and illegal drugs. He argues that drug prohibition is justifiable only because people, especially young people, need protection from the consequences of potentially imprudent decisions, which may limit their future opportunities. This argument is paternalistic

Table 1.2 Drug deaths per annum per 10,000 weekly users in the USA[16]

Cannabis	0
Alcohol	21
Cocaine	29
Tobacco	83

because it 'limits the liberty of individuals for their own good'. He accepts that most illegal drug use is defensible enjoyment and hence that drug prohibition sacrifices the liberty of many to benefit the imprudent few.[18]

An objection to this view is that it is illiberal to prohibit imprudence. Imprudent drug use can damage future opportunities, but so can imprudent alcohol use, gambling, sex, dangerous sports and religious or political fervour. To think that imprudence justifies legal prohibition undervalues individual freedom and autonomy. De Marneffe says that alcohol is more harmful than any illegal drug and accepts that his case for heroin prohibition makes alcohol prohibition justifiable in principle, but he thinks it is not justified in practice mainly because, unlike heroin, the alcohol industry is legal and alcohol is socially accepted.[19] This is to argue that heroin but not alcohol *ought* to be prohibited because heroin but not alcohol *is* prohibited. Even if paternalistic prohibition of imprudence were acceptable, a second objection to de Marneffe's view is that it is unjust to criminalize and punish prudent drug users because *others* might be imprudent. Imprudence ought not to be illegal but, if it is, those innocent of it ought not to be punished for others' imprudence.

Drug use is immoral even if harmless
(appeal to legal moralism)

It might be claimed that drug use is immoral irrespective of any harmful effects and this justifies its prohibition. This argument can be stated thus:

1   The law should prohibit harmless immorality (legal moralism).
2   Drug use, even if harmless, is immoral.
3   Therefore, the law should prohibit drug use.

An objection to legal moralism is that 'harmless immorality' is an oxymoron: If no one is harmed, then no one is wronged, so harmlessness is sufficient for moral permissibility. However, this reply may be too quick because it can be argued that there can be harmless immorality (see chapter 6, fourth section). The next three kinds of argument against the permissibility of drug use do not appeal to harm (to self or others).

Argument from Kantian duties to oneself

Kant argued that how one treats oneself is a moral question. Rational beings have a capacity to govern themselves which, according to Kant, they have a duty to respect in themselves as well as in others. Corresponding to that duty is a moral right to self-government, which might imply a right to use drugs. However, some drug use, especially addiction, reduces one's rationality and autonomy, one's capacity to govern one's life rationally, thus disrespects one's rational capacity and violates a duty to oneself. This argument might be summarized thus:

1 One has a duty to respect one's own rationality and autonomy.
2 Some drug use undermines one's rationality and autonomy.
3 Therefore, some drug use is morally wrong.

It may be objected that this argument does not support the legal prohibition of drugs. First, the idea of duties to oneself may be questioned. Second, the argument applies to legal as well as illegal drugs. Rationality may be hard to define, but we know it dissolves in alcohol. And tobacco, being so addictive, undermines autonomy in the sense that many addicts say they want to give up but cannot. So, this argument does not justify the differentiation between the legal and the illegal drugs. Third, despite Kant, one can, without self-contradiction, rationally and autonomously choose to do something that reduces or even ends one's rationality and autonomy. Kant himself concedes that medicinal use of opium and moderate use of alcohol are permissible[20] and he observes that, in extreme circumstances, our reason and autonomy entail a duty to choose death rather than serious wrongdoing (see chapter 11, penultimate section, text to note 20).[21] Fourth, even if the virtue of autonomy supports the immorality of (especially addictive) drug use, it opposes its illegality. To legally prohibit disrespect for one's own capacity for rational self-government would thwart that very capacity. So, a Kantian view might be that immoderate or addictive use of drugs, including alcohol, is immoral but should not be illegal.[22]

Arguing from the Kantian duty to respect one's rational capacity, Samuel Freeman denies that liberalism excludes *all* prohibition of voluntary, self-destructive conduct. It permits restrictions against conduct that permanently destroys one's capacities for rational agency and moral responsibility. Any activity that destroys those capacities is, he argues, impermissible. Existing drugs may not do this, but any that did would be justifiably prohibitable. He thus clarifies the *limits* of a right to use drugs.[23] However, since existing drugs do not permanently destroy those capacities, this argument does not justify existing drug laws, and could possibly justify prohibition not of any potentially destructive substance (for example, alcohol) but only of self-destructive *use* of it.

Argument from an ideal of human excellence (appeal to legal perfectionism)

Another kind of argument for drug prohibition appeals to an ideal of human excellence and the idea that government should improve the character of its subjects. This kind of argument might be stated thus:

1   The law should promote virtue and prohibit vice (legal perfectionism).
2   Drug use is stupefying, dehumanizing, degrading, a vice, a character defect, not part of a good way of life.
3   Therefore, the law should prohibit drug use.

The first objection to legal perfectionism is the observation that there is reasonable disagreement about ideals of human excellence and of the good life. Liberals infer from this that the state should not enforce any such ideal, which would be oppressive, but allow individuals to pursue 'our own good in our own way'.[24] For many people, drug use is part of their conception of a good life. A second objection is that, even if there were agreement that drug use is not part of a good way of life, that it is a vice, this would be an argument for its immorality but not for its illegality. This is because the criminal law enforces minimum standards of behaviour, not ideal or virtuous behaviour.[25]

Argument from the community's traditional way of life and/or the majority's values (traditional conservatism, communitarianism)

Traditional conservatism and communitarianism hold, respectively, that government has a duty to maintain the community's traditional way of life and to enforce the community's prevailing values. Although these are two distinct claims, the arguments and the replies run parallel so can be put together, thus:

1   The state should maintain the community's traditional way of life and/or enforce the majority's values.
2   Drug use deviates from the traditional way of life and/or from the majority's values.
3   Therefore, the state should prohibit drug use.

Either of the principles appealed to here is question-begging, because neither being traditional nor conforming to the majority's values makes something (for example, the impermissibility and non-use of the illegal drugs) right. Their practical implication, the legal enforcement of a way of life on individuals who reject it, is oppressive (because it does not allow individuals to live according to their own values), futile (because belief is unenforceable) and self-condemnatory (because if a tradition is valuable, it needs no coercion to gain adherents).

An interim conclusion might be that none of the arguments from liberty-limiting principles justifies legal prohibition of adult drug use.

*   *   *

A second kind of debate about our drug laws, and, despite widespread belief in personal freedom, the one that prevails in politics and the media, is concerned not with the liberty rights of the individual but with the welfare of society as a whole. The focus of controversy thus shifts from moral principles to factual claims – to the question of which policy – prohibition or legalization – will have the better consequences. Both sides to this debate thus implicitly presuppose the utilitarian principle that policy ought to maximize benefits and minimize harms to all affected. Given this principle, which policy – prohibition or legalization – is more likely to minimize drug-related harm?

A utilitarian argument for prohibition

It is argued that prohibition minimizes drug use by various means. First, although illegal drugs are widely available, they are less available than they would be were they legal. Second, many people are deterred by their illegality because they do not want to break the law or fear the consequences of doing so. Third, compared to legal trade, prohibition increases the price of drugs (because of the high profits necessary as a sufficient incentive to bear the risks of illegal production and commerce) and thus reduces demand. Fourth, prohibition denounces drug use unambiguously, while legalization would undermine drugs education and encourage drug use. An objection to this last point is that legally permitting something does not mean encouraging or advocating it (for example, adultery, attempted suicide, smoking). However, the reply from prohibitionism is that legalization would *appear* to condone drug use and would thus send the wrong signal, especially to young people, and would undermine efforts to discourage drug use. So, it is argued, in those four ways (availability, deterrence, price and denunciation) prohibition minimizes drug use and thus minimizes its associated harms – stupefaction, ill health, addiction, death, child neglect and abuse, property crime and violence. So, it is concluded, it is the policy with the best consequences for the welfare of society as a whole and thus the right policy.[26] The argument might be summarized thus:

1 The policy that minimizes the harms of drug use is the right policy.
2 Prohibition minimizes drug use:
    (a) it reduces drug availability;
    (b) it deters many people;
    (c) it increases the price of drugs;
    (d) it denounces drug use.
       Objection: Allowing is not advocating.
       Reply: Allowing *appears* to condone.
3 By minimizing drug use, prohibition minimizes the associated harms.
4 Therefore, prohibition, by minimizing the harms of drug use, is the right policy.

Even if premises 1 and 2 are accepted, it does not follow that minimizing drug use necessarily minimizes drug-related harm. The utilitarian counterargument is that legalization, even if it increased drug use, would reduce drug-related harm. Let's turn to that argument.

A utilitarian argument against prohibition

The utilitarian case against prohibition shares the premise that the policy that minimizes the harms of drug use is the right policy. However, it is argued that prohibition causes or increases the harms associated with drugs[27] in a number of ways.

The prohibitionist claim that legalization would greatly increase drug use presupposes that many people would want to take drugs and be willing to take the risks. Prohibition thus frustrates satisfaction of those wants, which, provided they would be well informed, is a harm to welfare.

By associating drug use with rebellion, daring and being outside the law, prohibition may make drugs more attractive, especially to young people, as 'forbidden fruit', and thus increase drug use. Evidence for this claim is that, prior to prohibition, drug consumption was no greater, and less problematic, than it is now[28] and that decriminalization of cannabis in the Netherlands and in some US states did not result in increased use.[29] However, while illegality may be attractive to some people, it probably deters more.

A third harm of prohibition is that it is futile and thus brings the law into disrepute. People have experimented with drugs for millennia and, despite decades of prohibition, many people continue to use illegal drugs, despite their illegality, and the risk of criminal conviction and imprisonment, and of addiction, overdose and death. Despite the world-wide efforts of police, customs officers, the intelligence services and, in some countries, the armed forces, and despite increasingly harsh penalties including, in some countries, the death penalty, the supply of illegal drugs continues and they have become increasingly widely available, cheaper and purer, proving that there is no shortage of supply.[30] Furthermore, the numbers of people using illegal drugs has steadily increased over the decades.[31] So, it is claimed, prohibition is futile and brings the law, police and government into disrepute. Yet the more prohibition fails, the more governments advocate it, citing the evidence of its failure as reason to redouble efforts yet again.

As with prohibition of other goods and services for which there is a demand (alcohol, pornography, prostitution, gambling), prohibition of drugs in effect invites organized crime to supply a lucrative market. The United Nations Office on Drugs and Crime estimates the international illegal drug trade to be worth $321 billion a year.[32] By making illegal trade so lucrative relative to legal occupations, prohibition encourages others to engage in criminal activity. Prohibition cannot prevent a market in drugs; the question is whether it should be a legal market or an illegal market supplied by criminals.

Supply by criminals greatly increases the harms associated with drugs in several ways. It results in drugs being supplied in their most concentrated and addictive forms,[33] in drugs being adulterated, sometimes with more toxic substances, and thus made more dangerous, and in the supply of drugs of unknown and variable strength, making them more dangerous and leading to deaths from inadvertent overdoses when a batch is unusually pure. Illegality thus makes dangerous drugs even more dangerous. (This is also true of illicit alcohol.) Even heroin, when supplied unadulterated and of known strength, can be taken for years with little physical harm, but becomes much more dangerous when supplied illegally. Supply by criminals, which prohibition creates, also promotes continual expansion of the drug market. Ruthless criminals have a lucrative incentive to create new users by offering or giving away drugs to create new users dependent on them, targeting ever-younger people. In contrast, legalization could create licensed suppliers who would be more restrained in order to keep their licence. Criminal supply also results in violence – gang warfare between rival suppliers and the settling of debts between illegal traders. The huge profits from the illegal trade also lead to widespread bribery and corruption of police and customs officers, bankers and politicians.[34]

Prohibition greatly increases the price of drugs, which leads many habitual users to fund their drug use through theft, burglary and robbery. In Britain, an official estimate is that crime to fund drug use amounts to 36 million crimes each year, or 56 per cent of the total number of crimes, including 80 per cent of domestic burglaries and 54 per cent of robberies.[35] This represents enormous harm to the victims, which is a consequence mainly of prohibition, not of the drugs themselves. Legal supply to dependent users reduces their property crime. Legalization would bring down the price of drugs and so curb the tendency of drug users to steal to pay for drugs.

Another way habitual users fund their drug use is by recruiting new users to sell to. Prohibition creates 'pyramid selling' whereby drug users sell to new users who in turn recruit yet more users and sellers. This is another reason an illegal market has a greater tendency to expand than a legal one, and thus to spread to ever-younger people. Legalization would eliminate the tendency of drug users to sell drugs to pay for their own.

Prohibition pushes many drug users into a chaotic lifestyle, which undermines their employability and family life; many become trapped. When drug dependants are legally supplied, they can be employed and maintain a family life, despite their addiction, and living a fuller life makes it more likely that they will give up drugs.

The enforcement of prohibition adds further harms. Prohibition criminalizes many otherwise law-abiding people, undermining respect for the law, police and courts. Punishment of victimless drug offenders inflicts enormous non-retributive harm on them and their families. Expenditure on enforcement (customs, police, courts and prisons) could be better spent, perhaps on drugs education and treatment services for dependent users. Enforcing the drug laws leads to many innocent people being subject to stop and search by police and customs officers and raids on pubs and clubs. Enforcement falls on blacks and whites unequally and on rich and poor unequally. The presumption of innocence has been compromised as convicted drug dealers can have their assets seized unless they can prove that they are not financed from dealing. The privacy of bank accounts has been compromised, as banks are legally required to report suspicious accounts. Sentences for drug offences have become increasingly harsh. Employers have introduced compulsory drug testing, not always to test fitness to do the job but to check on employees' leisure activities. So, in various ways, enforcement of drug laws harms civil liberties.

Prohibition gives criminals control of the quality, purity, price and proceeds of drugs. But criminals give no information about how to use the drugs with least risk. In a legal market, like those for alcohol and tobacco, government could license sellers in order to enforce regulations on the quality and purity of drugs, to prevent adulteration with more harmful substances, on compulsory labelling, so users know the strength of a drug instead of the unknown and variable strength of illegal drugs, and on compulsory health warnings and advice on least harmful use (for example, safe doses, avoiding mixing with alcohol), as with medicines. Government could also tax the drugs trade and divert into public funds the billions of dollars now going to criminals. Through taxation, government could control the price of drugs and thus influence overall levels of consumption (as with alcohol and tobacco). Because licensed sellers are less likely to sell to children than illegal sellers are, legalization might reduce the availability of drugs to children.

Prohibition distorts drugs education. Exaggerations (of the dangers, of addictiveness, and of the difficulty of giving up) and falsehoods are counterproductive because people know from their own experience they are false and do not believe them, but may disregard the real dangers. Legalization would allow better drugs education, based on facts not myths, about how to minimize the dangers of drug use (for example, by not mixing drugs and alcohol).

So, for all these reasons, anti-prohibitionists argue that prohibition causes or increases the harms associated with drug use, and legalization would reduce those harms. This argument may be summarized thus:

1   The policy that minimizes the harms of drug use is the right policy.
2   Prohibition causes or increases the harms associated with drugs:
    (a) Prohibition presupposes people want drugs and frustrates those wants.
    (b) Prohibition may make drugs more attractive.
        Objection: More people deterred than attracted by illegality.
    (c) Prohibition inevitably fails to suppress drug use, so brings the law into disrepute.
    (d) Prohibition creates lucrative criminal opportunities and invites organised crime to supply the market. Criminal supply results in:
        (i) drugs supplied in their most concentrated and addictive forms;

   (ii) drugs adulterated, so more dangerous;
   (iii) drugs of unknown and variable strength, so more dangerous;
   (iv) ruthless expansion of the market to ever-younger people;
   (v) violence – settling debts and gang warfare;
   (vi) bribery and corruption.
 (e) Prohibition increases price, turns many drug users into thieves.
 (f) Prohibition increases price, turns many drug users into suppliers.
 (g) Prohibition produces a lifestyle that undermines some users' employment and family life.
 (h) Enforcement of prohibition:
   (i) criminalizes many, undermines respect for the law;
   (ii) punishes victimless offenders;
   (iii) takes resources from drugs education and treatment;
   (iv) harms civil liberties.
 (i) Prohibition gives criminals control of quality, purity, price and proceeds. Legalization allows government control, through licensing, of quality, purity, price, proceeds, labelling, availability, and advertising.
 (j) Prohibition distorts drugs education.
   In all these ways, prohibition causes or increases the harms associated with drug use.
3 Therefore, prohibition is the wrong policy.

Prohibitionists may object that legalization would be a dangerous gamble. It might reduce the harm associated with drug use, but might also lead to many more people using drugs, and consequently more harm. And if legalized drugs became widely used, in a democracy legalization would be difficult to reverse. A utilitarian anti-prohibitionist reply would be that the risks of legalization could be controlled by gradual legalization, starting with the least dangerous drugs, to allow evaluation of the consequences.

This survey of the arguments about our drug laws suggests that there is a case for a moral right to the freedom to use drugs, which none of the arguments from liberty-limiting principles defeats, and that drug prohibition may well cause more harm than it prevents. So, whether considered in terms of individual liberty rights or societal welfare, our drug laws, and the extensive punishment they entail, may be unjustified.

Questions for discussion

1   Do adults have a moral right to the freedom to use drugs?
2   Which, if any, of the following arguments against a right to use drugs are convincing?
    (a) Drug use harms others.
    (b) Drug use harms oneself.
    (c) Drug use disrespects one's rational capacity.
    (d) Drug use is not part of a good way of life.
    (e) Drug use deviates from the traditional way of life.
    (f) Drug use deviates from the majority's values.
3   Which policy minimizes the harms associated with drug use: prohibition or legalization?
4   Who benefits from legal prohibition of drugs?

2

JUSTIFICATIONS OF PUNISHMENT

The question of how society ought to treat criminals is always topical and controversial. Most people agree that criminals ought to be punished, but disagree *why* they should be. People give different, perhaps conflicting, justifications. What *justifies* punishment? Is punishment justified because wrongdoers deserve it, or is it justified as a means to reduce crime? And what determines the right *kind* and *amount* of punishment? Is it what fits the crime committed or what will most effectively reduce future crime? These are the questions that theories of punishment address.

Punishment involves an authority deliberately harming someone found to have broken a rule, for example, by depriving them of some of their freedoms or property.[1] Deliberately harming someone is usually wrong. So what makes this harm right? There are two main kinds of justification of punishment: retributivism, which justifies punishment as retribution for wrongdoing; and utilitarianism, which justifies punishment as a means to reduce crime. Perhaps the greatest moral philosopher to advocate retributivism was Immanuel Kant. These two kinds of justification of punishment, then, illustrate two main kinds of general moral theory, Kantianism and utilitarianism (the subjects of chapters 10 and 11).

This chapter examines each of those justifications of punishment, the criticisms they make of each other, and attempts to combine them. It will be assumed that lawbreaking is wrongdoing (as it typically is). That is, I shall set aside the questions of unjust laws, when, if ever, it is morally permissible to break the law and whether justified lawbreaking ought to be punished. (These questions are discussed in relation to civil disobedience in chapter 3.)

Retributivism

What *justifies* punishment? The retributivist answer is simply the crime itself. Punishment is justified as paying back the offender for their crime. Wrongdoers *deserve* punishment, the innocent do not, and justice requires that each person receives his or her due. It is unjust if the guilty are not punished, because they would not receive what they deserve, just as it is unjust if an innocent person is punished. Punishment of the guilty is deserved, therefore just, therefore morally good, independently of its consequences.

What determines the right *kind* and *amount* of punishment? Again, the retributivist answer is simply the crime itself. Justice requires punishment that fits the crime, that is, is proportionate to the seriousness of the crime.[2] The worse the crime, the more severe the punishment deserved. Justice requires punishment to be neither too lenient nor too harsh. 'An eye for an eye, a tooth for a tooth.' Retribution is sometimes thought to mean harsh punishment, but this is mistaken – punishment must not be more severe than the offence justifies, even if that would reduce crime.

Joel Feinberg[3] summarizes retributivism thus:

1 Guilt is necessary for justified punishment.
2 Guilt is sufficient for justified punishment, independently of any good consequences.
3 The amount of punishment should fit the crime, that is, be proportionate to its seriousness.

Some retributivists say that the kind of punishment ought to *resemble* the crime. Punishment should be retaliation in kind. This implies death for murder, corporal punishment for violence, fines for theft. (Imprisonment resembles few crimes.) However, it would be impossible for punishment to resemble some crimes (for example, those involving deception) and wrong for it to resemble some others (for example, rape or torture). The idea that punishment ought to be proportionate to the crime is essential to retributivism, but the idea that punishment ought to resemble the crime is not. Retributivism requires that the worst crime – murder – receives the most severe punishment available in a system of punishment, but it does not require that punishment to be death.

Kant's retributivism[4]

Kant adopted the retributivist view of punishment. What justifies punishment is the crime itself:

> Punishment by a court … can never be inflicted merely as a means to promote some other good for the criminal himself or for civil society. It must always be inflicted upon him only *because he has committed a crime*.

Punishment is a 'categorical imperative', that is, an unconditional duty irrespective of our desires, and must not be waived or reduced in order to promote happiness or other advantages. For Kant, then, guilt is necessary and sufficient for justified punishment, the first two elements in Feinberg's characterization of retributivism.

What determines the right kind and amount of punishment is 'equality'. This might be interpreted as equivalence between the seriousness of the crime and the severity of the punishment. However, the seriousness of crimes and the severity of punishments are not susceptible to cardinal measurement in common units, which equivalence presupposes.[5] Rather, by 'equality' Kant means punishment that *resembles* the crime, the principle of 'like for like': 'whatever undeserved evil you inflict upon another …, that you inflict upon yourself', if you insult, steal from, strike or kill another, you insult, steal from, strike or kill yourself. Only the law of retaliation 'can specify definitely the quality and quantity of punishment'. A thief makes everyone's property insecure and therefore deprives himself of security in his own property. Every murderer 'must *die*'. No other punishment 'will satisfy justice'. No other punishment is similar to the crime. Punishment is justified, Kant says, when it resembles the crime. Although Kant claims that the right of retaliation is the principle for the right kind of punishment, he recognizes that it would be impossible or wrong for some crimes. It also conflicts with his suggestion that punishment may be made useful for the offender or for society.[6] So, the idea of retaliation *in kind*, and thus the death penalty, is not essential to Kantian retributivism, which is more convincing if it requires only that punishment ought to be proportionate to the crime.

Even if Kant is right that some murderers deserve the death penalty, there are Kantian objections to its availability. First, Kant recognized that it would be wrong for the punishment to resemble some crimes, for example, it would be wrong to rape rapists or torture torturers. Similarly, perhaps, it would be wrong to imitate deliberate killing; indeed, it is claimed that capital punishment is worse than most murders because few murder victims live with the knowledge that they are going to be killed. Second, in any criminal justice system, miscarriages of justice inevitably occur. Any punishment of the innocent is an injustice but, in a death penalty case, it becomes unrectifiable. The availability of the death penalty inevitably leads to the killing of innocent people. To legislate for the availability of the death penalty is knowingly, if unintentionally, to legislate to kill innocent people. Such legislators do what they claim to abhor.

Kant's arguments for retributivism

Kant argues that justice requires punishment, because wrong-doers *deserve* to suffer a penalty. Every crime deserves to be punished, simply because it has occurred and not because punishment has good consequences.[7] When a wrongdoer is punished, the harm inflicted on him is considered good 'even if nothing further results from it', that is, even if it has no good consequences, and the wrongdoer 'must acknowledge, in his reason, that justice has been done to him'.[8] The reason that Kant thinks that punishment of the guilty is a categorical imperative, an unconditional duty (and not, as some other retributivists say, merely a right, which may be waived when it would not have good consequences), is that justice requires punishment. And, Kant exaggeratedly claims, 'if justice goes, there is no longer any value in human beings' living on the earth'.[9] It is for this reason that he says that even if a society were to dissolve itself (for example, if islanders left their island), every murderer ought first to be executed so that each receives 'what his deeds deserve'. Failure to punish is a 'violation of justice'.[10]

James Rachels[11] gives two additional arguments that relate retributivism to Kant's two main formulations of 'the supreme principle of morality', which he calls the Categorical Imperative. Kant's first formulation of the Categorical Imperative is this: 'Act only according to that maxim whereby you can at the same time will that it should become a universal law.'[12] According to Rachels, part of what Kant means by this is that a person's action expresses a judgement about how people are to be treated. If that person is treated the same way in return, he is treated in accordance with his own judgement. By his deeds, he has decided how he is to be treated.[13] As Kant puts it, 'he brings his misdeed back upon himself, and what is done to him ... is what he has perpetrated on others.'[14] Even if the kind of punishment does not resemble the crime, the fact of punishment is similar to crime in that it infringes the (former, forfeited) rights of those who infringed the rights of their victims. Thus, punishment treats offenders as they treated their victims. It harms harmdoers. It thus treats offenders in accordance with their own actions.

Kant's second formulation of the Categorical Imperative is: 'Act in such a way that you treat humanity, whether in your own person or in the person of another, always at the same time as an end and never simply as a means.'[15] This formulation is sometimes called the formula of respect for persons. The 'humanity' of persons is their moral capacity, which their *rational* capacity enables. Their rational capacity gives each person the power of *choice* over her actions. This makes each person *responsible* for her voluntary actions and, therefore, *accountable* for them. Retributive punishment presupposes that the criminal is accountable and, therefore, responsible for her actions, and, therefore, that her actions were voluntarily chosen. Retributive punishment thus respects the criminal as a person. (Infants and people who are severely mentally ill or severely mentally disabled do not fully possess rationality, the power of choice, responsibility or accountability, so retributivism does not apply to them.)

Criticisms of retributivism

It may be objected that the idea of proportionality between crime and punishment is vague. Judgements differ over the relative seriousness of crimes and the relative severity of punishments. Violent crime may be judged more serious than property crime, but at some point large-scale theft is more serious than a minor assault. Even if a scale of crimes were given, proportionality requires only that a more serious crime is punished more severely than a less serious one, but it does not determine the right kind or amount of punishment. What kind and amount of punishment 'fits' theft? Judgements about what is a fitting punishment for a crime vary between individuals – sentences are often criticised as too harsh or too lenient. Judgements vary between cultures – for example, adultery is punishable by death in some societies, but is not even a crime in others. And they vary historically – torture and the death penalty used to be thought appropriate for many crimes, but now are widely thought to be appropriate to none. Even comparisons of magistrates' courts in Britain at any one time find wide variations in sentences for similar offences. So the idea of a 'fitting' punishment is problematic. Retributivism can reply that alternative justifications of punishment are also vague about the right kind and amount of punishment. The right punishment is not capable of precise determination.

A utilitarian criticism of retributivism is that it is not concerned with doing good by reducing crime and the suffering it causes. Rather, it is concerned only to make offenders suffer too. Even if punishment were to *increase* future crime (say, by embittering offenders), retributivism would still insist on punishment as right. The final paragraph of this chapter suggests a retributivist reply to this criticism, but let us now turn to the utilitarian theory of punishment, which justifies punishment only as a means to reduce crime and the suffering it causes.

The utilitarian theory of punishment

What makes an action (or policy or set of rules) right or wrong? According to consequentialist moral theories, an action is made right or wrong only by its probable consequences. The right action is the one which has the best consequences. What makes consequences good or bad? According to utilitarianism, which is the main consequentialist ethical theory, pleasure, happiness or the satisfaction of wants or interests (these are alternative definitions of utility) is intrinsically good. Conversely, pain, unhappiness or the frustration of wants or interests (disutility) is intrinsically bad. Utilitarianism uses its definition of good and bad to determine right and wrong. The right action (or policy or set of rules) is the one that would maximize utility and thus have the best consequences for all affected.

Punishment involves deliberately harming someone (and perhaps unintentionally harming that person's family). For utilitarianism, harm is bad. However, if it has sufficiently good consequences, it can be right. Thus, punishment is justified only when its probable good consequences outweigh the harm involved. Punishment is justified only as a necessary means to good consequences, namely, reducing crime and the harm and suffering it causes.

So, what *justifies* punishment? Punishment is justified if it has good consequences for society. What is the right *kind* and *amount* of punishment? Whatever produces the best consequences for all affected.

How might punishment reduce crime and/or the harm it causes, and thus have good consequences?

- Punishment may *prevent* crime by reducing the offender's capacity to commit further crimes (for example, by imprisonment or curfew).
- The credible threat of punishment may *deter* people from breaking the law, so punishment is justified to make its threat credible. Utilitarianism would justify the death penalty if, but only if, it deters more effectively than long-term imprisonment. (According to Hugo Bedau, there is no convincing evidence that the death penalty does deter more effectively than long-term imprisonment.)[16]
- Punishment may *rehabilitate* (reform or correct) the offender by tackling causes of their crime, such as psychological problems, drug or alcohol dependence, lack of job skills or moral deficiency, by providing appropriate therapy, treatment, training or moral education. The response to crime is thus tailored to fit the criminal rather than the crime. This response to crime is claimed to be more humane, because it condemns the crime but not the criminal, more rational, because it aims to respond to crime on the basis of knowledge of its causes, and more constructive, because it aims to help rather than harm the offender. Rehabilitationists observe that imprisonment, far from reforming, often worsens offenders, because in prison they acquire

or develop criminal skills, attitudes, associates and identity, resulting in high rates of recidivism.

- Punishment may force the offender to make *amends* to their victim or to the community, for example, by paying compensation, repairing damage or doing unpaid work. Here punishment is justified as restitution (restoration or reparation), as correcting the offence rather than the offender. Justice is conceived as righting wrongs rather than as harming wrongdoers. This approach is more plausible as a response to property crime than to violent crime, for which it is impossible to make amends. (This justification of punishment as restitution is not among the standard utilitarian justifications. It could be presented as a third kind of justification, distinct from both retributivism and utilitarianism, or as an alternative to punishment. However, its forward-looking, consequentialist character is the reason for its tentative inclusion, for simplicity, within utilitarianism here.)[17]

The first three ways aim to reduce future crime, the fourth aims to reduce the harm done by crime once it has been committed.

Joel Feinberg summarizes the utilitarian theory of punishment as follows:

1   Utility (for example, prevention or deterrence of crime) is a necessary condition for justified punishment.
2   Utility is a sufficient condition for justified punishment.
3   The right kind and amount of punishment is that which has the best consequences for all affected.[18]

Utilitarianism is a forward-looking justification of punishment: to justify punishment it looks forward to its good consequences. In contrast, retributivism is a backward-looking justification: to justify punishment it looks back to the crime that has been committed.

Utilitarianism regards punishment as only *instrumentally* valuable, as a means to reducing crime. The harm done to the offender is bad, but this may be outweighed by its good consequences, which make it right. In contrast, retributivism regards justified punishment as *intrinsically* valuable, as deserved, as just, as right in itself, independently of its consequences. The harm done to the offender is good, because it is right. Their justifications of punishment thus illustrate a fundamental contrast in the structures of utilitarian and Kantian ethical theories: for utilitarianism, the good is prior to, and determines, the right; for Kantian ethics, the right is prior to, and determines, the good.

Because utilitarianism justifies punishment only as a means to reduce crime, it can question, while retributivism accepts, the centrality of punishment to society's response to crime. Since punishment leaves unchanged social causes of crime, such as poverty and unemployment, it is not very effective at reducing crime. Utilitarians may argue that tackling such causes would reduce crime more effectively than punishment does.

Criticisms of the utilitarian theory of punishment

Utilitarianism falsely assumes that all harm is bad. Consequently, in deciding whether and how much to punish, it requires that the punitive harm done to the criminal be less than the criminal harm it will prevent. This is objectionably neutral between the criminal harm, which is morally wrong, and the punitive harm, which is morally right (and therefore good harm).

A second objection to utilitarianism is that it would justify punishment of the innocent in certain circumstances. For example, a terrorist atrocity causes public anger that threatens revenge against innocent members of the religious or ethnic community from which the terrorists come. Framing a few innocent individuals could prevent reprisals against many more and could thus be justified according to utilitarianism. According to retributivism, this would be a grave injustice. It would be wrong to punish an innocent person, whatever the good consequences of doing so.

A utilitarian reply to this objection is to define punishment as penalizing the guilty.[19] On this definition, 'punishing the innocent' is an oxymoron. The utilitarian justification of punishment by definition justifies punishing the guilty and not the innocent. One rejoinder to this is that this definition is contentious, because saying that someone was punished for a crime they did not commit is not incoherent. But the main rejoinder is that utilitarianism would nevertheless justify deliberately harming the innocent when to do so would have the best consequences. Whether this harm is called 'punishment' is less important.

A Kantian objection to the utilitarian theory of punishment is that punishing someone to prevent or deter crime, or to rehabilitate them, is to treat the criminal as a mere means to society's end, namely, reducing crime. According to Kant's second formulation of the Categorical Imperative, we must never treat a person as a mere means to our ends. Kant's reason for saying that punishment should 'never be inflicted merely as a means to promote some other good for the criminal himself or for civil society' is that 'a human being can [that is, ought] never be treated merely as a means to the purposes of another'.[20] A non-utilitarian reply to this objection is that, by breaking the law, the criminal *consents* to the risk of being treated in those ways, which are publicly known, and so is not treated as a mere means. A rejoinder is that warning of unjust treatment does not justify it.[21]

A fourth criticism is that utilitarianism, in attempting to bring about the best consequences, prescribes the wrong amount of punishment. The aims of preventing or deterring crime or reforming offenders or making amends would justify punishments that would be effective means to those ends, but would be disproportionate to the crime:

- The aim of preventing reoffending by a persistent petty criminal would justify prolonged imprisonment. Under 'three strikes and you're out' laws, life imprisonment is imposed for a third conviction, even if it is for a minor offence. This is unjust because it is disproportionate and because the offender is punished again for previous offences for which they have already paid the penalty.
- The aim of deterring crime would justify harsh or cruel penalties (or even harming the criminal's innocent family) if it would deter enough crime to outweigh the harm done. Exemplary sentences are sometimes imposed in order to deter other people from committing similar crimes. This is disproportionate because the individual receives not only punishment for what he has done but also additional punishment for what others might do.
- Crime carries only a risk, not the certainty, of punishment (and, for most crime, the probability of conviction is low). Criminals

gamble on not being caught and convicted. The lower the probability of conviction, the greater the amount of prospective punishment needed to deter. Factoring in this probability (which varies among different crimes, areas and periods) entails that the punishment needed to deter deviates systematically from proportionality to the crime.

- The punishment just sufficient to deter property crime varies inversely with a person's socio-economic position.[22] For most affluent people, small-scale property crime would be deterred merely by a high probability of conviction independently of any punishment, apart from disgrace in their milieu. For some poor people, small-scale property crime is more tempting and may be more tolerated in their milieu, so greater punishment is needed to deter. The aim of deterrence thus permits unjustly punishing similar offences dissimilarly.
- The aim of rehabilitation requires tailoring the punishment to fit the offender rather than the offence. This leads to similar crimes receiving dissimilar punishments, depending on judgements about the offender's attitude, background or character. Such judgements may be influenced by stereotypes about good and bad families, schools and jobs.
- The aim of making amends for property crime (criminal damage or theft) by restitution of property would be appropriate for *innocent* damage or loss, but insufficient for *wrongful* damage or theft.
- Utilitarianism would require no punishment in cases where its consequences would not be good. For example, prosecution of elderly Nazi war criminals is said to do no good. Punishment of fanatical terrorists may not deter other fanatics willing to die for their cause, or may cause reprisals, and thus do more harm than good. In both cases, retributivism says that justice demands punishment, because it is deserved, even if it has no good consequences.

Thus, prevention, deterrence, rehabilitation and restitution can each justify the wrong amount of punishment, according to retributivism. The retributivist principle of punishment to fit the crime is needed to determine the right amount of punishment.

Attempts to reconcile retributivist and utilitarian justifications of punishment

Retributivism and utilitarianism each has its attractions and flaws. Attempts have been made to combine and reconcile them. John Rawls proposes one such reconciliation. He argues that utilitarianism can avoid criticisms of its justification of punishment if utilitarianism is understood as applying not directly to each action (act-utilitarianism) but to institutions, that is, to systems of rules to be applied and enforced (rule-utilitarianism). Utilitarianism would not justify an institution of punishment that gave officials discretion to decide particular cases on utilitarian grounds – for example, to 'punish' the innocent when it would probably have good consequences. This is because such discretion would probably have unintended bad consequences (abuse, doubt about the guilt of convicts, fear of being wrongly punished). Utilitarianism would justify an institution of punishment that punishes only those found guilty by due process, and punishes them proportionately to their crime. Thus, utilitarianism justifies an institution of punishment whose rules are not utilitarian but retributivist. Legislators, in establishing a system of punishment, look forward to its benefits for society. Judges, in imposing particular punishments on particular individuals, look back to their crimes. Utilitarianism thus justifies the institution of punishment, in which retributivism justifies particular acts of punishment.[23] Rawls's proposal avoids the criticism that the utilitarian justification of punishment would justify 'punishing' the innocent. However, it would not, as Rawls claims, lead to the severity of penalties (the 'prices' of crimes) being proportional to the seriousness of offences in order to deter crime. Deterrence requires the price of each crime to be proportional not to its moral seriousness but to its attractiveness, and inversely proportional to the probability of conviction. So, the criticism remains that even a rule-utilitarian system of punishment would systematically prescribe disproportionate punishment.

Herbert Hart proposes that the justifying aim of the general practice of punishment is its beneficial consequences, namely preventing crime. However, pursuit of this utilitarian aim should be qualified or restricted by retributivist principles of justice, which require that only those who have voluntarily broken the law may be punished, and the amount of punishment should be proportionate to the gravity of the crime. Hart thus proposes a compromise between utilitarian and retributivist principles in which utilitarianism supplies the aim of punishment and retributivism supplies moral constraints on the means to that end.[24] Unlike Rawls, Hart regards the retributivist principles as valid independently of any utilitarian justification. His proposal avoids the criticisms that the utilitarian aim would permit harming the innocent and excessive punishment. However, since the retributively just amount of punishment, proportionate to the crime, will not suffice as a deterrent because of the low probability of conviction, Goldman argues that hybrid theories like Rawls's and Hart's combine inconsistent principles.[25]

Rawls and Hart propose incorporating retributivist principles within a utilitarian framework. Kantian retributivism perhaps permits incorporation of consequentialist considerations in the following way. Retributivism insists that what justifies punishment and the amount of punishment is only the crime itself. However, Kant remarks that once someone has been found guilty and therefore punishable, then 'thought can be given to drawing from his punishment something of use for himself or his fellow citizens'.[26] Once freed from Kant's idea that punishment ought to resemble the crime, Kantian retributivism can allow that, in deciding the form of punishment, usefulness to the offender or to society is pertinent. Retributive punishment may be designed to encourage offenders to reform. (Kant remarks that a wrongdoer, as a moral being, always retains the capacity to improve.)[27] If, as the evidence suggests, imprisonment worsens offenders and non-custodial punishment does better at reform, the latter is a morally better form of retribution from a Kantian perspective. For some offenders, retribution may take the form of being required to make amends to their victim or their community by doing unpaid work (which may also reform them). For some violent criminals, retribution may take the form of imprisonment in order to protect the public. In each case, the fact and amount of punishment is justified only as retribution, but its form may be designed for its beneficial consequences (reform, restitution or incapacitation). This version of Kantian retributivism avoids the criticism that it is not concerned with reducing crime or the harm it causes. Since it makes no appeal to deterrence, it avoids Goldman's criticism of inconsistency because the just amount of punishment is insufficient to deter. It also illustrates how Kantian ethics does not disregard consequences, as it is sometimes claimed, but can incorporate consideration of consequences in a subsidiary way, constrained by duties and rights.

Questions for discussion

1   Which justification of punishment do you find more convincing – retributivist or utilitarian? Why?
2   Do wrongdoers deserve to be punished? Or do psychological and social factors cause choices such that the criminal could not have chosen to act differently?
3   Does justice require, or only permit, punishment of wrongdoers? Is punishment a duty or a right, which can be waived?
4   Which of the utilitarian aims of punishment do you find most convincing as a justification of punishment?
5   Can retributivist and utilitarian justifications of punishment be convincingly reconciled?
6   What might be the causes of crime? Is punishment an effective way to reduce crime?

3

CIVIL DISOBEDIENCE: IS THERE A DUTY TO OBEY THE LAW?

Anti-war protesters illegally damage military equipment. Animal liberationists illegally damage cages. Environmental protesters illegally damage logging or road-building equipment. Is it ever right to break the law? In particular, is it ever right for political action to break the law? These are questions that civil disobedience raises.

Definitions and varieties of civil disobedience

Hugo Bedau defines civil disobedience as 'any act in violation of the law done with the intention of frustrating or changing the law, conducted... not to involve intentional violence... and done... to achieve social justice or some other fundamental moral goal'.[1] Essentially, civil disobedience is *illegal* non-violent political action, done for *moral* reasons (this distinguishes it from crime). Civil disobedience may be distinguished from conscientious objection, which is refusal to participate in perceived wrongdoing such as military action, rather than an attempt to change a policy or a law.

Some definitions of civil disobedience include its being done publicly, not covertly. Bedau earlier said that appealing to the public conscience requires the illegal conduct to be done publicly.[2] However, a non-violent, illegal conscientious political act may be done covertly, and perhaps later publicized, especially if frustrating injustice requires secrecy – for example, hiding Jews from Nazi persecution or freeing animals from cages.

So, including public performance in the definition of civil disobedience is questionable.

Civil disobedience is often defined as non-violent. Other definitions allow an act to qualify as civil disobedience even if it involves some violence, provided that the violence was not instigated by the protesters but by opponents or the police, or was solely against property[3] (if damage to things, rather than persons, can properly be called 'violence' – a usage that flouts a morally important distinction). Examples include protesters' damage to animals' cages or to vivisectionists' equipment, to road-building equipment and to warplanes destined for a repressive regime or an aggressive war. (The damage to warplanes was borderline civil disobedience because it was arguably legal, as attempted prevention of crime.)

Examples of civil disobedience include the following: Thoreau, who coined the term 'civil disobedience', withheld his tax in 1846 to protest against slavery and the United States' war against Mexico; the Suffragettes' campaign for votes for women; the campaign for India's independence, led by Gandhi; the campaign against racial segregation and discrimination in the USA, led by Martin Luther King; campaigns against nuclear weapons; animal liberationists' freeing animals from laboratories or fur farms; environmentalists' trespassing to try to prevent environmental damage.

Civil disobedience may vary in several ways. It may be individual or collective. It is typically collective action but examples of individual civil disobedience are Mordecai Vanunu revealing Israel's secret possession of nuclear weapons and Katherine Gun's revealing secret American plans to spy on members of the UN Security Council in the run-up to the war on Iraq.

Civil disobedience may be direct, where the law broken is the law protested against, or indirect, where one law is broken in protest against another. Protesters may withhold tax to protest directly against that tax or indirectly against another government policy, refuse conscription to protest directly against conscription or indirectly against a war, or trespass to protest directly against trespass laws or indirectly against something being done on the private property.

Civil disobedience may be co-operative or uncooperative with the authorities. Some activists (for example, Martin Luther King) and philosophers (for example, John Rawls) think that justified civil disobedience requires informing the authorities in advance and accepting arrest and lawful penalty. Others (for example, Ronald Dworkin) argue that justified civil disobedience requires no such co-operation with the authorities or accepting punishment, which may reduce its effectiveness in ending injustice.

Is there a duty to obey the law?

Civil disobedience is controversial because it is illegal. It is widely assumed that, at least in a democracy, we have a moral duty to obey the law, that is, to do as the law requires because the law requires it. It is said that we cannot pick and choose which laws to obey, because that would lead to anarchy. The duty to obey the law may be only prima facie, that is, one that can be overridden in some circumstances by another duty. But if we have such a duty, civil disobedience, being illegal, is morally questionable. So, in order to consider whether civil disobedience is ever justifiable we must consider the wider question of whether we have a moral duty to obey the law. It is important to get that question clear. Independently of the law, there are often moral reasons to act as the law requires. For example, we are morally obliged not to steal, assault or drive dangerously. Such actions are not wrong because they are illegal; they are illegal because they are wrong. If they were legal, they would still be wrong. The question of whether we have a moral duty to obey the law is not whether we have a duty to act in the ways that the law requires, but whether we have a duty so to act *because* the law commands it. Where morality and law coincide, it is easy to confuse the moral duty to act as the law happens to require with the putative moral duty to obey the law. Where morality and law differ, the distinction becomes clear. Suppose the law forbids conduct that you believe is morally permissible, would you be morally obliged to obey it? For example, suppose the law forbids a religion, or a sexual practice between consenting adults in private, or a drug (say, alcohol), would there be a moral duty to obey the law? Let us consider the strongest arguments for the duty to obey the law.[4]

Socrates originated two of the main arguments for the duty to obey the law, even unjust laws.[5] He was sentenced to death, unjustly. His friends urged him to flee. Socrates argued that he had a moral duty to obey the law, and hence to accept his unjust death sentence. First, he argued, receipt of benefits from the state entails a duty to *reciprocate*. Receipt of the protection of the law incurs a duty to obey the law. An objection to this argument is that even if beneficiaries owe something to their benefactors, they do not incur the duty to obey them, and benefactors do not acquire the right to command beneficiaries.

Second, Socrates argued, if one does not accept the laws, one can emigrate. By not emigrating, by living in a state, one voluntarily undertakes, 'in deed if not in word', to obey its laws. That is, by living in a state, one gives tacit *consent* to its laws; one voluntarily, if implicitly, agrees or promises to obey its laws. One thus incurs a moral duty to obey the law. It may be objected that, although this argument may be plausible in relation to someone voluntarily entering a state, native residents do not promise or agree to obey the law; mere residence in a state is not a promise. Most native residents have no reasonable alternative to continued residence in their state because emigration is very costly, if not impossible. (And there is no alternative to living in some state.) So, the supposed consent to the law is not voluntary and hence not binding.

A variant of the reciprocation argument is that voluntarily participating in co-operation incurs an obligation to do one's fair share, because one benefits from others doing theirs. One benefits from others obeying the law, so *fairness* demands that one does the same. This obligation is owed to one's fellow citizens, not to the state. Disobedience unfairly takes advantage of others' obedience. This argument applies to voluntary co-operation. For example, if one chooses to drive on public roads, one benefits from others' obeying some traffic laws, so one incurs a moral duty to do so too. However, it may be objected, being born in a state is insufficiently voluntary for this argument to apply to all laws. Living in a law-abiding society is not a voluntary act, so does not incur a duty to reciprocate. It might be replied that the duty of fairness applies to *non*-voluntary co-operation too. Mere receipt of benefits from the state incurs a duty to obey the law because disobedience unfairly takes advantage of others' obedience. For example, there is a duty to pay taxes because evasion is unfair to fellow citizens. However, not all law-breaking takes unfair advantage of fellow citizens, so the duty of fairness does not support a general duty to obey the law.

A fourth argument for the duty to obey the law starts from the *consequentialist* principle that one ought to do what has the best consequences. (For utilitarians, the best consequences are those that maximize happiness or welfare.) The second premise in this argument claims that disobeying the law risks bad consequences, even anarchy. So, there is a duty to obey the law because it is necessary in order to prevent harmful consequences. Socrates also suggests this argument, saying that disobeying the law intends to destroy the law and the state. An objection to this argument's second premise is that selective, conscientious disobedience does not have dire consequences. Acts that are morally permissible do not wrongfully harm others when those acts are illegal. Indeed, in some circumstances, disobeying the law has better consequences than obeying it. Socrates' escape might have been better than his death.

A response to this objection acknowledges that sometimes acts that disobey the law would have better consequences than obeying it, but insists that a *rule* of obedience to the law will, if generally followed, have better consequences than each person deciding, act by act, whether or not to obey. This rule-utilitarian response is vulnerable to the objection that, in circumstances in which disobeying the rule would have better consequences than obeying it would have, there is no utilitarian reason for following the rule. Any consequentialist argument for a duty to obey the law is vulnerable to the objection that it can justify obeying the law only when doing so has the best consequences. It cannot justify a general duty to obey.

Another argument for the duty to obey the law appeals to the duty of *justice*, that is, the duty to respect others' moral rights (for example, not to steal, assault or endanger others). This implies a duty to uphold and support the coercive institutions that enforce those rights, hence a duty to obey the law. An objection to this is that the duty of justice entails a duty to respect others' moral rights, but not a general duty to obey the law. A duty to respect others' moral rights often requires acting in the way that coincides with what the law commands, but not because the law commands it.

Moral rights provide an argument against the duty to obey the law. Ronald Dworkin[6] argues that, if there are moral rights, there cannot be a duty to obey every law. If you have a moral right to do something, it would be wrong for the government to try to stop you from doing it. Moral rights, such as the freedoms of speech and religion, place moral limits on legislation. When a law wrongly invades someone's moral rights, they have a right to break that law. If a government enforces an unjust law, it does a further wrong, so it can be right not to prosecute breakers of unjust laws. And if the law is wrong, any penalty is wrong, so the breaker of an unjust law has no duty to accept the penalty. A government's harsh treatment of civil disobedience counts against the sincerity of its claim to recognize individual rights. Dworkin's argument justifies direct civil disobedience against laws that invade moral rights.

Simmons and Smith find all the arguments for the duty to obey the law unconvincing and so conclude that there is no such duty.[7] Feinberg observes that the fact that an act is illegal has no tendency whatsoever to make that act wrong (although most acts that are illegal are wrong on other grounds, because they harm, endanger or exploit others). So, there is no obligation to obey any unjust laws – for example, Nazi laws against helping Jews or nineteenth-century American laws against helping fugitive slaves. The fact that helping was illegal was morally irrelevant – it was the right thing to do.[8]

If there is not a moral duty to obey the law, this does not imply that one may generally act contrary to the law. When the law enforces moral requirements, there is a moral duty to act in the way the law commands, but not because the law commands it. We should normally act as the law requires also when voluntarily participating in co-operation (for example, some traffic laws), when fairness requires it (for example, tax laws) and when morality leaves open the details of duties, which law fills in (for example, property rights).[9] But when the law's requirements are not moral requirements, there is no duty to act as the law requires. On this view, if the law prohibits a religion, a consensual sexual practice or a drug, there is no moral duty to obey it.

So, we have seen that one view is that we have an unconditional duty to obey the law, including unjust laws. This view implies that civil disobedience is always wrong. The opposite view is that we have no duty to obey the law, so unjust laws may be broken. This implies that injustice permits recourse to civil disobedience (although this must be weighed against the duty of fairness to fellow citizens and the duty to support just institutions, so not done precipitately).[10] Leading justifications of civil disobedience adopt intermediate views, for which there is a moral duty to obey the law, but one that can be overridden by other moral duties. John Rawls thinks that the argument from justice supports a duty to obey the law, at least in a democracy, but that serious injustices can justify civil disobedience even in a democracy if certain conditions are met. Peter Singer argues that the consequentialist argument supports a duty to obey the law but that preventing serious harm can override that duty and justify civil disobedience.

Justifications of civil disobedience

John Rawls offers a Kantian justification of civil disobedience in a democracy, which is the most influential theory of civil disobedience (as part of the most influential theory of social justice, which is the subject of chapter 12). Rawls is concerned with civil disobedience in a democracy. The problem of civil disobedience arises only in a democracy, he says, because in undemocratic societies there is 'no difficulty' about civil disobedience, 'along with militant action and resistance, as a tactic for transforming or even overturning' an unjust political system.[11]

Rawls rejects the two unconditional views, namely, that we are *always* obliged to obey the law even when it is unjust and that we are *never* obliged to obey unjust laws. The constitutional validity of a law is insufficient to require obedience and the injustice of a law is insufficient to justify disobedience. He argues that in a democracy there is normally a duty to comply with an unjust law. This is because there is a duty to uphold just institutions, and as democracy is a just institution there is a duty to uphold it. Upholding democracy implies we must accept majority rule so in a democracy we normally have a duty to obey the law, even unjust laws, provided they are not *too* unjust. *Small* injustices do not nullify the duty to comply with the law. Whether non-compliance is justified depends on the extent of the injustice. In a democracy, we must not oppose *all* unjust laws by illegal means.[12]

However, we also have a natural duty to oppose injustice. So, there is a conflict of duties. This gives rise to the problem of civil disobedience in a democracy: 'At what point does the duty to comply with the laws ... cease to be binding in view of ... the duty to oppose injustice?'[13] This is the problem Rawls tries to solve.

Rawls defines civil disobedience as 'a public, nonviolent, conscientious yet political act contrary to law', usually intended to change the law or government policy.[14] He says that civil disobedience is a form of address. It addresses a democratic society's sense of justice, appealing to the democratic ideal of citizens as free and equal persons, to urge reconsideration of laws or policies. For example, the US civil rights movement against racial segregation and discrimination appealed to 'white' Americans' own democratic ideals of freedom and equality. Rawls defines civil disobedience as conscientious, that is, done for moral reasons rather than grounded solely in self-interest. He defines civil disobedience as political in the special Rawlsian sense that it is guided by public, political principles of justice that all citizens can accept, not appealing to personal morality or religious doctrines that other citizens can reasonably reject. Rawls defines civil disobedience as done in public, not covertly, because it is 'a form of address, an expression of profound and conscientious political conviction'. And he defines it as nonviolent (that is, as trying to avoid violence, especially against persons) because it is a mode of address intended to *convince* the majority that holds political power, not to threaten or force them. It is nonviolent also because, although it breaks the law, it does so 'within the limits of fidelity to law', that is, respect for the law in general. Fidelity to the law 'is expressed by the public and nonviolent nature' of civil disobedience and by a willingness to accept arrest and punishment. Kent Greenawalt adds that accepting punishment also demonstrates depth of conviction, which is more likely to convince others, and inhibits irresponsible resort to civil disobedience.[15]

According to Rawls, there are two main conditions for civil disobedience to be justified. First, civil disobedience should be limited to instances of 'substantial and clear injustice', namely violations of equal basic liberties or of equality of opportunity (that is, the first two principles in Rawls's conception of social justice). Such injustices are sufficiently substantial and clear to justify illegal protest. In contrast, unjust pay or unjust tax is less certain, so the resolution of such issues is normally best left to legal politics, provided that the equal basic liberties are secure.[16] (The third principle in Rawls's conception of social justice defines economic inequalities as just only if they are necessary to make the worst-off group as well off as possible – this principle guides just pay and just taxation.)

The second condition for civil disobedience to be justified is that legal means have been tried and have failed. Legal means need not have been exhausted – if past actions have shown the majority does not care about an injustice, further lawful actions may be futile. (In cases of 'outrageous violation of equal liberty', there may be no duty to try legal means first.) Satisfaction of these two conditions establishes a right to civil disobedience. It is another question 'whether it is wise or prudent to exercise this right'. It may not be if it risks 'harsh retaliation'.[17] If civil disobedience fails, if nonviolent 'appeal against injustice is repeatedly denied', forceful resistance may become justified even in a democracy. To 'employ the coercive apparatus of the state' to maintain injustice is illegitimate use of force, which people 'have a right to resist'. The crushing of basic liberties is unacceptable even if it is by a democratic majority.[18]

Civil disobedience in a democracy helps to maintain, strengthen and stabilize just institutions, which establish equal basic liberties and equal opportunities. By resisting injustice, it inhibits departures from justice and corrects them when they occur.[19] Although civil disobedience breaks the law, it appeals to the fundamental democratic principles of freedom and equality. By publicizing injustice, forcing the state to re-examine its policies, and by being vigilant against injustice, civil disobedience may make the state more just and so may be 'an act of good citizenship'.[20]

An objection to civil disobedience is that it 'invites anarchy' by encouraging everyone to decide for themselves when they may break the law. In reply, Rawls accepts that each person must decide whether civil disobedience is justified, but notes that it is not justified by personal interests but by democratic principles of freedom and equality; if 'the conditions for resorting to civil disobedience are respected', there is 'no danger of anarchy'.[21]

An objection to Rawls's theory of civil disobedience is that limiting justified civil disobedience to violations of the principles of equal basic liberties and equal opportunities is too restrictive. There are other great evils (cruelty to animals, environmental destruction, military aggression, poverty abroad) which demand urgent action and which may justify civil disobedience. This omission in Rawls's theory derives from its being part of a theory of justice that is deliberately restricted in scope to the main institutions of society and political in the Rawlsian sense, rather than a comprehensive moral theory. The objection here is not to Rawls's restriction of the scope of his theory of social justice, but to his thinking that this restricts justifications for civil disobedience. Moral questions that the theory of justice deliberately avoids are not thereby disqualified from justifying civil disobedience. Another objection is to his insistence on civil disobedience being done in public and on willingness to accept arrest and punishment. It may be objected that, if the duty to oppose injustice can justify breaking the law, it can also justify doing so secretly and avoiding arrest if that would be more effective.

Peter Singer gives a utilitarian justification of civil disobedience that avoids these objections.[22] Singer accepts an obligation to obey the law, because obedience contributes to others' respect for the law while disobedience encourages others to break the law, and because breaking the law imposes law enforcement costs on society. So, for Singer, the law has some moral weight. However, the reasons for generally obeying the law may be outweighed in a particular case by the reasons for disobeying it. For Singer, as a utilitarian, the end justifies the means. So, a sufficiently weighty end can justify illegal means. Illegal acts are justified if they are the only or most effective way to prevent some great harm, for example, persecution of minorities, dire poverty, cruelty to animals or environmental destruction. The importance of the ends may justify breaking the law. Whether civil disobedience is justified depends on how wrong the target is and on how likely success is.[23]

Whereas Rawls's theory of justice is concerned with justice among citizens, and so limits the issues that can justify civil disobedience, utilitarianism is a comprehensive moral theory, which includes relations with non-citizens and non-humans; it thus allows any serious wrong to justify civil disobedience. For Rawls, justifiable civil disobedience in a democracy appeals to principles of justice that a liberal-democratic society already accepts, but for Singer it may appeal to moral principles that are not generally accepted, such as animal rights or environmentalism.

An objection Singer considers is that, while breaking the law may be justified in a dictatorship, in a democracy there are legal means to right wrongs. This makes the use of illegal means unjustifiable. Singer's reply is that this shows only that the legal means should be tried first. But the legal means may be ineffective or slow, while the wrong continues. Illegal means may end it sooner. In trying to stop evil, we should adopt the most effective means.[24]

A rejoinder is that, if legal means fail to achieve reform, this shows that the majority disagrees with the protesters. Use of illegal means violates the democratic principle of majority rule. Thus, civil disobedience is anti-democratic. Singer has two replies to this. First, in a democracy, the majority view does not always prevail, for various reasons. Voters cannot usually vote on single issues but only for parties or candidates. Governments are influenced by powerful interests, especially large corporations and the media. Voters and governments may be unaware of an issue or of strong feelings about it and illegal action may be necessary to draw attention to it; for example, illegal action draws attention to cruelty to farm and laboratory animals, which the public is otherwise unaware of. So, illegal actions, far from being anti-democratic, may make government more democratic by raising public awareness or by counteracting powerful interests. By remaining nonviolent and by accepting the legal penalty, civil disobedients show respect for the rule of law and for democracy. Singer's second reply to the objector's appeal to the principle of majority rule is that, although we should be reluctant to act against it, a majority may be seriously wrong. Grave wrongs are not made right by a majority's support for them.[25] So, illegal means may be justified, even in a democracy.

Questions for discussion

1   How convincing is each of the following arguments for a duty to obey the law?
    (a) Receipt of benefits from the state implies a duty to obey the law in reciprocation.
    (b) Living in a state implies consent to its laws.
    (c) Fairness requires one's obedience to the law in return for fellow citizens' obedience.

    (d) A duty to obey the law has better consequences than each
        individual deciding what morality requires.

    (e) A duty to respect others' moral rights and the institutions
        that enforce them implies a duty to obey the law.

2   Do moral rights, such as to the freedoms of religion and
    expression, establish a right to break any law that violates such
    a right?

3   In a democracy, do we have a duty not to oppose *all* unjust laws
    by illegal means?

4   Is civil disobedience justified if (a) it is to protest against viola-
    tions of equal basic liberties or equal opportunities, and (b)
    legal means of protest have been tried? Is it justified in other
    cases?

5   How might civil disobedience *strengthen* democracy?

6   Are illegal means justified whenever they are the most effec-
    tive means to right wrongs?

7   Does justified civil disobedience require accepting lawful
    arrest and penalty?

4

GLOBAL POVERTY

Facts about global poverty and affluence[1]

In rich countries there is relative poverty – some are poor relative to others who are affluent. In poor countries there is absolute poverty – people do not have enough income to meet their basic needs for food, clean water, clothing, shelter, sanitation, health services and education. Millions of people in poor countries are absolutely poor. As a result, they suffer hunger and malnutrition, which cause vulnerability to disease, from which millions, especially children, die. Thus, poverty causes high infant mortality, shorter life expectancy, stunted child development, misery and premature death for millions of people in the world today. 'Absolute poverty is probably the principal cause of human misery today.'[2]

Hunger is not caused by insufficient food production. The world produces enough food to feed everybody. However, rich countries feed most of their grain to farm animals. Most (about 90 per cent) of the calories are lost in converting grain to meat. If we stopped animal farming, the amount of food saved would be more than enough to end human hunger. Hunger is caused not by lack of food but by poverty.[3] Poor people are hungry because they cannot afford to buy the food produced by farmers in rich countries. Poor farmers cannot afford to invest to increase their productivity. Transferring money from rich to poor countries could change this.[4]

Consider these facts:[5]

- 2.8 billion people (46 per cent of world population) live below the World Bank's poverty line of $2 a day.
- 18 million each year die prematurely from poverty-related causes – one third of all human deaths, each of which could be

prevented cheaply. That's 50,000 preventable deaths every day, including 34,000 children under the age of five, or 2,000 each hour, including 1,400 children under the age of five.

- 2.8 billion (46 per cent of world population) receive 1.2 per cent of global income.
- 0.9 billion (the rich countries, 15 per cent of world population) receive 80 per cent of global income.
- Shifting a mere 1 per cent of global income from the rich countries to the poor could eradicate severe poverty worldwide.

Many people in rich countries, Thomas Pogge notes, do not see global poverty as morally important and assume that there is nothing wrong in our conduct, policies and institutions.[6] The daily death toll from global poverty, which is the equivalent of a 9/11 every two hours, is not even deemed newsworthy.

Now consider some facts about affluence. People in rich countries spend a lot on luxuries – expensive food, clothes, cars, holidays, jewellery, large houses and electronic gadgets. We could give more to help the poor without seriously harming our welfare. Yet we give very little – almost all rich countries fail to achieve even the modest UN target of giving 0.7 per cent of GNP in development aid.[7] By not giving more, we allow poor people to suffer absolute poverty, malnutrition, preventable diseases and premature death. To buy luxuries is to allow people to die.

We shall consider two kinds of moral and political response to these facts – the view that there is a duty to help the absolutely poor and the view that global poverty is an injustice, which we have a duty to end.

Is there a moral duty to help the distant poor?

Some moral and political theories can be appealed to in order to argue that there is no duty to help the poor. Some theories imply that there is a duty not to harm others but no duty to help others (except those to whom we have special obligations, such as our family and friends). One theory that implies this view is contractarianism, which conceives morality as the set of rules that rational, self-interested people would agree to. Purely from rational self-interest, we would agree to a duty not to harm each other and perhaps a duty of mutual aid, but not a duty to help distant strangers who cannot reciprocate. If starvation is not our fault, there is no duty to help.[8]

Another moral and political theory that denies that there is a moral duty to help distant strangers is libertarianism. This starts from the premise that individuals have a fundamental, natural right not to be harmed (by force, theft or fraud), but not a right to receive help. A right to receive help would violate others' rights over their property. People are entitled to whatever property they acquire from their own productive activities and from voluntary transactions. They have a right not (to be forced) to help others. Poverty and starvation violate no libertarian rights, so are not unjust.[9]

These views are vulnerable to the following objections. First, contractarianism conflates morality with rational self-interest. It takes account of other people's interests only insofar as they have the power to harm or benefit us. The mere fact that it is in our self-interest not to help the needy does not make it morally permissible not to do so. Second, against libertarianism, it may be observed that rights may be exercised rightly or wrongly. Even if there is a libertarian right not to be forced to help, refusal to help may still be wrong. Third, it may be objected that the contrast both theories draw between harming and not helping is not as morally significant as these theories assume. Letting people suffer or die is morally equivalent to harming them.[10] Fourth, the rich do harm the poor – for example, rich countries protect and subsidize their agribusiness and thus impoverish poor farmers, consume most of the world's natural resources and contribute most to atmospheric pollution and global warming. This point will be developed below in support of the view that global poverty is unjust.

Let us turn now to moral theories that can be appealed to in order to argue for a duty to help the poor. Utilitarianism (the subject of chapter 10) claims that the fundamental principle of morality is that we ought to maximize utility. Utility may be interpreted as happiness or the satisfaction of preferences or interests. Money and most goods have diminishing marginal utility, that is, the more you have, the less you gain from an increase. For example, the extra utility gained from a sum of money varies inversely with the amount of money you already have (other things being equal). Given this fact, maximizing utility requires redistribution from rich to poor – the poor would gain more utility than the rich would lose. Millions of people die from preventable causes each year. Transferring money from the rich to the poor would prevent painful deaths at comparatively little cost. According to utilitarianism, we ought to prevent those deaths; it is seriously wrong not to do so.[11]

Another theory that can be appealed to in support of a duty to help the distant poor is Kantian moral theory (the subject of chapter 11). Kant aimed to identify the supreme moral principle, which he called the Categorical Imperative. He gave two main formulations of this principle. First, the Formula of Universal Law states: 'Act only according to that maxim whereby you can at the same time will that it should become a universal law.' Kant argued that a maxim of indifference, that is, recognizing a duty not to harm others but denying a duty to help, could not be willed to be a universal law. The indifferent person may themselves need help in the future so could not will universal indifference. This argument supports a duty to help those in need. Second, the Formula of Humanity states: 'Act in such a way that you always treat humanity, whether in your own person or in the person of another, always at the same time as an end and never simply as a means.'[12] The duty to treat persons as ends entails a duty to help those who need our help. This is an imperfect duty – we have discretion over whom, how, when and where, but not whether, to help. Thomas Hill suggests the general duty to help others could be made more specific as a duty to 'help others with basic needs, at least when their need is great and the cost to us is proportionately small'.[13]

Peter Singer's argument for a duty to help the distant poor

Although Singer is a utilitarian, his argument for a duty to help the distant poor is deliberately not specifically utilitarian in order to make his view widely acceptable. Imagine, Singer says, you see a child drowning in a shallow pond; you ought to rescue her. Someone who refused to help because it wasn't their fault she was drowning would be thought monstrous. Singer proposes that a plausible principle that would support the judgement that you ought to rescue her is this:

> If it is in our power to prevent something very bad from happening, without thereby sacrificing anything of comparable moral significance, we ought to do it.[14]

Singer formulates this principle to be acceptable to non-consequentialists, that is, to those who deny consequentialist moral theory (for example, utilitarianism) according to which actions or rules are made right or wrong only by their good or bad consequences. Non-consequentialists should accept Singer's principle because the qualification about not 'sacrificing anything of comparable moral significance' means that this principle cannot lead to serious violations of individual rights or other injustices, as means to prevent bad events. This contrasts with Peter Unger's act-utilitarian view that, when necessary to reduce serious suffering such as absolute poverty, it is morally right to do what is typically wrong (for example, lying, breaking a promise, cheating or stealing).[15]

Singer's principle applies not just to the rare chance to save a drowning child but to the everyday opportunity to save starving children. The principle implies that we all have an obligation to help the absolutely poor, just as we have an obligation to rescue a drowning child. Singer's principle denies that helping is 'praiseworthy to do, but not wrong to omit'. Helping is something 'everyone ought to do'; it is wrong not to. Most people in rich countries have income they could use to reduce absolute poverty without giving up basic necessities. People could and should forgo luxuries to save hungry people. Choosing to spend money on luxuries is choosing to let people die.

Singer considers various objections to his argument. First, his qualification of 'comparable moral significance' is vague.[16] However, it is deliberately vague – his principle and its application to poverty are designed to be widely acceptable, not only to utilitarians, so he allows each of us to fill in our own version of what is morally significant. On any serious account of moral significance, most people in rich countries spend money on things that are not comparable with saving lives. Different accounts of moral significance affect how much help we ought to give, not whether we have a duty to do so.[17]

A common second objection to Singer's view is that we should look after our own families and then the poor in our own country, rather than the distant poor. In reply, Singer agrees that parents do have special obligations to their children – to feed, clothe and educate them. But their wants for luxuries are less urgent than the needs of the absolutely poor. Greater need takes priority.[18] Similarly, we have a special obligation to our fellow citizens to eliminate relative poverty, but we also have a duty to eliminate absolute poverty (wherever it occurs), which is more urgent. We could and should do both.[19]

A third objection is that helping the poor now will result in more poor people being born and thus bring about more poverty in future. In order to prevent even greater suffering, we should let the poor die.[20] This assumes that overpopulation is the cause of absolute poverty and hunger. This is mistaken. The world produces enough food to feed its population. Hunger is caused not by overpopulation but by poverty, by wastefully converting grain into meat, and by rich countries' policies of protecting and subsidizing their agribusiness. Nonetheless, global population is a serious problem. However, absolute poverty causes a high birth rate. As living standards rise above a certain level, birth rates fall. Education, health care and better opportunities for women also reduce the birth rate. So, helping poor countries' development reduces population growth. Singer advocates designing aid to promote economic and social development – higher productivity, better health care, contraception, housing and education. If a poor country's government's policies make aid ineffective, it is better directed elsewhere.[21]

A fourth objection is that overseas aid is a government responsibility. Charity allows government to escape its responsibilities. Singer agrees that governments should give much more aid – that is the surest way of increasing total aid and would share the cost fairly (according to ability to pay). But individuals should give too. Individuals' donations demonstrate public concern about world poverty and thus encourage governments to give more. We should campaign, Singer says, for more public and more private aid, and for fairer international trading arrangements. These are not alternatives.[22]

A fifth objection is that the obligation to help the poor is too demanding. In reply, it may be observed that to forgo luxuries is far less demanding than to forgo necessities. The obligation to help the poor may be demanding on the affluent, but denial of the obligation is much more demanding on the poor. To forgo luxuries to help the hungry is not too demanding. 'We can all give much more than we do give.'[23]

A sixth objection is that each person in the rich countries should give only their fair share of aid and not give more to make up for non-contributors. Taxation for aid is the fairest way. Singer's reply is that, since many people are not doing their fair share, children will die preventably unless we do more than our fair share, so we ought to do more than our fair share.[24] If one can save a life at little cost, the fact that others fail to help does not justify one's failure to do so.[25]

How much should we give? Strictly, according to Singer's principle, we ought to give until giving any more would sacrifice something of moral significance comparable to absolute poverty. However, allowing for our natural inclination to give priority to self-interest, Singer seeks a less stringent standard. He has made various suggestions. He proposes that people in rich countries could give at least 10 per cent of their income. Poor families may be unable to do so. Affluent people could and should give much more. But people with average incomes in rich countries ought to give 10 per cent to reduce absolute poverty. This 'is the minimum we ought to do, and we do wrong if we do less'.[26] In a later article, addressing Americans, Singer says that each household should give all money not required for necessities: 'whatever money you're spending on luxuries, not necessities, should be given away'.[27] Recognizing that this may be so demanding as to be counterproductive, Singer advocates a public policy of affluent people giving at least 1 per cent of income as the minimum donation, one's fair share of global responsibility, failure to do which is seriously morally wrong, but we ought to give much more.[28]

Richard Arneson considers various attempts to place moral limits on the duty to help, rejects them and accepts Singer's principle. Nevertheless, he says, the intuitive recoil from its demandingness remains. In response, he distinguishes between what is morally right and wrong and what is morally obligatory and forbidden. Helping the absolutely poor at significant cost to oneself is right and failing to do so is wrong. However, given our natural inclination to favour ourselves and our family, it is very hard to adhere to Singer's principle, and failure to do so fully is excusable and so not blameworthy. Making moral obligations too demanding may alienate some people altogether and so produce worse results than a less demanding standard. The optimal level of obligation is the one that would have the best results in practice, but it is unlikely that people should be obliged to do what is right, which is what in theory would have the best consequences. Nevertheless, affluent people are obliged to give 'enormously more than they do at present' to relieve absolute poverty, misery and premature death, and failure to do so is blameworthy.[29]

Global poverty as injustice

Another kind of moral and political response to global poverty and the extreme inequality of income and wealth is to argue that they are an injustice. This view implies that redistribution of income from rich to poor is not only a humanitarian duty, as Singer argues. Rather, the poor have a right to such redistribution. Justice demands it. It is a matter not of rich societies giving away money that rightfully belongs to them, but of transferring money from those to whom it does not rightfully belong to those to whom it does.

One reason for regarding absolute poverty as an injustice is that human rights are a minimum requirement of justice, and poverty violates, threatens and restricts human rights. The Universal Declaration of Human Rights (UDHR)[30] includes a right to a standard of living adequate for health and well-being (article 25), which absolute poverty violates, and the right to life (article 3), which absolute poverty threatens. Absolute poverty also restricts the exercise of other rights in the UDHR: the rights to freedom of movement and residence, to marry and found a family, to own property, to free choice of employment, to just and favourable conditions of work, to education, to impart ideas through the media and to participate in political activity (articles 13, 16, 17, 19, 21, 23, 26). The poor may have these rights in a formal, legal sense, but may be unable to exercise them. By violating, threatening and restricting human rights, absolute poverty is unjust.

Who has the duties corresponding to human rights? The UDHR is addressed primarily to governments. It provides minimum standards for how governments are to treat their citizens, 'a common standard of achievement for all peoples and all nations' (Preamble). It also states that 'Everyone is entitled to a social and international order in which the rights and freedoms set forth in this Declaration can be fully realized' (article 28). This implies that international organizations, policies and practices too are responsible for realizing human rights.

Thomas Pogge notes three kinds of reasons that may be given for the view that global poverty is an injustice. First, historical injustices (conquest, plunder, imperialism, colonialism, slavery) are major causes of present global inequality. As a result of them, the societies that perpetrated them became, and remain, rich, and the societies that were victims of them became, and mostly remain, poor. These facts refute the argument that present global inequality is not unjust because it results from a history of voluntary actions. Second, the rich use most of the world's natural resources and thus exclude the poor from their fair share. These facts refute the argument that present global inequality is not unjust because it might have resulted, counterfactually, from a history of voluntary actions. Third, global institutions and policies, imposed by rich states, cause absolute poverty and thus cause those human rights violations. These facts show that absolute poverty is unjust because it is a violation of human rights that preventably and foreseeably results from institutions and policies to which there are feasible and reasonable alternatives that would eradicate much poverty. All three approaches may support the view that extreme global inequality and massive avoidable poverty are unjust, and justice demands reforms to redistribute global income.[31]

Pogge develops the third argument, that global institutions and policies, imposed largely by rich states, cause global poverty. Rich societies are thus causally and morally responsible for much global poverty. A common objection to this view is the observation that poverty is mainly caused by national factors – bad (incompetent, corrupt, oppressive, tyrannical) governments, indifferent to their poor. Of course, a country's government, institutions and policies are important determinants of its national income and its distribution. However, in response to this objection it must be asked: why do so many poor countries have bad governments? Pogge argues that these national factors, which are the proximate causes of poverty, are themselves caused by global institutions and policies, which are thus a fundamental cause of poverty. He identifies the following global institutions and policies as causes of bad government in poor countries and thus of global poverty.[32]

- International recognition of dictatorships: Whoever rules a country is internationally recognized as the legitimate government, regardless of how it came to power, how it exercises power and whether it is supported or opposed by the population. The practice of recognizing whoever has effective power in a territory as the legitimate government affirms the principle that might is right.[33]
- The international resource privilege: The rulers of a country are internationally recognized as having the right to dispose of the country's natural resources (for example, oil, diamonds and other minerals). When they sell resources, the buyer is legally recognized worldwide as the legitimate owner. If an armed gang takes control of a warehouse or an oil depot, they are not recognized as the legitimate owners; if they sell the contents, the buyer is not legally recognized as the legitimate owner. However, if an armed group takes control of a whole country, they are internationally recognized as the legitimate owner of its resources, and companies that buy them are internationally recognized as legitimate owners; their ownership is protected by the courts and police in all other states.[34] This policy provides a powerful incentive for coups and civil wars in resource-rich countries. Whoever takes power, by whatever means, is enriched. Dictatorships do not depend on popular support and so do not pursue economic development or tackle poverty. It is often observed that resource-rich countries are especially liable to coups, civil wars, dictatorships, incompetent government, corruption and low economic growth. (Africa, the Middle East and South-East Asia provide many examples.) It is because of the international resource privilege that this is so. This is why resource-rich countries tend to be poverty-stricken. Without the international resource privilege, natural resources would not handicap democracy, economic

growth and the eradication of poverty.[35] In the colonial era, rich countries gained control of natural resources such as oil directly, by military force and direct rule, but now do so indirectly, by paying local dictators who control natural resources by military force.

Who benefits from the international resource privilege? Rich countries benefit by ensuring a secure supply of natural resources, irrespective of who is in power, how they gained power, how they rule and how unpopular they are. Rich countries' corporations benefit, since they acquire legally recognized rights of ownership of the resources they buy from dictators. The dictators benefit, since they enrich themselves. Who is harmed? The people of resource-producing countries – they suffer coups and civil wars and tyrannical and corrupt government, their natural resources are taken but they do not receive the proceeds.[36]

- The international borrowing privilege: Whoever is recognized as the legitimate government is conferred with the privilege to borrow in the country's name, thus imposing the obligation to repay on the whole country. This provides another lucrative incentive to coups and civil wars. It enables dictators to buy arms for repression and to buy the support of the army. Many poor countries have huge debt burdens which previous dictators incurred, and which rich countries' banks and governments insist they repay. Who benefits from this policy? Rich countries' banks gain profitable business from lending to dictators. Other firms profit from selling them arms and luxuries. Rich countries' governments gain financially-dependent allies. Dictators enrich themselves. Who is harmed? The people of indebted countries, who have to repay the debts.

- Rich countries' governments have permitted, and even encouraged by tax deductibility, their companies' bribery of foreign officials, to win exports. This encourages corrupt and wasteful government in poor countries, indifferent to their people's needs.[37]

- Rich countries' lucrative sale of arms to poor countries facilitates repression, fuels civil wars and diverts funds from tackling poverty.

- Rich states use their vastly superior bargaining power to negotiate international economic treaties that favour rich, rather than poor, countries.[38]

- Rich countries protect their own agribusiness by excluding cheaper products of poor farmers. They subsidize their own agribusiness, so poor farmers cannot compete even in their own countries. They thus impoverish poor farmers.

So, Pogge argues, the national factors that cause poverty are themselves largely caused by the policies of the rich states. Rich countries want natural resources such as oil and so recognize, finance and arm any regime that controls them. This produces bad government and poverty in those countries. Rich countries protect and promote their own companies' interests despite the harm to the interests of the poor. Rich countries' policies thus cause severe harm to the global poor. Preventable premature deaths from poverty-related causes over 15 years exceed the combined death toll from all the wars, civil wars, genocides and other repression of the entire twentieth century. Rich countries are thus 'guilty of the largest [not the gravest] crime against humanity ever committed'.[39]

The moral debate over whether affluent societies have an obligation to help the global poor ignores the fact that affluent societies impose, support and benefit from global institutions and policies that substantially cause their poverty, and thus millions of preventable deaths each year, and thus harm the poor. This is a grave injustice, which we have a duty to work to change.[40]

In response to Pogge's argument, it may be argued that we have a duty to help the needy independently of whether our state has contributed to causing their poverty, and independently of whether their poverty is unjust. If poverty is not caused by our policies (for example, starvation in North Korea), we still have a duty to help. If dire need is due to natural circumstances, hence not unjust, we still have a duty to help. The mere fact of absolute poverty, together with Singer's principle, entails a duty to help, irrespective of whether we caused it and of whether it is unjust. It may be concluded that these two moral and political responses to global poverty are not mutually exclusive or even opposed to one another. There is a duty to help the poor and a duty to work to end injustice.

Questions for discussion

1 Is there a moral duty to help the poor?
2 'If it is in our power to prevent something very bad from happening, without thereby sacrificing anything of comparable moral importance, we ought to do it.' Do you accept Singer's principle?
3 Should almost everyone in rich countries give at least 10 per cent of their income to help the absolutely poor? Should we give away all money not required for necessities?
4 Are global poverty and extreme inequality an injustice?
5 How do rich countries' policies cause global poverty?
6 Is global poverty a matter of humanitarianism or of justice, or both?

5

LIBERTY

The value of freedom or liberty (I shall use the terms interchangeably) is often appealed to in moral and political discourse. People with diverse moral and political views value freedom. However, the idea of freedom is interpreted in various ways. This chapter looks at some leading philosophers on liberty. We begin with John Stuart Mill's advocacy of individual liberty, consider his utilitarian case for freedom and an alternative, contractualist argument, and which freedoms are especially important. We then turn to two influential analyses of the concept of liberty: Isaiah Berlin's and Gerald MacCallum's. Examples illustrate how MacCallum's analysis clarifies disputes over the meaning of liberty. His analysis is then applied to competing political views of the relationship between the state – especially the welfare state – and freedom.

John Stuart Mill on liberty

John Stuart Mill's *On Liberty* (1859) sets out the classic case for liberty. Mill is concerned with the limits of the power that society and the state may legitimately exercise over the individual (chapter I, paragraph 1). Democracy attempts to limit the power of rulers to what the community or its representatives consent to (I, 2). However, 'limitation ... of the power of government over individuals loses none of its importance' in a democracy, because a majority may oppress a minority; society must guard against 'the tyranny of the majority' (I, 4).

Society may tyrannize individuals not only by laws but also, Mill claims, by 'the tyranny of the prevailing opinion and feeling'. Society tends to impose its ideas and practices on dissenters and thus fetters the development of their individuality (I, 5). So it is vital to establish the limit to the legitimate interference of society with individual independence (I, 5).

Law and public opinion must impose some rules, but 'what these rules should be is the principal question in human affairs' (I, 6). Mill proposes a principle to govern society's control of the adult individual, whether by laws or by the 'coercion of public opinion' (I, 9):

> That principle is, that the sole end for which mankind are warranted, individually or collectively, in interfering with the liberty of action of any of their number, is self-protection. That the only purpose for which power can be rightfully exercised over any member of a civilised community, against his will, is to prevent harm to others. His own good, either physical or moral, is not a sufficient warrant. He cannot rightfully be compelled to do or forbear because it will be better for him to do so, because it will make him happier, because, in the opinions of others, to do so would be wise, or even right. These are good reasons for remonstrating with him, or reasoning with him, or persuading him, or entreating him, but not for compelling him...
>
> (I, 9)

The individual is accountable to society for actions and omissions that may harm the interests of others, and *may* (not must) be subject to social or legal punishment; but is not accountable for actions or omissions that concern only his own interests (V, 2, 3; I, 11). In conduct that concerns only himself, 'his independence is, of right, absolute. Over himself, over his own body and mind, the individual is sovereign' (I, 9). (Chapter 6, on liberty-limiting principles, discusses Mill's principle, which permits coercion to prevent harm to others but not to oneself, and his idea that the individual is sovereign, along with other proposed reasons to limit freedom.)

So for Mill conduct that directly affects only oneself and consenting others is the domain of liberty (I, 12). It includes, first, liberty of conscience, thought, feeling and opinion on all subjects, and the liberty of expressing opinions. Second, it 'requires liberty of tastes and pursuits; of framing the plan of our life to suit our own character; of doing as we like' as long as we do not harm others. Third, this liberty of each individual implies the liberty to unite voluntarily for any purpose unharmful to others (I, 12).

A society is free to the extent that these freedoms of expression, harmless action and association exist. 'The only freedom which deserves the name, is that of pursuing our own good in our own way', consistent with others' similar freedom. Humankind gains more by tolerating 'each other to live as seems good to themselves, than by compelling each to live as seems good to the rest' (I, 13).

In support of liberty of thought and discussion, Mill argues that no opinion should be suppressed, for two reasons. First, because we can never be sure that an opinion is false. Every age has held opinions later deemed false and many opinions now accepted will be rejected in future. Unrefuted opinions may be assumed to be true only if there is complete liberty to disprove them. Free discussion is necessary to rectify mistaken opinions and practices. Second, even if we could be sure that an opinion is false, stifling expression of it would still be an evil because it would deprive everyone of consideration of it (II, 1–5). So, everyone ought to be free to form and express their opinions (III, 1).

People should also be free to act on their opinions. With regard to actions that concern only oneself, the same reasons that support freedom of opinion support freedom of action. In relation to actions as well as opinions, diversity is good: 'there should be different experiments of living', from which all can learn about the worth of different activities and ways of life (III, 1).

In things that primarily concern oneself, 'individuality should assert itself'. Individuality is a principal ingredient of human happiness and of individual and social progress (III, 1). For the individual, liberty is valuable because the free development of their individuality is essential to their well-being (III, 2). Conformity to custom, even a good one, does not develop the faculties of observation, reasoning, judgement, discernment or self-control, which are exercised, and thus developed, only in making choices (III, 3, 4). For society, cultivating individuality makes human life 'rich, diversified, and animating' (III, 9); uniformity of beliefs and practices would be drab and dull. Others' liberty gives us new and better ideas, practices and taste. Liberty is the most reliable source of improvement (III, 11, 12, 17). Mill's claim that liberty produces diversity, innovation and improvement applies widely – to the arts, science, technology, the economy and politics.

In matters that concern only oneself, people should be free to act on their opinions but, Mill adds, 'at their own risk and peril', free to act 'and stand the consequences' (III, 1; IV, 3: also I, 12; V, 8). An implication of personal freedom is responsibility for one's choices and their costs, risks and consequences.

A counterpart of individual freedom is toleration of each other's opinions and harmless practices, despite one's disagreement or disapproval. Toleration, Thomas Scanlon argues, involves accepting as equals people whose practices we disapprove of, not only as possessing equal legal and political rights but also equal entitlement to define and shape society. Tolerance is valuable, he continues, because it contains inevitable disagreement over beliefs, values and ways of life within a framework of mutual respect, and expresses recognition of common and equal membership of society that is deeper than those conflicts.[1]

Mill's distinction between conduct concerning oneself only ('self-regarding') and conduct concerning others (other-regarding) may be questioned. Most actions affect other people. If someone harms their body or mind, they harm their family, they contribute less and may become a burden, and so indirectly harm others (IV, 8). Mill sometimes formulates his distinction loosely as being between actions that do or do not 'affect' others, which is a factual distinction. Elsewhere, he formulates it as being between actions that do or do not 'concern' others, which may be a normative distinction. You may be affected by conduct that is no concern of yours. Mill's reply to the objection to his distinction is that when conduct violates an obligation, it is not self-regarding. If, through extravagance, someone fails to repay a debt or to support their children, they deserve censure and perhaps punishment, but for the breach of duty, not for their extravagance. If the resources had been misdirected into prudent investment, 'the moral culpability would have been the same' (IV, 10). 'No person ought to be punished simply for being drunk, but a soldier or policeman should be punished for being drunk on duty' (IV, 10). Whenever conduct harms or endangers others, it is 'taken out of the province of liberty, and placed in that of morality or law' (IV, 10). Mill often refers loosely to the duty not to harm others' interests, but he also more carefully restricts this to interests that 'ought to be considered as rights' (IV, 3) and to harm not justified by one's own rights (IV, 6). As a utilitarian, Mill seeks to found his moral principles on the non-moral concept of utility or interests (I, 11), that is, to found an account of what is morally right on an account of what is non-morally good. However, it is noteworthy that his apparently non-moral concepts of self- and other-regarding actions presuppose an account of moral obligations and his apparently non-moral concept of harm to interests presupposes an account of moral rights.[2]

Mill claimed that his liberalism was founded on utilitarianism (I, 11), and his case for the value of liberty refers to its good consequences for individuals and for society. However, utilitarianism justifies liberty only if and insofar as liberty maximizes happiness. Mill's principle of liberty and the utilitarian principle of maximizing happiness may conflict. For example, limiting the freedom of an unpopular minority (a cultural, racial, religious, political or sexual minority) may, in certain circumstances, increase overall happiness; limiting the freedom of individuals to harm themselves (for example, by smoking) may increase their long-term happiness. Utilitarianism would prescribe limiting the freedom of minorities or individuals when it would maximize happiness.[3] Mill's liberalism thus conflicts with his utilitarianism. Mill's claim that his liberalism was founded on his utilitarianism, despite the latter's illiberal implications, seems to be a case of utilitarian arguing backwards,[4] that is, contriving a utilitarian justification for a commitment that is held independently of its supposed utilitarian justification.

Contractualism and liberty

Contractualism offers another argument for Mill's freedom of 'pursuing our own good in our own way' and tolerating 'each other to live as seems good to themselves' (within the limits of each other's rights). According to contractualism, morality is a matter of agreement; the most reasonable moral principles are those that rational and reasonable people would agree to. (Being rational is the non-moral idea of choosing effective means to one's ends; being reasonable is the moral idea of being fair to the interests of others in pursuing one's ends, and thus being ready to compromise self-interest.)[5] People disagree over what is a good way to live, because of their different beliefs and values. Such disagreement is inevitable. Despite this, rational and reasonable people could agree on the principle of freedom to live according to one's own judgements of what is good, and toleration of others' different judgements and of different ways of life that do not harm others. It would not be rational to agree to compulsion to live according to others' beliefs and values, or to prohibition of living according to one's own. Those who would deny to others freedom of harmless action could not accept denial of their own freedom to live harmlessly according to their own beliefs and values. It would not be reasonable to expect others to agree to compulsion to live according to alien beliefs and values or to prohibition of living harmlessly according to their own. The primary example of this general contractualist argument is conflicting religious, and irreligious, beliefs. No one could agree to being compelled to live according to religious beliefs that are not their own, or to their own harmless religious practices being prohibited, but people with different religious beliefs can agree on principles of religious liberty and toleration. The argument has been extended to different sexual preferences.[6] No one could accept being compelled to live according to sexual preferences that are not their own, or to prohibition of their consensual sexual preferences, but people with different sexual preferences can agree on a principle of sexual freedom and toleration among consenting adults.[7]

A crucial difference between the contractualist and Mill's arguments for liberty is this. Mill proposes a conception of the good, that is, a conception of what is valuable in human life, in which liberty and individuality are essential. But some rival conceptions of what is good for humans deny this; some conceive a good life as one that is obedient to religious authority. The contractualist argument for liberty does not offer a conception of the good. Rather, it starts from the fact that people hold diverse and conflicting conceptions of the good, for example, the Millian liberal one and religious illiberal ones. Given this diversity, contractualism seeks moral principles that reasonable persons holding diverse conceptions of the good could accept, and argues that only principles of liberty and toleration are acceptable to all reasonable and rational persons.

An implication of the contractualist argument for equal individual freedom and toleration is state neutrality on conceptions of a good way of life. If individuals are to have equal freedom to decide how to live, within legal and moral rules that define equal individual rights, the state should not intentionally promote particular beliefs, values or ways of life, or discourage others. For example, the state should not promote religion, or a particular religion, or discriminate against other beliefs, or promote heterosexuality or marriage, or discourage other lifestyles.

John Rawls and Thomas Scanlon provide contemporary examples of contractualism. Rawls's contractualism seeks moral principles that it would be rational to agree if one did not know what one's particular beliefs and values, and hence one's particular interests, are.[8] This imagined ignorance is a device to exclude one's own particular interests in order to seek principles that are impartial among persons with diverse beliefs and values. Not knowing one's particular beliefs and values, it would be rational to agree to a Millian principle of liberty to pursue one's own good in one's own harmless way and toleration of others' different harmless ways of life. It would be irrational to agree to any principle that would risk being compelled to live according to others' beliefs and values or being prohibited to live according to one's own.

In relation to laws, Rawls says that citizens exercise state power legitimately when its exercise is justifiable to fellow citizens with diverse beliefs and values. Legislative questions that concern basic questions of justice, of which liberty is one, should be settled as far as possible by principles and ideals that all free and equal citizens may reasonably be expected to endorse.[9] Given that citizens disagree over what is a good way to live, it would be unreasonable to use state power to enforce any particular conception of the good or to prohibit any other conception that does not violate other citizens' rights. However, free and equal citizens may reasonably be expected to endorse principles of liberty and toleration.

Scanlon's contractualism conceives morality as 'rules for the general regulation of behavior which no one could reasonably reject as a basis for informed, unforced general agreement'.[10] One could reasonably reject being compelled to live according to another's conception of the good way of life or being prohibited from living according to one's own (provided it would not violate others' rights). But a Millian principle that allows each the freedom 'of pursuing our own good in our own way', consistent with others' similar freedom, is not reasonably rejectable.

Which freedoms are especially important?

So far, we have mostly discussed freedom in general, but are all freedoms equally valuable? A good way to approach this question is a thought-experiment of Charles Taylor's.[11] Imagine two countries, identical in every respect except these. Country A has freedom of religion but many traffic laws (compelling people to stop at red lights, wear seat belts and crash helmets, prohibiting parking in innumerable places, and so on). Country B has no such traffic laws – its people can drive and park freely – but has a law that compels one religion's practices and forbids other religions' practices. In which country are people more free? In quantitative terms, country A has many extra restrictions, forbidding many acts, affecting everyone, everyday. Country B has only one extra law, forbidding a few acts, affecting perhaps a few people, perhaps one day a week. But country B is not more free than country A. When we compare freedoms, Taylor says, we must judge their value. What matters is not how many freedoms there are, but which freedoms. Some freedoms, of religion for example, are very important; others are comparatively trivial.

John Rawls notes that, throughout the history of democratic thought, the focus has been on achieving not liberty in general but certain specific liberties as found, for example, in declarations and bills of rights. Rawls identifies certain 'basic liberties': political liberty (the right to vote and to hold public office), the freedoms of thought, conscience, speech, association, assembly, occupation and movement; the freedoms from physical assault, psychological oppression, arbitrary arrest and arbitrary seizure; and the right to hold personal property.[12] These are the vitally important freedoms, in which all human beings have a fundamental interest. Rawls's first principle of social justice requires that each citizen be guaranteed equal basic liberties.

Analysing interpretations of liberty: how many concepts of liberty?

The word 'freedom' is used with different meanings. Isaiah Berlin and Gerald MacCallum have produced two very influential analyses of the different interpretations of liberty.

Berlin claimed that in Western social and political thought there are two broad concepts of liberty: negative and positive liberty. Negative liberty is the area within which the individual or group is or should be left to do or be what they are able to do or be, without interference by others or coercion. It is freedom from interference by others, freedom from coercion. It is concerned with the questions 'What am I free to do?' 'How far does government interfere?' 'How much am I governed?' Mill's idea of freedom to pursue one's own good in one's own way illustrates the idea of freedom from interference, of an area of private life over which the state and society must not trespass.

But there is another concept of liberty – positive liberty – which is concerned with the questions 'Who governs me?' 'Who says what I may do?' Positive liberty is the idea of self-government, self-determination or autonomy. It may be applied to the individual or to a society. An individual may have negative liberty to decide how to live, but may mindlessly conform to the dictates of custom, parents or religious authorities, and thus lack self-determination. Similarly, there is no necessary connection between negative liberty and a society's democratic self-government or positive liberty. A democracy may deprive individuals of liberties – Mill's 'tyranny of the majority' – and a dictatorship may allow its subjects personal freedom. Nevertheless, democracy provides the best guarantee of negative liberties.[13]

Berlin may have identified two very broad ideas of liberty but his analysis forces various ideas of freedom into just two concepts; in particular, his 'positive liberty' includes diverse ideas.[14] MacCallum provides a much better analysis of liberty and its various interpretations.[15]

MacCallum denies Berlin's claim that there are two kinds or concepts of freedom. There is only one: freedom is always of someone, from something, to do something. Freedom is always the same relation between three elements:

X (an agent)
is free from Y (a constraint/restriction/obstacle)
to do/omit/have/become Z (an action/condition/goal)

Any freedom is both freedom from something (a constraint) and freedom to do something. Disagreements about freedom are not about what freedom *is* but about the range of the three variables, especially about what counts as a constraint. There are many (not two) conceptions of freedom, but they are all variants of this one concept.

Competing conceptions of freedom

Some examples can illustrate the sources of different conceptions of freedom in different ideas about what counts as an X, Y or Z in MacCallum's formula.

What should count as the agent (X) – actual or ideally rational persons? One conception of freedom is that 'true freedom' consists not in doing what one actually wants to do but in control by one's ideally rational self.[16] On this conception, stopping someone from doing what they want to do does not restrict their freedom when, if they were ideally rational, they would not want to do it. For example, it might be said that a law against using heroin does not restrict freedom because a rational person would not want to risk addiction. Or a religious regime might say that, as its religion is the way to salvation, banning false religions does not restrict freedom because a rational person would not want to follow a false religion. Or a one-party state might claim that, because the party represents the true interests of the people, banning other parties does not restrict freedom because rational people would not want to support a party that was against the interests of the people. On this conception of freedom, as Berlin observed,[17] the state may force you to act against your wishes in the name of your 'freedom'. These considerations suggest that agents should be conceived as actual, not ideally rational, persons.

What should count as a goal (Z) – *actual* or *possible* wants? Is freedom being allowed to do what you *actually* want to do or what you *might* want to do? Here are three reasons why possible, rather than actual, desires are what are important. First, someone who lacks options lacks freedom even if they can do what they want. For example, someone locked in a room is unfree to leave even if they want to stay. Or someone forced (for example, by a threat) to do something lacks freedom even if they would have done it anyway.[18] If only one political party is legally allowed, you lack political freedom even if you support that party. Or if you're allowed to preach only one religion, you lack religious freedom even if you don't want to preach any other religion. Second, conversely, someone who has diverse options (not merely many, if similar, options) has freedom even if they cannot do what they want. For example, you have a political freedom if you can choose among diverse political parties even if your ideal party does not exist. Similarly, you may have much freedom of speech even if you are not allowed to slander or libel someone as you wish. Third, if freedom were being allowed to do what you actually want, then adapting your wants to what is allowed, by eliminating disallowed desires, would increase your freedom.[19] For example, if you were allowed only to practise one religion or to support one political party, then cultivating the desire to do so would give you religious or political freedom. This absurdity results from conceiving freedom in terms of what you actually want to do rather than what you might want to do. So for these three reasons, freedom should be conceived as having diverse options, not just being allowed to do what you happen to want to do. Freedom (or unfreedom) is a feature of a person's situation, which is independent of their (ordinary)[20] desires.

What should count as a constraint or obstacle (Y)? This is the most interesting and controversial variable. Different conceptions of freedom often depend on different conceptions of what counts as a constraint. We will discuss various kinds of constraint, but a preliminary general point is that it is important to avoid moralized conceptions of freedom or constraints, which conflate the questions of what one *is* free to do and what one *ought* to be free to do, what *is* a constraint and what is a *justified* constraint.[21]

Physical constraints, such as handcuffs, shackles or imprisonment, uncontroversially restrict freedom by making certain actions impossible. Coercion too is almost[22] uncontroversially a constraint. Coercion occurs when something is done or not done because of lack of a reasonably acceptable alternative, not lack of any alternative (there is usually an alternative even if it is 'your money or your life'). Typically, threats make alternatives unacceptable. For example, laws that compel or prohibit, with the threat of punishment, constrain freedom, as do criminals who compel or prohibit with threats. But does public disapproval or peer pressure restrict freedom, as Mill claimed? Does poverty restrict freedom? Must constraints be external? Or can one's freedom be restricted by one's own mind? Do natural conditions restrict freedom, or only human actions and institutions?

On MacCallum's definition of freedom, anything that prevents you from doing what you might want to do can be regarded as a constraint on freedom. However, conceptions of freedom variously restrict which constraints should count.

Berlin distinguishes 'between liberty and the conditions of its exercise', for example, income, knowledge and health. Poverty, ignorance and ill-health are said to reduce the value of liberty, not liberty itself. This implies that these factors should not be counted among constraints on liberty. In Berlin's case, this restriction does not express indifference to poverty, ignorance and ill-health, or opposition to government action to combat them. On the contrary, he says that freedom is 'worth little without sufficient conditions for its active exercise'. His objection is only to describing such conditions as constraints on freedom and remedial government action as promoting freedom. Promotion of education, health and prosperity, he says, is right, but is not promotion of liberty: 'liberty is one thing, the conditions for it are another. ... Everything is what it is: liberty is liberty, not equality or fairness or justice ...'[23]

John Rawls notes that lack of means (for example, poverty or ignorance) is sometimes counted among the constraints on liberty, as defining liberty. Rawls instead thinks of these things as affecting the worth or value of the basic liberties to individuals. Everyone may have the same freedoms by law, but the worth of liberties varies with one's means (money, knowledge and authority) to achieve one's ends. Social justice, on Rawls's theory, requires equal basic liberties for all citizens. It allows unequal wealth and income, and thus allows unequal worth of those liberties. However, it requires making the worst-off group as well off as possible, which has the effect (Rawls says the aim) of maximizing the worth of the basic liberties for the least advantaged.[24]

So, Berlin and Rawls say that poverty, ignorance and ill-health affect not liberty but its value to individuals. They thus imply that these things should not be counted as constraints on liberty. The thought behind this may be a distinction between not being *allowed* by other people (for example, by law) to do what you might want to do and not being *able* (due to poverty, ignorance or ill-health) to do so. The former, but not the latter, is unfreedom. (Some who make this distinction are indifferent to disabling

social conditions and oppose enabling policies, but Berlin and
Rawls oppose only their conception and description in terms of
freedom.) Laws are morally and politically important constraints
on liberty, especially on the basic liberties, but other constraints,
even if less important, are still constraints. So, it may be objected,
it is artificial to exclude them. On a broader conception of constraints, this exclusion obscures the fact that you are really (not
merely legally) free to do something only if you are both allowed
to do it and able to do it. Poverty, ignorance or ill-health can each
disable you from doing innumerable things, and thus make you
unfree to do them. Ordinary language permits use of 'unfree' to
include inability due to lack of resources; the poor may be said to
be unfree to do innumerable things, despite their legal freedom
to do them. Inability due to poverty is a limitation on freedom
and, conversely, enabling by increasing resources is a means to
enlarge freedom. Similarly, freedom of occupation, or freedom to
work at all, can be restricted not only by law, but also by prejudice
or economic conditions. Social facts other than the law can limit
freedom.

Some conceptions of freedom count only external factors as
constraints. However, a broader conception accepts that internal
factors such as ignorance, false belief or inability can constrain
freedom, implying that education can increase freedom. Adam
Swift argues that education can increase personal freedom.
Education directly develops abilities to do things and indirectly
abilities to get jobs that require those skills, and thus increases
freedom by giving more options. Education also develops critical abilities and thus enables better choice and more control over
one's life.[25] This is especially true of critical reflection on ethical
values, on what is good and what is right, which enables better
decisions about the most important choices.[26] Liberal philosophy
of education has long regarded education as increasing freedom
of thought and action by removing the constraints of ignorance,
superstition and prejudice, and it is artificial to exclude these constraints because they are internal.

If constraints can be internal, can one's own desires restrict
one's freedom? Charles Taylor[27] uses the distinction between
first-order desires, which are ordinary desires, and second-order
desires, which are desires about our first-order desires. While we
want, or accept, most of our wants, some we may prefer not to

have – for example, addictions, neurotic obsessions, compulsions, cravings and phobias. Our ordinary wants do not meaningfully restrict our freedom, but wants that we would prefer not to have may be counted as constraints on our freedom. They force us to act, or not act, in certain ways. Treatment that frees someone from addiction or obsession frees them to do many things. Since wants that we do not repudiate should not count as a constraint on freedom, one's desire to comply with one's moral or religious beliefs should not be regarded as a restriction on one's freedom of action. But wants that one does not desire may be counted as internal constraints on freedom.

It is argued that natural conditions should not count as obstacles to freedom, only human actions and institutions should. We are naturally unable to do innumerable things, and it would be unhelpful to say that we are unfree to do them. Constraints on freedom should be restricted to human deeds and exclude natural conditions. However, an objection to this is that an obstacle restricts your freedom (for example, of movement) whether it is natural or human. This exclusion obscures the fact that technology that removes natural constraints enlarges options and thus freedom. It might be replied that such technology increases ability, not freedom, but this would be a false contrast because increasing ability is the means by which it increases freedom. In ordinary language it is said, for example, that effective contraception increases sexual freedom, that improved means of transport increases freedom to travel, that the internet increases freedom of communication, and that reproductive technology increases infertile people's freedom to have children. Technology that removes natural constraints enlarges human freedom. The development of human productive power, as Marx observed, enables the enlargement of human freedom. So, natural conditions may be counted as constraints on freedom.

The broad conception of constraints is controversial, but a simple example illustrates that ordinary language permits it. A person lacks the option of walking to a mountain summit and so lacks the freedom to do so if they are imprisoned, prevented by an effectively enforced trespass law, lack or cannot afford the necessary transport, do not know the route or are bed-ridden or agoraphobic. They are unfree to do it if boulders block the only route, whether they were placed there by the landowner or fell there naturally. Constraints on freedom can, then, include physical constraints, coercion, poverty, ignorance, ill health, phobias, and human and natural obstacles. Conversely, options, and hence freedom, are enlarged by release from imprisonment, a legal right to roam, money, knowledge, health or removal of a phobia or an obstacle.

The question of what should count as a constraint on freedom is controversial but is a matter of definition, about which we should be relaxed. A range of conceptions of freedom results from admitting a more or less wide range of constraints. Different conceptions may be appropriate in different contexts. For moral and political purposes, it is appropriate to focus on social rather than internal or natural factors that constrain freedom. These include other people's actions, such as coercive threats, and laws. Mill also includes others' opinions, which inhibit or enforce actions. Social constraints also include the distribution of income, wealth, education, employment, health and health care, since the distribution of these resources produces a distribution of freedoms.

Freedom and the state

Conflicting political views over the relationship between freedom and the state, especially the welfare state, illustrate how different ideas about what counts as a constraint (MacCallum's Y factor) generate different conceptions of freedom. The Left and the Right in politics each appeals to freedom, but mean different things.

A right-wing view says that only coercion, particularly by the state, limits freedom. Friedrich Hayek 'defined freedom as the absence of coercion' and so 'the only infringement on [freedom] is coercion'.[28] On this view, if there is no law against something, and nobody is forcibly preventing you from doing it, then you are free to do it. This is a narrow conception of the constraints on freedom. Its political implication is that, to promote freedom, we should minimize government regulation (for example, health and safety, environmental, anti-discrimination and minimum wage laws) and minimize state welfare provision in order to minimize taxation (which is coercive).

The Left objects that coercion is not the only constraint on freedom. People may be prevented from doing what they might want to do by poverty or involuntary unemployment, or by lack of resources such as education or health. This is a much broader conception of constraints. On this view, freedom is a matter both of what you are allowed to do and of what you are able to do. Freedom must be not merely formal or nominal (that is, no law compelling or prohibiting something) but effective or real – a matter of what you are able, not merely allowed, to do. For example, if you lack the money to do something, you are not really free to do it even though no law prohibits it – thus, poverty limits freedom. Similarly, if there are no jobs available, you are not free to work, even though no one is preventing you from working. Similarly, lack of education or ill-health may prevent you from doing things you might want to do. Thus you may be unfree to do things even though there is no law against doing them.

The political implication of this view is that promoting freedom requires government action, not the minimal state but the welfare state, because this can enable people and thus increase their freedom. State provision of employment, social security, education, housing and health care enables people to do things they would otherwise be unable to do and thus increases their freedom. Government regulation can also enable freedom from unsafe and unhealthy working conditions, pollution, discrimination and very low pay.

The Right replies that the Left's objection confuses freedom, which it defines as the absence of interference, and ability. Poverty diminishes ability but not freedom.

Gerald Cohen's rejoinder is that, even on the Right's definition of freedom as the absence of interference, which contrasts freedom with ability, poverty restricts freedom. Money confers freedom of access to the innumerable goods and services that are for sale or for hire. Lack of money – poverty – imposes lack of that freedom. Without payment, access is prevented (by owners, the police and the courts). Lack of money to pay for something is not inability to have it; it is being prevented, by law, from having it. The law prevents non-payers from doing what they would otherwise be able to do.[29] So, the distribution of money (and, therefore, the distribution of saleable wealth) is a distribution of freedom of access to goods and services.

In relation to property in general, not just money, owners are free, and non-owners are unfree, to use their property. Again, what

prevents non-owners is not in ability but the law. So, the distribution
of wealth is a distribution of freedom and unfreedom.[30]

On the Left's view, the welfare state's redistribution of resources
(from the more to the less affluent) is a redistribution of freedom.
Taxpayers lose some freedom to dispose of their money as they
would choose, but beneficiaries of state-provided social security,
education and health care gain freedom to do things they would
not otherwise be free to do. Do the gains and losses cancel each
other out, with no overall effect on freedom? No, because the freedom to satisfy basic needs is more valuable than the freedom to
satisfy less important wants. Thus, state welfare provision, despite
necessitating taxation, can promote freedom.

Questions for discussion

1 Is liberty valuable to individuals? If so, why?
2 Are other people's liberties valuable to us? If so, why?
3 Which freedoms are particularly valuable?
4 What should count as a restriction on freedom:
   (a) Coercion (for example, by laws)?
   (b) Public disapproval?
   (c) Poverty?
   (d) Involuntary unemployment?
   (e) Lack of education?
   (f) Ill health?
   (g) One's own thoughts (desires, cravings, fears, phobias)?
5 How does education increase freedom?
6 How does the welfare state enlarge freedom?
7 How does the welfare state restrict freedom?
8 Overall, does the welfare state reduce or increase freedom?

6

LIBERTY-LIMITING PRINCIPLES

Should the law prohibit prostitution, pornography, homosexuality, sadomasochism, consensual polygamy, dangerous drugs, consensual maiming or consensual killing? Should the law compel the wearing of seatbelts or motorcycle helmets? Or should adults be legally free to decide for themselves about such matters? Such controversial laws raise the question of what justifies laws that limit liberty. In chapter 5 it was suggested that freedom is valuable to individuals and to society, and that reasonable people who disagree about what is a good way to live could nonetheless agree on a principle of individual freedom to pursue one's own good in one's own way and toleration of each other's harmless ways of life. Because freedom is so valuable, there is a presumption in favour of liberty, that is, the burden of proof rests with those who would limit freedom. Although it is debatable what should count as a constraint on freedom, one thing that uncontroversially limits freedom is the law, because it prohibits and compels actions with the threat of punishment. What kinds of actions may the law rightly prohibit or compel? What kinds of reasons should support laws that limit liberty? Liberty-limiting principles are proposed answers to these questions. A liberty-limiting principle proposes a reason for coercive laws. It is neither a necessary reason, if more than one liberty-limiting principle is valid, nor a sufficient reason, because freedom, privacy or other values may outweigh it. The reasons we shall consider are harm to others, offence, harm to self, harmless wrongdoing, and, briefly, provision of public goods, and social justice.[1]

Harm to others

Joel Feinberg's harm principle states that it is always a good reason in support of penal legislation that it is probably necessary to prevent harm to persons other than the person whose action is prohibited or compelled.

Virtually everyone agrees that prohibition of causing or risking harm to others is a good reason for restricting liberty, that it is right for the law to prohibit and thus prevent serious harm to others – for example, laws against assault, murder, theft, dangerous driving. John Stuart Mill thought that the *only* purpose for which power can be rightfully exercised over the individual is to prevent harm to others, by action or by inaction (see chapter 5, first section).

To harm someone is to impair their interests.[2] People have important interests in their bodies, personal relationships, property, privacy and reputation. Not all harms to interests hurt, that is, cause physical or mental pain. One can be harmed but not know about it and so not be hurt. One can be unaware of theft of one's property, of harm to one's reputation, of adultery or other deceit, or of invasion of one's privacy by a snooper. These are harms to one's interests independently of one's awareness of them. So, it is not true that what you don't know can't harm you. You can be harmed without knowing about it. All hurts are harms but not all harms are hurts.[3]

Only harmful acts that are also morally wrong may justifiably be legally prohibited. Not all harm is wrong; some harms are justified by other principles. For example, just punishment, fair competition (for example, for jobs, customers or lovers), self-defence or defence of others from unjustified harm, truthful harm to reputation, or harm or risk to which one has voluntarily consented (for example, surgery, boxing). The harm principle applies only to wrongful harms. Both Mill and Feinberg restrict it to harms to others' rights.

According to Mill, actions that harm others' rights, which may be prohibited and punished, include deception, unfair use of advantage and failure to protect from injury. The individual may also be compelled to perform acts that benefit others, such as giving evidence in court, bearing their fair share of burdens and helping others by saving a life or protecting the defenceless. For Mill, then, both action and inaction can cause wrongful, prohibitable harm (I, 11; IV, 3, 6).[4] Mill sometimes suggests that his harm-prevention principle justifies only prohibiting conduct that causes harm, but his examples confirm that it also justifies compelling conduct to help others and to co-operate.[5] Feinberg similarly argues that the harm principle covers non-consensual, but not consensual, exploitation and failure to prevent harm.[6] Mill's and Feinberg's harm-prevention principles would permit laws that require easy rescue of someone in danger.

Feinberg distinguishes between private and public wrongful harm. Private harm is harm to specific individuals (for example, assault, theft); public harm is harm to institutions that are in the public interest. Examples of public harm are failing to give evidence in court (Mill), perjury, contempt of court, counterfeiting, tax evasion and social security fraud. These harm institutions that are in the public interest, so they indirectly harm everyone collectively.[7]

Preventing wrongful private or public harm is always a good reason for legislation, according to the harm principle, but not always decisive. Prohibition reduces liberty and enforcing laws reduces privacy and costs public resources, so not every wrongful harm ought to be illegal. Legislators must take account of the seriousness of the harm, its probability and the value of the harm-risking activity.[8] Preventing serious harm to others, or the risk of it, may justify legal limits even on the basic liberty of freedom of expression. Mill thought that expressing an opinion in a way likely to incite violence is prohibitable and punishable (III, 1). Similarly, preventing harm justifies laws against defamation, fraud and conspiracy to commit crime, which limit freedom of expression. The legal prohibition, in Britain, of incitement to racial hatred is justifiable because such incitement risks serious harm to individuals and to society. Similarly, prohibition of violent pornography may be justified on the ground that it may make violent sex crimes more likely; although the causal link is unproven, the seriousness of the risk outweighs the value, if any, of the material.

So, prevention of serious, probable wrongful harm to others is a good reason for laws that limit liberty.

Offence

Feinberg's offence principle states that it is always a good reason in support of a proposed criminal prohibition that it is probably a necessary and effective way to prevent serious offence. Offence refers to unpleasant mental states such as disgust, shock or embarrassment.

Some experiences cause offence and, for this reason, imposition of them may be morally wrong. The conduct or material need not itself be morally wrong, but the imposition of the experience of it on unwilling victims is wrong and so is a candidate for legal prohibition. Examples include sexual activity, defecation and, perhaps, nudity in public, prostitutes soliciting in a residential area, public displays of pornography, drunkenness in public and public display of symbols of mass murder (Nazi or Ku Klux Klan regalia). It might be thought that offence is never a good reason to limit liberty, but few people will think that none of these examples ought to be legally prohibited. (If unconvinced, see Feinberg's lurid examples.)[9]

In contrast, knowledge, not perception, of supposed wrong-doing is sometimes said to cause offence. For example, some people say they are offended by bare knowledge of unwitnessed homosexuality, racism or pornography. However, in such cases the action is held to be wrong independently of being witnessed and independently of the offence resulting from knowledge of it. Offence is not the reason for the action being held to be wrong. In such cases, the argument for prohibition really appeals not to offence but to harm to others or self or to harmless wrongdoing. The offence principle is concerned with things that are held to be wrong because they cause offence, not with things that cause offence because they are held to be wrong.

Mill said that preventing harm to others is the only justification for coercion, but he must have included offence within harm because he accepts that many acts that are permissible may be prohibited from being done in public, for example, indecent acts (V, 7). Since harm is an impairment of an interest, and people have an interest in not being offended, offence is a kind of harm.[10] However, offence lacks the objective character of harm to a person's body, property, privacy or reputation. Much, but not all, offence is subjective in that it depends on the individual's beliefs and attitudes. This difference warrants its separate treatment.

Many things offend people. Some people claim to be offended by books, magazines, plays, films or television programmes they have not seen. Some religious believers are offended by anything that mocks, challenges or even questions their religious beliefs. Some patriots are offended by desecration of their national flag. Some racists are offended by 'interracial' couples. Some people are offended by homosexuality. People who are offended often demand that the offending conduct or material be legally prohibited. They may assert a 'right not to be offended'. This obviously threatens other people's liberties. Preventing offence must be balanced against liberty.

In applying the offence principle, Feinberg argues, legislators and judges should weigh the seriousness of the offence against the reasonableness of the offending conduct.[11] The seriousness of an offence is determined by four factors. First, its intensity and duration; intense and prolonged offence is obviously a stronger candidate for prohibition than trivial or fleeting offence. Second, the seriousness of offence depends on how widespread it is likely to be. (In assessing the offensiveness of an insult to a particular individual or to a particular racial, ethnic or religious group, one must consider the offensiveness of a similar insult to others.) Offence need not be so widespread as to be universal within a society, as Feinberg once thought.[12] The standard of universality would not protect particular racial, ethnic or religious groups from offensive insults. Third, the seriousness of offensive conduct or material depends on how avoidable it is. Offensive conduct or material in public places is not easily avoidable, so may be prohibited in such places and restricted to private or designated places. Those who would be offended by, say, nudity, sex, prostitution or pornography can then avoid those places. Similarly, people who would be offended by them can easily avoid particular books, magazines, plays, films, television programmes and websites, so their potential offence (because they contain nudity or sex or because they question, challenge or mock religious beliefs) is not a good reason for censorship. Fourth, if offence is voluntarily experienced or risked (campaigners for censorship sometimes deliberately view the material they will be offended by), then it is not wrongful offence, because the offended person consented to it.

The reasonableness of the offending conduct is determined by its importance to the actor and to society, by the availability of less offensive places for it and by whether the offence is deliberate or unintended. The fundamental importance of freedom of expression, to both the producer and consumers of material, and the threat to everyone's freedom of expression of giving the state the power to censor material that it deems offensive, outweigh the interest in prohibition of offensive material that is easily avoided. In relation to offensive opinions, Feinberg judges that the importance of the individual's interest in the free expression of their opinion and the importance of the public interest in open discussion (of, for example, religious, moral, social and political questions) are such that these interests can never be outweighed by the offensiveness of an opinion. However, an offensive way of publicly expressing an opinion, given that less offensive alternatives are available, may be a candidate for legal prohibition – for example, public desecration of a religious symbol or public display of a racist symbol.[13]

So, prohibition of the imposition of serious, public, unreasonable offence is a second good reason for laws that limit liberty.

Harm to self

Legal paternalism is the principle that 'it is always a good reason in support of a prohibition that it is necessary to prevent harm (physical, psychological, or economic) to the actor'.[14] Paternalism means acting like a father or parent – parents typically do not allow their children to harm or endanger themselves. Legal paternalism is the idea that the law should not allow competent adults to harm or endanger themselves, that it should limit one's liberty for one's *own* good, not to protect others from harm or offence. Examples of laws whose justification may appeal to paternalism (although there are also non-paternalist justifications) are laws that compel the wearing of seatbelts and motorcycle helmets, compulsory participation in a social insurance scheme and laws that prohibit certain drugs, voluntary euthanasia, prostitution and gambling.

Legal paternalists may argue that harm is bad and ought to be prevented. Prevention of harm to others is accepted as a good reason for coercion and this should extend to harm that one causes or risks to oneself. Anti-paternalists insist that there is a morally significant difference between harm to others and harm to oneself.

In support of legal paternalism, it may be argued that harming oneself is immoral. Derek Parfit argues that great imprudence is immoral. If someone chooses short-term benefits (for example, unhealthy or profligate behaviour) at the cost of greater long-term harms (to their health or wealth), they do not do what has the best consequences. On a consequentialist moral view this is wrong, even when the harms are borne by that person alone. Imprudence is wrong because it does not produce the best consequences. Independently of consequentialism, it could be argued that a person has special obligations to their future self. Parfit argues that we may think of our future selves as like other people. Harming one's future self is like harming another person. 'We ought not to do to our future selves what it would be wrong to do to other people.' If either of those arguments establishes that great imprudence is immoral, this could support paternalistic intervention to prevent it; for example, prohibiting smoking to protect the future self's health or enforcing saving to prevent future poverty. Nevertheless, Parfit notes, there remain the objections to paternalism that it is better to learn from one's mistakes and that others cannot know that they are mistakes.[15] So even if great imprudence is immoral, it may not justify paternalism.

Despite his utilitarianism, which would support paternalism when it would have the best consequences, Mill objects to coercing an adult for their *own* good; that is a good reason for advice and persuasion, but not for compulsion or prohibition (I, 9; V, 1). Objecting to paternalism, Mill says that the individual is the person 'most interested' in their own well-being, and most knowledgeable about their own feelings and circumstances. So, interference to overrule their own judgement of their interest is liable to be misguided (IV, 4). 'His voluntary choice is evidence that what he chooses is desirable ... to him, and his own good is on the whole best provided for by allowing him to take his own means of pursuing it' (V, 11). Consequently, the 'strongest' argument against interference with purely personal conduct, he says, is that it will probably interfere erroneously, neglecting the pleasure or convenience of the person interfered with (IV, 12). In addition, Mill observes, deciding for oneself develops one's mental powers and individuality, which promotes one's well-being (III, 3, 4). So, paternalistic interference, despite its good intentions, is likely to have worse consequences for the individual than allowing them to decide for themselves.

This objection, Feinberg observes, regards personal self-determination (autonomy, self-rule, self-government) – that is, deciding for oneself – as instrumentally valuable, as conducive to one's own good. This instrumental view of the value of self-determination allows the possibility that paternalistic interference would be justified, perhaps rarely, if it was known that an exercise of autonomy was against a person's interest. Thus, Mill thought that voluntary slavery ought not to be permitted.[16]

A more fundamental objection to paternalism is that self-determination is intrinsically valuable, independently of whether the decision is conducive to one's own good (as Mill suggests it typically is). Mill also says that a person's own way of life is best 'not because it is the best in itself, but because it is his own' (III, 14). Thus, Feinberg regards personal sovereignty or self-determination as a fundamental right, not derived from a person's own good. Even when self-determination risks self-harm, others do not have the right to intervene coercively for one's own good. Preventing harm to self does not justify interference with genuine choices. The harm and offence principles protect the right of personal sovereignty from violations by others. Paternalistic interference is a violation of the right to sovereignty, and is typically indignantly resented as such. Few people welcome their own judgement of their self-interest being overruled.[17] Mill also expressed this non-instrumental and non-utilitarian view of the value of self-determination. In conduct 'which merely concerns himself, his independence is, of right, absolute. Over himself, over his own body and mind, the individual is sovereign' (I, 9). On this view, paternalism is never justified.

One way of determining the boundaries of inviolable personal sovereignty is to restrict it to especially important decisions, for example, in relation to religion, education, sex, occupation, marriage, suicide and euthanasia.[18] On this view, safety laws, such as those requiring the wearing of seatbelts and motorcycle helmets, affect unimportant interests and so do not invade personal sovereignty. However, it may be objected that the distinction between those decisions that are sufficiently important to be within the domain of personal sovereignty and those that are not is vague and arbitrary. Is it an important interest to have the freedom to participate in a dangerous sport, smoke cigarettes, take other dangerous drugs or have an unhealthy diet? If these are deemed insufficiently important interests to be protected by the right to personal sovereignty, paternalistic prohibition remains objectionable, especially to its victims. Moreover, the importance of an interest varies among individuals. For some, motorcycling without a helmet is a matter of mere convenience, for others it is a central lifestyle choice.[19] For some, taking hallucinogenic drugs is a trivial pleasure easily forgone, to others it is as important as religion is to believers. These problems vitiate this way of limiting personal sovereignty.

Another way of determining the boundaries of personal sovereignty is the distinction between self- and other-regarding actions. The personal domain over which the individual ought to be sovereign includes:

> all those decisions that are 'self-regarding', that is which primarily and directly affect only the interests of the decision-maker. Outside the personal domain are all those decisions that are also other-regarding, that is which directly and in the first instance affect the interests or sensibilities of other persons.[20]

On this view, the right to personal sovereignty does not allow even 'trivial' interferences, such as paternalistic safety regulations: 'a trivial interference with sovereignty is like a minor invasion of virginity'.[21]

The right to self-determination presupposes the capacity for self-determination. Children only gradually gain the experience, knowledge and capacity to be the best judges of their own interests, so may need to be protected from their own unwise choices, for example, by making education compulsory. Adults who are severely mentally ill or mentally disabled may lack the capacity to be the best judges of their own interests and so are vulnerable to self-harm or exploitation that is not genuinely voluntary, and so may rightly be protected by state paternalism. But when the state prohibits competent adults from voluntarily risking harm to themselves it treats adults as children ('the nanny state'). Adults who have the capacity to judge their own interests and to decide how to live have the right to live by their own judgements and to risk self-harm. Kant and Mill both regarded paternal government as 'despotic', treating adults as children, and Feinberg calls paternalism arrogant, demeaning and patronizing.[22]

Strong (hard) paternalism must be distinguished from weak (soft) paternalism. Strong paternalism, paternalism proper, is prevention of *voluntary* self-harm. Weak 'paternalism' is prevention of *nonvoluntary* self-harm. Weak 'paternalism' is really *non*-paternalism, Feinberg points out, because it does not stop someone doing what they *want* to do; on the contrary, it stops them doing what they *don't* want to do and so does not violate their personal autonomy.

Weak 'paternalism' is the principle that 'the state has the right to prevent self-regarding harmful conduct when but only when it is substantially nonvoluntary, or when temporary intervention is necessary to establish whether it is voluntary or not', or when it can be presumed to be nonvoluntary.[23]

Voluntariness is a matter of degree. It may be reduced or eliminated by coercion – that is, lack of a reasonably acceptable alternative – misinformation, deception or incapacity (for example, being drunk, drugged, mentally ill, mentally disabled, immature, or distressed).[24] It is right, according to weak 'paternalism', for the state to prevent people from seriously harming or endangering themselves if they are doing so involuntarily because they are coerced or nonvoluntarily because they do not know what they are doing, due to intoxication, misinformation, deception, mental illness, mental disability or youth. For example, prohibition of the sale of cigarettes without compulsory health warnings or to children prevents some ill-informed, hence nonvoluntary, risk-taking. Mill says that competent adults ought to be warned of dangers, not prevented from risking them; compulsory warning labels on poisons do not violate liberty because 'the buyer cannot wish not to know' the danger (V, 5). Sometimes, temporary intervention is necessary to establish whether an action is sufficiently voluntary or not. For example, giving the purchaser of an expensive financial product, such as a life insurance policy, the legal right to cancel the contract within a set period stops them from doing something that, on reflection, they do not want to do. Some self-endangering conduct is very unlikely to be voluntary and so may be presumed to be nonvoluntary (unless shown otherwise), which justifies interference. Mill (V, 5) gives the example of someone about to cross an unsafe bridge; if it was impossible to warn of the danger, it would be right to forcibly prevent them. There would be no real infringement of liberty because 'liberty consists in doing what one desires' and they were about to do what they presumably did not want to do.[25]

Feinberg regards the harm and offence principles as the only morally valid liberty-limiting principles. He also accepts weak 'paternalism'. This might be seen as a third valid liberty-limiting principle. However, it is not a liberty-limiting principle in the sense of a principle to guide legislators as to the kinds of reasons that may support criminal legislation. Weak 'paternalism' does not propose prohibiting and punishing nonvoluntary self-harm.[26] Indeed, since it prevents nonvoluntary harm or danger, it is a liberty-protecting principle.

There are some hard cases for anti-paternalists. If an adult voluntarily contracted to become a slave, should the law enforce the contract? Should the law permit adults to consent to being injured or killed? Consider these cases:

- Sadomasochistic sexual acts between consenting adults in private are, if they involve wounding or actual bodily harm, unlawful in Britain and punishable by imprisonment. 'People must sometimes be protected from themselves', said Judge Rant in a test case.[27] But should consent make such acts legally permissible?
- Some people have a strong desire for the amputation of a healthy limb. Others desire castration. Should surgeons perform the operation despite the absence of a (non-psychological) medical reason?[28]
- Should adults be allowed to consent to being killed? '[A]ll the evidence suggests that Sharon Lopatka, aged 35, knew exactly what she was doing' when she arranged for a man 'to fulfil her sexual fantasies by torturing her and then killing her.'[29]
- Bernd Brandes responded to an advert for a man 'who wanted to be eaten' (as did five other men) and voluntarily participated in being dismembered, killed and eaten.[30]

Should adults be allowed to consent to being enslaved, deliberately injured or killed? Or should the law prohibit serious voluntary self-harm?

Mill argued that a slavery contract should not be enforced. The reason for not interfering with voluntary acts, he says, is to protect liberty. But the voluntary slave abdicates liberty. So, Mill argued, the reason for non-interference is absent in this case. 'The principle of freedom cannot require that he should be free not to be free' (V, 11). However, Mill's argument is inconsistent with his principle that 'the individual is sovereign' over himself. As Feinberg observes, one can autonomously choose a life in which all further autonomy is forfeited; the choice, although not the subsequent life, could be autonomous.[31] There are, however, other reasons for not enforcing a slavery contract and not permitting consensual maiming or killing, that are consistent with the right to personal sovereignty.

Adults' right to personal sovereignty implies a right to forfeit voluntarily their life, limb or liberty. If a competent, fully informed, uncoerced adult consents, there is no wrong done. So, in principle, adults ought to be permitted to consent to being voluntarily killed, maimed or enslaved. However, the degree of voluntariness required for permissibility varies with the seriousness of the harm, its probability and its irrevocability.[32] Being enslaved, maimed or killed are seriously harmful and irrevocable. So the standard of voluntariness required must be very high. The voluntariness of apparently voluntary death, maiming or enslavement would be insufficiently certain, so it is safer to presume nonvoluntariness in order to avoid the risk of involuntary enslavement, maiming or killing. In particular, the desire to be murdered (let alone tortured or eaten too) suggests impaired rationality and hence insufficient voluntariness to be permitted. So, preventing nonvoluntary harm to others, not paternalism, can be appealed to in support of laws that prohibit consensual killing or maiming and the law's to refusal to enforce a voluntary slavery contract.[33] (Nevertheless, the right to personal sovereignty permits sadomasochism, where the injuries are well short of maiming, and active or passive euthanasia when the patient's request is demonstrably voluntary.)

Some other laws that may seem to be paternalistic may also have a non-paternalist justification, acceptable to the anti-paternalist. Laws making the wearing of seatbelts or motorcycle helmets compulsory on public roads can be justified on the non-paternalistic ground of preventing the harms to others of witnessing avoidable deaths and injuries on public roads, and bearing the costs of treating those who sustain easily avoidable injuries and of supporting them and their dependants.

Are laws enforcing health and safety at work or a minimum wage objectionably paternalistic limitations on adults' freedom of contract? Should adults be free to take dangerous or very low-paid jobs, as libertarians claim? Gerald Cohen argues that disadvantaged workers who take such jobs may be being forced to do so, and this leads to a non-paternalist justification of such laws. Someone is forced to do something when they do it because they lack a reasonably acceptable alternative. So, workers can be forced, by lack of a reasonably acceptable alternative, to take dangerous or very low-paid jobs. This makes their labour contract not fully voluntary. However, 'you cannot do what you are not free to do', so if you are *forced* to do something, you must also be *free* to do it.[34] (This calls into question Feinberg's assumption that 'it is beyond controversy that one cannot be both free and compelled to do the same thing'.)[35] So, a constraint that removes your freedom to do something can prevent you from being forced to do it. This gives a non-paternalist justification for health and safety and minimum wage laws that restrict freedom of contract.[36] If workers are not legally free to accept very low pay or hazardous conditions, they are less liable to be economically forced to do so. Such laws prevent *nonvoluntary* self-harm; they do not prevent workers from doing what they want to do, they prevent them from being forced to do what they presumably do not want to do. The employee's consent to very low pay or hazardous conditions is not fully voluntary. The harm-to-others principle justifies legally limiting the employer's freedom in order to protect the employee from nonvoluntary harm, by preventing the employer from wrongfully harming the employee's interests. Weak 'paternalism' justifies limiting the employee's freedom of contract in order to protect them from nonvoluntary harm.

Consumer protection laws that prohibit false advertising and unsafe products may seem to be paternalistic limitations on consumers' freedom to decide for themselves what to buy. However, they can be justified non-paternalistically by the harm principle in that they limit the liberty of businesses in order to protect consumers from nonvoluntary harm.[37]

Compulsory contributions to a social security scheme may seem paternalistic towards the imprudent. However, those who would choose to risk destitution in sickness, unemployment or old age would impose on the public the distress of witnessing their destitution and/or the cost of relieving it. So, the harm principle, not paternalism, can justify such compulsion.

So, laws that may seem paternalistic often have a non-paternalist justification acceptable to anti-paternalism. The reasonableness of such laws does not challenge the view that adults' right to personal sovereignty makes legal paternalism an unacceptable liberty-limiting principle.

Harmless wrongdoing

Legal moralism is the principle that 'It can be morally legitimate to prohibit conduct on the ground that it is inherently immoral, even though it causes neither harm nor offense to the actor or to others' (Feinberg).

Legal moralism claims that the law should prohibit harmless wrongdoing, that is, supposedly immoral conduct that causes no harm or offence (so has no victim). Examples of supposed harmless wrongdoing, which may be legally prohibited, include homosexuality, prostitution, sadomasochism, pornography, gambling, drunkenness or other drug-taking, each involving consenting adults in private, and adult consensual polygamy and euthanasia. (Other examples sometimes given – for example, cruelty to animals, adultery, treason, and mistreating corpses – are not harmless to others.)

Legal moralism is a misnomer because the controversial question is not whether the law ought to enforce morality. The harm, offence and paternalist principles are moral principles. Rather, the issue is whether harmless conduct can be immoral (and, if it can, whether the law ought to enforce that part of morality). An objection to legal moralism is that 'harmless wrongdoing' is an oxymoron. If no one is harmed, no one is wronged; and if no one is wronged, there is no wrongdoing. Each of those inferences can be questioned.

If no one is harmed, does it follow that no one is wronged? As examples of wrongs that are not harms, Feinberg suggests breaking a promise or trespassing that benefits the promisee or trespassee.[38] Another candidate is a beneficial lie. However, these wrongs are harms to the interests in not being let down, trespassed or deceived, even if that harm is outweighed by benefits. Perhaps every wrong to a victim can be described as a harm to their interest. If so, the fact that no one is harmed would entail that no one is wronged.

If no one is wronged, does it follow that there is no wrongdoing? Feinberg suggests various candidates for harmless wrongdoing that wrongs no one,[39] to many of which it may be objected that they are not harmless (for example, extinguishing a species), are not wrong (for example, consensual adult non-reproductive sibling incest) or are not doings (for example, evil thoughts, false beliefs).

However, Feinberg identifies two stubborn candidates for wrongdoing that wrongs no one.[40] One is a gladiatorial contest to the death with genuinely consenting adult participants and spectators. It would be difficult to establish that the gladiators' consent was genuine (well-informed and unforced) but, if it could, it might be argued that there would be no wrongdoing here because all involved consent. Other dangerous sports in which deaths occur, such as mountaineering, boxing and motorcycle racing, are accepted as morally permissible, so why not gladiatorial contests? However, the gladiatorial contest differs crucially in that here a death is *intended*. Would the fact that the vanquished consented to the risk make deliberate killing morally permissible? It might be thought that voluntary euthanasia shows that deliberate killing of consenting adults can be permissible, but there is a difference between deliberately killing someone who consented to being killed and deliberately killing someone who consented only to the risk of being killed. Even if it were accepted that the gladiators themselves would not be wronged because they consented to the risk, their recklessness would wrong their families and, even if they lack families, the possible brutalizaion of the spectators risks harm to, and thus wrongs, the wider society. So, it can be argued that this candidate could never be an example of wrongdoing that wrongs no one.

The other strong candidate for wrongdoing that harms or wrongs no one is knowingly conceiving a child that will be disabled, when a short delay would allow conception of one that would not. The disabled child's life is worth living, so it is not harmed or wronged by its conception. Is this a case of wrong-doing that harms or wrongs no one? Although no one is harmed or wronged, it may be said that the outcome is less good than it might have been. For consequentialism (for example, utilitari-anism), according to which the right action is that which has the best consequences, this suboptimal outcome makes the action morally wrong. However, given that the parents chose to have a disabled child, there is no one for whom the outcome is less good than it might have been. Non-consequentialists might insist that, because no one is harmed or wronged, there is no wrongdoing. Perhaps our intuition of wrongdoing is groundless.

In this case, the life of a future person is less good than the life of an alternative future person would have been. The outcome is less good than it could have been, but there is no one for whom it is less good. No one is harmed or wronged. Therefore, it might seem, there is no wrongdoing.

This conclusion may seem plausible in this case. However, if no one is harmed or wronged, does it follow that there is no wrong-doing? Derek Parfit provides other examples that suggest other-wise.[41] Suppose a policy of depletion of natural resources, after two centuries, makes the quality of life for many centuries much lower than it would have been had resources been conserved. The different economic and social consequences of depletion and conservation affect who meets whom, who mates with whom, the timing of conceptions, and thus who is conceived. After two centuries of depletion, none of those future people would have existed had we conserved resources (different people would have existed). So, depletion results in a lower quality of life, which is much worse than the alternative, but there is no one for whom it is worse. Would this policy be wrongdoing that harms or wrongs no one?

Suppose a policy of burial of radioactive waste results, after several centuries, in a catastrophe, which kills many people and which was a foreseeable risk. A different energy policy would have had economic and social consequences such that none of those people would have existed. So, the nuclear energy policy has an outcome that is much worse than the alternative, but there is no

one for whom it is worse. Would this policy be wrongdoing that
harms or wrongs no one?

In these two cases, the lives of future persons are less good
than the lives of alternative future persons would have been. The
outcome is less good than it could have been, but there is no one
for whom it is less good. No one is harmed or wronged, but is there
no wrongdoing?

Parfit's two cases refute the idea 'that a choice cannot have a
bad effect if this choice will be bad for no one'.[42] Since a choice can
have a bad effect even though it is bad for no one, it may be wrong
to make that choice. If so, this would be wrongdoing that harms
or wrongs no one.

Returning to the conception case, it must be conceded that
the fact that no one is harmed or wronged does not show that
there is no wrongdoing. So, it may be wrong to choose to conceive a child whose life will be less good than that of an alternative child. On the other hand, it may be that the impersonal
standard of the best outcome, regardless of who is conceived, is
appropriate for public-policy decisions, such as conservation or
energy policies, but not for the personal decision of when, and
thus whom, to conceive.

Parfit's examples show that harmless wrongdoing, that is,
wrongdoing that harms no one, is not an oxymoron. However,
Parfit's examples concern cases where our choices affect who is
conceived. The fact that harmless wrongdoing can exist in such
cases does not imply that any of the standard putative examples of
harmless wrongdoing (private, adult, consensual homosexuality,
prostitution, pornography, sadomasochism, gambling or drug-
taking and adult consensual polygamy or euthanasia) really are
wrongdoing. The conduct of consenting adults (hence no wrongful harm) in private (hence no wrongful offence) wrongs no one,
and so is within the sphere of personal autonomy and liberty. On
this view, none of those supposed examples of harmless wrongdoing is wrongdoing, so none should be illegal. (Legal regulation
may be required to ensure that such activities involve only consenting adults and are easily avoidable.)

Feinberg argues that the only morally valid reasons for criminal
prohibition are preventing harm or offence to others. Harm and
offence to others have victims, who are wronged. The harm and

offence principles protect rights. With harms to self and supposed harmless wrongdoing, no one is wronged, so these are not good reasons for criminal laws.

However, the possibility that harmless wrongdoing may exist leads Feinberg to distinguish bold and cautious liberalism. Cautious liberalism holds that only harm and offence are reasons that are always good and often decisive for criminalization, but concedes that harmless wrongdoing may rarely be a good reason. (It is conceivable that legislation should prohibit using reproductive technology deliberately to conceive a child that will be disabled.) Bold liberalism insists that harm and offence are the *only* kinds of reasons that are ever good or decisive.[43]

Public goods

A different kind of justification for state coercion, in the form not of prohibition but of taxation, is the provision of public, or partly public, goods. Public goods are things that almost everyone wants and, once provided, almost everyone benefits from. Examples are national defence, police, courts, prisons, the fire service and street lighting. Public goods won't be supplied voluntarily through the market because everyone would benefit from them whether or not they paid, so few would pay. This is an obstacle to the freedom to have those goods, which the state removes by supplying them and forcing everyone who can to contribute to the costs by taxation. Some other goods, which are only partly public, can be provided voluntarily through the market, but because many people could or would not buy them are better provided publicly. Examples are roads, schools, health care, social security, libraries and parks. Again, the only practical way to have these things sufficiently is for the state to provide them and force everyone to contribute to their cost. So, provision of public and partly public goods is another justifiable limitation of liberty – the state forces people to pay for them. The compulsion enables the public to achieve a collective good that it wants but cannot otherwise obtain efficiently.[44] State provision of public goods both limits taxpayers' freedom to dispose of their money and increases citizens' freedom to have those public goods.

Social justice

Another justification of laws that limit freedom is social justice. There are competing conceptions of social justice, but we shall take John Rawls's (see chapter 12), as it is the most systematic and influential one, to illustrate how principles of social justice may justify laws that limit liberty for some people in order to protect and equalize liberties for all. Rawls's principle of equal basic rights and liberties is implemented by standard criminal laws that prohibit violations of individuals' rights but also by constitutional or legislative provisions that protect those equal rights and liberties and thus limit political freedom, for example, the political freedom of a majority to discriminate against a racial, ethnic, religious or sexual minority. Political equality is promoted by laws that limit donations to political parties or candidates, and thus limit the freedom of the rich to buy political influence. Equality of opportunity is promoted by anti-discrimination laws, which limit the freedom of employers, businesses and educational institutions over whom they employ or promote, buy from or sell to, or admit. It also requires universal access to education, health care and social security, and thus taxation, which limits taxpayers' freedom to dispose of their money. It may also justify limiting the freedom of the rich to obtain unequal opportunities for their children through private education or inheritance of wealth. Making the worst-off group (the lowest paid) as well off as possible further justifies minimum wage and health and safety laws, which limit the freedom of contract of employers and employees. So, principles of social justice are also liberty-limiting principles that limit some freedoms in order to protect and equalize other freedoms.

Questions for discussion

1 Is preventing the imposition of offence to others a good reason for prohibiting conduct? What kinds of offensive conduct ought to be prohibited? Does offence ever justify censorship or prohibition of offensive material (books, magazines, plays, films, television programmes, lyrics, websites, and so on)? Consider this in relation to pornography, the mocking of religious beliefs, racism and homophobia.

2   Should competent adults be permitted to make informed and voluntary choices that may seriously harm them?

3   Do minimum wage and health and safety laws limit adults' freedom for their own good or do they prevent people from being forced to do what they presumably do not want to do?

4   Is harmless wrongdoing a contradiction in terms? Which, if any, of the suggested candidates are convincing examples of harmless wrongdoing?

5   Does state provision of public goods justify forcing people to pay for them through taxation?

6   Does promotion of social justice justify limiting freedom in order to

    (a)   ensure equal basic rights and liberties?

    (b)   promote political equality?

    (c)   promote equality of opportunity?

    (d)   make the worst-off group as well off as possible?

7

RIGHTS

The idea of rights is now central to moral and political thought in liberal-democratic societies. Domestically, assertion of rights has become the usual way to advance interests and causes. This is because the language of rights adds moral force to claims.[1] Internationally, liberal-democratic governments claim that their foreign policy is based on support for human rights (although the support is too selective, according to state interests, for the claim to be convincing). So, the idea of rights is prominent both domestically and internationally.

Rights are linked to other central moral and political values in liberal-democratic societies – liberty, equality and justice. Certain liberties are held to be so important that everyone is thought to have a right to them, for example, the freedoms of religion, opinion, expression, association, assembly and movement. Whichever set of basic rights is advocated, they are held to belong equally to all citizens or to all human beings. A plausible way of spelling out the idea of equality of persons is as equality of rights. Rights characterize principles of criminal justice – for example, the rights to be presumed innocent until proven guilty and to a fair trial – and principles of social justice – for example, the rights to vote, to non-discrimination and to a fair wage.

The idea of equal natural rights – rights that each person has independently of the state and the law – from which the current idea of human rights has developed is modern in origin. It is not found in ancient Greece or Rome or in the Middle Ages. The modern idea of equal rights implies a society of equal citizens (rather than a hierarchical society); that the state has a primary duty to respect and protect citizens' rights; and that the natural rights of individuals limit the legitimate authority of the state. This implies that a government that violates individuals' rights lacks legitimacy and may legitimately be resisted or overthrown. These were revolutionary ideas and were used to justify the American and French Revolutions in the eighteenth century. Influenced by the seventeenth-century English philosopher John Locke, who argued for the natural rights to life, liberty and property, the American Declaration of Independence proclaimed inalienable rights to life, liberty and the pursuit of happiness. The French Revolution declared the Rights of Man and the Citizen, which it was the function of government to secure.

In 1948 the General Assembly of the United Nations proclaimed the Universal Declaration of Human Rights (UDHR)[2] 'as a common standard of achievement for all peoples and all nations'. Almost all states (with the exception of a few conservative Islamic regimes)[3] accept the UDHR in theory if not in practice. The many regimes that violate human rights rarely admit to doing so – and so do not deny the *idea* of human rights. So, despite its modern origin and its democratic-revolutionary implications, the idea of equal human rights is acknowledged internationally and cross-culturally.

What is a right? According to the *Oxford English Dictionary*, a right is a 'justifiable claim, on legal or moral grounds, to have or obtain something, or to act in a certain way'. If you have a right to do or to have something, others have a duty not to interfere with your doing or having it. Joel Feinberg says a right is an entitlement or valid claim. Laws or regulations validate or justify legal or institutional rights; moral principles validate or justify moral rights.[4] On Feinberg's account, 'a purported moral right is a genuine moral right if and only if it is validated as such by correct moral principles'.[5] (This account is neutral between the competing accounts of the correct moral principles and their basis offered by utilitarian, Kantian and contractualist moral theories.)

Rights are *strong* legal or moral claims, that is, they are more than requests, gifts, favours, permissions or privileges.[6] A right is an entitlement; it is what is due to you. Rights can rightly be demanded, insisted upon. When a right is met, there is no reason for gratitude for it is what is due; when a right is not met, the appropriate reaction is indignation.[7] Ronald Dworkin describes individuals' rights as political 'trumps' which normally beat or outweigh collective goals, such as utility-maximization, efficiency, public benefit or the satisfaction of majority preferences;

those things may be valuable, but if they conflict with individual rights, they must normally give way.[8] Individual rights limit the permissible means to pursue such collective goals. So, rights are very strong claims.

Some distinctions among rights

Moral rights must be distinguished from legal and institutional rights. This differentiates rights according to the form they take. Legal rights – for example, the legal right to the minimum wage – are explicit in law and can be enforced through the courts. Institutional rights are entitlements that derive from the rules of an organization (for example, a club, church, university or firm). They are conferred on individuals only because of the position they occupy within the organization; for example, an office-holder has the right to make certain decisions, or a registered student has the right to use the university library. Legal and institutional rights are matters of fact, conferred by consultable laws or rules, so what they are (as opposed to what they ought to be) is relatively uncontroversial. What moral rights we have, like other parts of morality, is more controversial.

Moral rights, which include human rights, are held to exist prior to, or independently of, legal or institutional rights.[9] They are held to exist whether or not they are expressed in laws or rules. Moral rights often provide the justification for legal rights. For example, a moral right to decent pay, which is held to exist independently of the law, justifies the legal right to the minimum wage; a moral right to education justifies state provision of schools. It is held that moral rights ought to be expressed in laws when they are not. For example, adults are held to have the moral right to vote even if they are denied the legal right to do so. Moral rights are thought to limit what governments and legislatures may morally do.

Moral or legal rights may be distinguished according to who bears the corresponding duties. Some rights are against specific persons, for example, contractual rights (landlord/tenant, employer/employee, creditor/debtor, etc.). The corresponding duties fall on those specific persons. Other rights are against everyone – rights against theft, trespass or assault. The corresponding duties fall on everyone.

Another distinction is between positive and negative rights. A positive right is a right to another person's *action* – for every positive right, someone has a duty to *do* something – a right to have a debt repaid entails a duty on the debtor to repay it. Negative rights are rights to *non-interference* by others – for every negative right, other people have a duty *not* to do something.[10] Negative rights are rights not to be interfered with, by other individuals or by the state. The natural rights proclaimed in the seventeenth and eighteenth centuries were generally negative rights. Security rights (for example, rights against being assaulted or killed) and liberty rights (for example, rights to the freedoms of association, religion or expression) are negative rights.

Negative rights can be subdivided. Active negative rights are rights to *act*, or not act, as one chooses, without interference. Liberty rights are active negative rights. Passive negative rights are rights not to be *done to* in certain ways, to be left alone. Security rights are passive negative rights – rights not to be assaulted, robbed, intruded upon or libelled, that is, rights against harm to one's body, property, privacy or reputation.[11]

Civil and political rights may be distinguished from economic and social rights. This distinguishes rights according to their contents, what they are rights to.

Civil rights (also known as civil liberties) are rights against the state and include the rights to the freedom of religion, expression, movement, assembly and association, rights to equal protection of the law, to equal treatment under the law, to a fair trial, to be presumed innocent until proven guilty and the right against cruel punishment. (Individuals and organizations other than the state can violate some of these civil rights.) These rights characterize the *liberal* state.

Political rights are rights to participate in control of the state – the rights to vote, to stand for public office and to the freedom to organize political meetings, demonstrations and parties. These rights characterize the *democratic* state.

Economic and social rights are rights to benefits provided or guaranteed by the state.[12] These are rights to have one's basic needs met – for example, rights to a minimum income, social security benefits, housing, health care and education – and are also known as welfare rights. These are positive rights since they are rights to receive something and entail a duty on the community, through the state, to provide these necessities. These rights characterize the *welfare* state. Economic and social rights are more recent than civil and political rights, being largely absent from seventeenth- and eighteenth-century declarations of rights, being demanded in the nineteenth and twentieth centuries, initially by the political Left, but later accepted much more widely by liberals and conservatives (though not by right-wing libertarians), and recognized in the UDHR (articles 22–26).

However, economic and social rights remain more controversial than civil and political rights. Right-wing libertarians deny that they *are* rights, and recognize only civil and political rights. One argument for the denial of welfare rights is that the only valid moral rights (apart from those arising from agreements) are negative ones, which require only non-interference on the part of others, whereas putative rights to welfare are positive rights, requiring action by the state to provide benefits and services. However, it is objected that the civil and political rights, which these opponents of welfare rights accept, are not purely negative rights. The rights to a fair trial and to vote require state action to organize fair trials and elections, so are positive rights. While security, property and liberty rights, which are standard negative rights, imply a duty on the state to provide police, courts and prisons to enforce laws in order to protect such rights, so they have a positive aspect too. It may be replied that security, property and liberty rights remain negative, requiring only non-interference to be respected, it being only their enforcement that requires state action.

Another objection to the denial of welfare rights is that people cannot fully exercise their civil and political rights unless their basic needs are met, so civil and political rights presuppose welfare rights. However, this objection implies that what is wrong with poverty is primarily its frustrating the exercise of civil and political rights, and that welfare is valuable primarily as a condition of exercising those other rights. However, poverty is bad and welfare is good independently of their effects on the exercise of civil and political rights. A more direct objection to the denial of welfare rights is that the basis of rights is that they protect morally important interests and welfare rights protect interests that are at least as important as those that civil and political rights protect. This raises the question of the basis of moral rights.

The basis of moral rights

What is the basis of moral rights? The standard view is that rights protect *interests* that are morally important. According to Joseph Raz, one has a right if one's interest is a sufficient reason to hold someone to be under a duty.[13] Strong candidates for interests that are sufficiently important to give rise to rights and the corresponding duties are the interests in physical security, basic liberties and, more controversially, basic necessities. Rights protect those interests that are sufficiently important from being overridden by less important interests of a greater number of people. For example, the right to freedom of expression protects the morally important interest in that freedom from being overridden by the lesser interest of a larger number of people in, say, silencing an unpopular opinion or prohibiting a political demonstration that delays traffic.

The idea that rights protect morally important interests, by imposing corresponding duties on others, is now widely accepted. The rival to the interest theory of rights is the choice theory. On this view, a right-holder is characterized as having a choice over whether and how the corresponding duty is discharged; for example, a creditor may waive a debt. However, although in many cases a right-holder does have choice over whether and how to exercise a right, this is not an essential feature of a right.[14] Another objection to the choice theory of rights is that it implies that beings incapable of choice (infants, animals, the comatose, the dead and future generations) cannot have rights. This would leave their important interests unprotected from unfavourable utility calculations, that is, liable to be overridden by the lesser interests of a sufficiently large number of people. If people incapable of choice lack rights, utility calculation could justify breeding infants for medical experimentation or rape of the comatose. It is people incapable of choice who are most vulnerable to such exploitation and so most dependent on moral rights to protect their basic interests.

In contrast, the interest theory of rights recognizes that beings incapable of choice, but having interests, do have moral rights. Infants have a morally important welfare interest in not being experimented on, treated cruelly or gratuitously killed, and so have a right not to be so treated, despite being incapable of choice. Similarly, some nonhuman animals (at least some other mammals) have similar welfare interests, and so have moral rights not to be so treated.[15] Future generations are incapable of choice now, but have important interests in what we do and so can have rights now. For example, planting a bomb with a timing device would violate the rights of its victims, even if the timer was set for a century hence. A person has a morally important interest in what happens to their body and property after their death, so dead people can have rights. So, the basis of moral rights in morally important interests avoids the choice theory's implausible restriction of rights to beings capable of choice.

Moral rights feature in diverse moral and political theories, but in different ways. They may be fundamental or derived. A theory may be rights-based. For example, Robert Nozick's libertarianism (see chapter 12, penultimate section) asserts that certain natural rights are fundamental. In other theories, rights are derived from more fundamental moral concepts – from duties, utility or ideals. Kantian moral theory (the subject of chapter 11) derives rights from the duty to treat persons as ends in themselves.[16] Utilitarianism (the subject of chapter 10) argues that recognizing certain rights maximizes utility (but perhaps permits overriding them when they do not). Rawls's theory of justice (chapter 12) is based on the ideal of society as a fair system of co-operation among free and equal citizens, from which he derives his principles of justice, which determine citizens' rights.

Rights and right conduct

Rights and right conduct must not be confused, although our language obviously lends itself to confusion here. Having a right often gives choice over whether and how to exercise it, and not all such choices need be morally right. Exercising one's rights is not necessarily doing what is morally right. Indeed, one can have a moral right to do something that is morally wrong. Since both what moral rights we have and what conduct is morally wrong are contentious, examples cannot be uncontentious, but here are some relatively uncontroversial ones. One may have a moral right to spend one's money as one chooses (within the law), but may choose to exercise that right in morally questionable ways, for

example, by extravagance or by never giving to charity; one has a
right to do so, but it would not be the right thing to do. Similarly,
one may have a right to spend one's leisure time as one chooses,
but one may choose to exercise that right in morally questionable
ways, for example, by getting drunk every evening and weekend.
One has a right to have a debt repaid but it may be wrong to insist
on one's right if it will cause severe hardship; rich governments
and banks may be morally wrong to exercise their right to have
debts of poor countries repaid, because of the poverty, suffering
and deaths it causes. One has a right to freedom of expression,
but deliberately insulting a religious or ethnic group is morally
wrong. One has a right to freedom of political opinion and to vote
as one chooses, but supporting a racist political party would be
morally wrong.[17] Jeremy Waldron points out that if someone exercises their right in a morally wrong way, their right makes them
immune from forcible interference, especially by the law, but not
from moral criticism.[18] So, exercising one's rights is not necessarily doing what is morally right.

Conversely, doing what is morally right is not necessarily upholding someone's rights. For example, giving money to charity may be
the right thing to do, but beneficiaries do not have the right to your
money in the same way a creditor does. More generally, helping
others, say by donating blood, may be morally right, but others do
not have a right to demand it of you. Developing one's talents may
be morally right, but no one has the right to demand it.

The distinction between having a right and morally right conduct shows that rights are only a part of morality, even if an important, perhaps fundamental, part. Raz argues that this implies that
morality cannot be rights-based. A rights-based morality, limited
to rights and the corresponding duties, would be impoverished
because it would have no place for oughts that do not amount to
duties (for example, to help strangers), for the praiseworthiness of
supererogation, that is, action beyond the call of duty, or for the
moral value of virtue and the pursuit of excellence.[19]

Rights and duties

What is the relationship between rights and duties? We shall
consider three ideas.[20] The moral correlation of rights and duties

is the idea that to have rights requires bearing duties, that is, only something capable of having duties can have rights. The choice theory of rights would support this. This idea is often invoked to argue that nonhuman animals cannot have rights because they cannot have duties. However, on the interest theory of rights, there are counterexamples. Human infants cannot bear duties, but they have rights, for example, the right not to be killed or tortured. Similarly, people who are severely mentally ill or disabled or unconscious cannot bear duties, but they still have rights. These counterexamples show that having rights does not depend on having duties. (So the fact that nonhuman animals cannot have duties does not show that they cannot have rights.)

The idea of the logical correlation of rights and duties is the idea that rights and duties are logically inseparable – one entails the other. The entailment could run from duties to rights or from rights to duties. Do all duties entail rights? There are counterexamples – some duties do not entail corresponding rights. It may be assumed that there are moral duties to give to charity, help others and develop one's talents, but no one has a right that one does so. Since there are duties without corresponding rights, not all duties entail rights. Do all rights entail duties? One person's right does entail others' duties. A positive right entails someone's duty to do something. A negative right entails other people's duty not to do certain things. So, rights do entail duties.

A putative exception is what Feinberg calls 'manifesto' rights. These are rights that cannot be met because of unfavourable circumstances. For example, a proclaimed right to have basic needs satisfied (UDHR, article 25) cannot be met in a very poor country. Such a right does not entail a duty on anyone to provide the necessities, but declares an aspiration to be striven for.[21] There are two ways of responding to putative counterexamples to the entailment of duties by rights. Either the supposed right is wrongly formulated if it asserts a right to something that is impossible, or the right is genuine and implies a duty to change the circumstances so that the right can be met. In Feinberg's example, it may be argued that the idea of a human right not to be in absolute poverty implies a duty on the state and the international community to eliminate such poverty. It is recognition of that right which raises the questions of who has what corresponding duties, and makes them duties of justice and not merely charity. The fact that that human right cannot be met under existing national and international institutions does not imply that the absolutely poor lack that right or that that right does not entail duties. Rather, it implies that human rights demand reform of those institutions.

As well as the logical priority of rights over the corresponding duties, in that all rights entail duties, there is also a moral priority of rights over the corresponding duties in that a right is the reason for the corresponding duty.[22] If a person has a right to have or to do something, others have a duty not to interfere with their having or doing it, *because* they have that right. If a person has a right not to be done to in a certain way, others have a duty not to so treat them, *because* they have that right. The corresponding duty derives from the right, which derives from the right-holder's morally important interest. To breach a duty that corresponds to a right is not merely to breach one's own duty, it is to infringe or violate another person's right. It is not merely to act wrongly, it is to wrong the right-holder. The wrongdoing has a victim, who has a grievance against the wrongdoer.[23] A moral theory that lacked rights but retained all the corresponding duties would lack recognition of the moral basis of those duties in the interests of others. 'The specific role of rights in practical thinking is…the grounding of duties in the interests of other beings'.[24]

Human rights

Feinberg defines human rights as 'moral rights of a fundamentally important kind held equally by all human beings, unconditionally and unalterably'.[25] Let's consider the elements in that definition. Human rights are *moral* rights, that is, people are held to have them whether or not they are recognized in law or in practice. Human rights are fundamentally *important* – they are about basic interests, not relatively trivial matters. They are said to be held *equally* by *all* human beings, regardless of citizenship, nationality, sex, 'race', religion, wealth, sexual orientation, ability, and so on. Human rights are said to be held by all human beings *unconditionally*, that is, they are rights people have simply *as* human beings. No further qualification (for example, citizenship) is required; they do not have to be earned. They are said to be held *unalterably*. This may involve exaggeration, because a

convicted criminal may forfeit the rights to the freedoms of movement, association and occupation (UDHR, articles 13, 20 and 23).
However, even the worst criminal retains certain human rights,
such as the rights to a fair trial and against torture; even a torturer retains the right not to be tortured. Richard Wasserstrom
says human rights are the *strongest* moral claims; they define and
protect what every human being is entitled to.[26]

Charles Beitz distinguishes between the 'orthodox' (or philosophical) and the 'practical' (or political) views of human rights.[27]
The orthodox view is that human rights are independent of their
expression in international doctrine. They reside at a deep level of
our moral beliefs. On this view, not necessarily all human rights
in international doctrine (for example, the UDHR) are properly
called human rights. This view regards human rights as natural
rights, that is, rights that are independent of institutions and conventions and are timeless. Joshua Cohen objects that the concept
of human rights is different from that of natural rights, if that
is understood as rights that individuals would have in a state of
nature, without social institutions such as the state. Institutions
are presupposed by many rights in the UDHR, such as rights to
a fair trial, equality before the law and participation in government.[28] In contrast, the practical or political view takes as basic
the doctrine of human rights as we find it in international practice. The role of human rights in international discourse is taken
as definitive of the idea of human rights. The framers of the UDHR
deliberately refrained from proposing any foundational theory,
believing that adherents of diverse moral traditions would find
reasons of their own to support those rights. Different philosophical or religious doctrines can agree to human rights for their own
reasons – there is no need for a single, commonly agreed justification of human rights.[29] Religiously, culturally and politically
diverse governments accept the UDHR. The global consensus on
human rights has developed and is developing despite, indeed
because of, this lack of a single philosophical foundation.

Various arguments for human rights have been given.[30] It has
been asserted that they are self-evident. It has been argued that
they are implicit in the intrinsic value of each human individual,
in each individual's self-ownership, in the individual's capacity
for agency, in the individual's capacity for self-determination or in
respect for the individual's capacity for moral agency. It has been

argued that they would be agreed by rational contractors or are justified by their good consequences. People can share the idea of human rights but differ over why all humans have such rights. The idea of human rights can be widely shared because it does not presuppose any particular moral theory.[31] Any one human right may have plural justifications, and different rights may have different foundations.[32] For example, the right to freedom of thought, conscience and religion (UDHR, article 18) is related to humans' rational capacity, but the rights against torture and to basic necessities (articles 5 and 25) are related to humans' sentient capacity. There is no need to identify a single basis for the diverse interests that human rights protect.

Although the idea of human rights is widely accepted, it is not unproblematic (and a few philosophers question whether there are any human rights).[33] We shall consider the questions of the universality of human rights, their equality and whether they are absolute.

Human rights are claimed to be *universal*, held by all human beings whatever their culture. It is objected that the idea of the universality of human rights conflicts with the fact of cultural diversity, that human rights are alien to some non-Western cultures and that the claim to universality is merely arrogant, Western moral imperialism. There are several replies to this. First, the idea of human rights is not peculiarly Western.[34] Second, even if it were, the origin of an idea is irrelevant to its validity. Third, the idea of universal human rights presupposes that all human beings, whatever their culture, have morally important interests in not being killed, tortured, enslaved, impoverished, tyrannized, exploited or coerced to conform to others' religious or political beliefs. The critic of the universality of human rights implies either that individuals in some cultures lack these interests or that they are not morally important, so those individuals are not entitled to protection of those interests by human rights and may be treated in those ways. It is this view, not the claim that human rights are universal, which is arrogant towards people in other cultures. Fourth, a culture that supports slavery, torture, racial, ethnic or sexual hierarchy, or compulsory religion is the culture only of that society's powerful members, not of the victims of those practices. The claim that culture overrides human rights sides with the powerful against their victims. Fifth, the human rights to freedoms of thought, conscience, religion, opinion, expression, assembly and association foster cultural diversity within and among societies. It is opposition to universal human rights that seeks to enforce cultural homogeneity. For these reasons, the fact of cultural diversity does not refute the universality of human rights.

Human rights are thought to be held *equally* by all, regardless of abilities or deeds. What could be the basis of equality of rights? Gregory Vlastos argues that equality of human rights is based on the idea of the equal intrinsic worth or dignity of each individual. This equal value of each person is distinct from their unequal merit, based on their abilities, qualities and deeds.[35] Thus, the UDHR affirms the 'dignity and worth of the human person', dignity which is 'inherent' and 'equal' (Preamble and article 1). However, this only reformulates the question: What is the basis of equal human worth? In what morally important respect are all human beings equal?[36]

One answer refers to humans' capacities for rationality, rational agency or moral agency. Although it may be objected that people are unequally rational, everyone has at least a minimum level of rationality. However, some people (infants, the severely mentally ill or the unconscious) lack even that. This answer would imply that non-rational people lack equality of intrinsic worth and equal human rights. So, it may be objected that basing equality of worth and equality of human rights on humans' rational capacity links them to normal adults to the exclusion of non-rational people.

Another answer, suggested by the idea that interests are the basis of rights, is that all human beings, including non-rational people, have certain fundamental interests in common: interests in satisfaction of basic needs, in physical security and in basic liberties. Human rights protect these fundamental interests that all humans have in common. In this respect, all humans are equal, having the same basic interests. It is because all human beings have a fundamental interest in not being destitute, enslaved, killed or tortured that all have a right not to be destitute, enslaved, killed or tortured. (Some of our fundamental interests – in not being killed or treated cruelly – are shared with members of some other species. So, if fundamental interests are the basis of equal human rights, they can also found animal rights.)

A third question about human rights is whether they are *absolute*, that is, never rightly overridden in any circumstances. For rights to be absolute, they would have to be carefully formulated such that conflicts between them could never occur. Declarations of rights leave the details unsettled but more careful definition of rights, building in qualifications, can reduce conflicts of rights, but probably not eliminate them altogether. Negative rights, since they require only inaction, could be formulated so as not to conflict. But positive rights, because they require action, are likely to conflict. Welfare rights, because they require resources, which are limited, are especially likely to conflict. The most plausible candidates for exceptionless human rights would be passive negative rights, that is, rights not to be done to in certain ways. The right not to be tortured is a strong candidate for a human right that is absolutely exceptionless in all circumstances, a right that can never be overridden.[37] A frequently suggested counterexample is the torture of a suspected terrorist when this is the only way to prevent a terrorist outrage. Would that be permissible? Or would permitting any exceptions be too dangerous, because states all too readily find exceptional cases? If human rights were limited to passive negative rights, they could perhaps be absolute. Robert Nozick asserts natural rights only against force, theft and fraud, which he conceives as absolute constraints on action, which may not be violated even to prevent more extensive violations of those rights.[38] However, even among negative rights, conflicts of rights are familiar. The right against detention without trial may conflict, in the case of terrorist suspects or dangerous psychopaths, with the security rights of the public. A hostage's right to life may conflict with others' right not to be taken hostage in the future. The right to freedom of the press may conflict with the right to privacy. Conflicts of rights are unavoidable, especially if welfare rights are acknowledged, so rights cannot be absolute and may be overridden if necessary to prevent a catastrophe or greater violations of rights. This is accepted in relation to everyday moral rights. For example, an unforeseen emergency can override the right of a promisee. Similarly, it has to be accepted that situations can arise in which it is impossible to uphold everyone's human rights, so they cannot be absolute. L. W. Sumner observes that a right insulates its holder to some extent against competing moral considerations, but it also typically has a threshold above which it gives way. 'Rights raise thresholds against considerations of social utility, but these thresholds are seldom insurmountable.' Some rights (for example, those against torture, slavery or murder) may be absolute, but most are not.[39]

A fourth question about human rights is which rights are human rights? Does the UDHR list too many or too few? Some philosophers object that the UDHR's economic and social rights (to work, just pay, a standard of living adequate for health and well-being, including housing and medical care, social security and education) are better thought of as citizens' rights rather than human rights. It might be replied that there is a human right against absolute poverty and a citizenship right against relative poverty.[40] Allen Buchanan observes that justification of the assertion of a human right must show that the right protects an interest that is important enough to trump what would maximize utility and must show that the interest that the right protects is one shared by humans generally, regardless of culture, religion, and so on.[41] Arguably, all the rights in the UDHR satisfy these conditions.

The importance of moral rights

Various overlapping reasons may be given for the importance of moral rights. Wasserstrom notes that rights provide security from arbitrary arrest, torture and other kinds of ill-treatment. Rights proclaim *entitlement* to decent treatment; it is not a matter of kindness or benevolence on the part of others, it can be demanded as everyone's due.[42] Feinberg observes that rights proclaim all persons as deserving respect. Respecting persons *is* respecting their rights. Rights promote mutual respect and thus support self-respect.[43] Dworkin says that rights protect the equal concern and respect to which each citizen is entitled from government. They set boundaries beyond which governments may not go in pursuit of their aims. Rights limit the legitimate power of government, constrain what may be done even for the benefit of society as a whole. They protect individuals from having their fundamental interests sacrificed for the benefit of others. Saying that individuals have rights against the government means that government may not override them just because doing so would produce more benefit than harm and benefit society as a whole. Otherwise, there is no special protection of the interest the right is supposed to protect. If individuals have rights, then governments may override them only when necessary to protect the rights of others or to prevent a catastrophe, but not merely to produce overall benefit for society. Individual rights represent 'the majority's promise to the minority that their dignity and equality will be respected'.[44]

Turning to the international role of human rights, Thomas Scanlon observes that human rights can be agreed on by many different political theories (liberals, conservatives and socialists all value human rights), cultures and social groups.[45] For this reason, like Scanlon, Rawls argues that human rights can and ought to inform international relations and foreign policy. Human rights set a minimum standard of decency required of governments: regimes that meet this minimum standard ought to be free from forceful intervention by other governments, by diplomatic or economic sanctions or military force; they have a right to sovereignty over their territory. But regimes that systematically violate human rights are illegitimate, and this violation may justify principled intervention in their internal affairs to help the victims of the regime. Human rights thus specify the limits to a regime's internal sovereignty – a government's right to govern its territory is not absolute but limited by individuals' human rights.[46] On this view, human rights ought to provide a moral basis for foreign policy, one that ought to constrain pursuit of national self-interest.

Criticisms of the idea of moral rights

Proliferation

It is objected that there has been a proliferation of claimed rights, from Locke's rights to life, liberty and property to the UDHR's 30 articles.[47] The idea of rights has been extended from fundamental interests against torture, murder and enslavement, to less important things, such as 'holidays with pay' (UDHR, article 24). It is said that mere wants are claimed as rights and this devalues the term, making it empty rhetoric. However, this is a criticism not of the concept of moral or human rights but of possible misuse of the term. The example of a human right to holidays with pay is not a mere want but protects a universal human interest in respite from work,[48] which many people are denied.

Individualism

The rights of individuals to various liberties are criticized by communitarians and traditional conservatives as being at the expense of the ideal of community, with a shared, traditional way of life. It may be replied that individual liberty rights make possible a community characterized by mutual respect among its members, while a community without such rights would oppress its members.

Egoism

Rights protect individuals' interests and so are open to the criticism that they encourage assertion of self-interest and selfishness. In contrast, duties, obligations and responsibilities attend to the interests of others.[49] Individuals are naturally inclined to pursue self-interest, and morality is needed to restrain that inclination and should not encourage it. It is claimed that Western societies have increasingly developed a culture in which people demand rights, but shirk responsibilities and duties. It is claimed that we ought to attend less to demanding rights for ourselves and more to our duties towards others. Whatever their merit as cultural criticism, these claims are misplaced as criticism of rights. The security, liberty and welfare interests that human and citizenship rights protect are not selfish.[50] Claiming a human or citizenship right for oneself implies a similar right for one's fellow humans or fellow citizens, and thus the corresponding duties for oneself.[51] Rights may be exercised selfishly or unselfishly – for example, the right to free speech may be exercised to advocate one's own interests or others'. Organizations and individuals campaigning for rights are typically concerned with the rights of others, whether humans or animals. So, rights, their assertion, exercise and advocacy are not necessarily linked to selfishness.

Disutility

Utilitarianism criticizes rights for blocking the pursuit of the best consequences for society as a whole. Supposed individual rights ought to be overridden for the collective good. Jeremy Bentham said that 'there is no right which, when the abolition of it is advantageous to society, should not be abolished'.[52] However, individual rights are necessary precisely to protect individuals' morally important interests (for example, in life, liberty and security) from being sacrificed for a greater sum of lesser interests.

* * *

Despite the criticisms and the competing interpretations of the idea, it is important to remember why the idea of moral rights, particularly human rights, is so important. Many governments imprison, torture and murder people because of their political or religious beliefs or their culture, and they claim that this is justified by the public interest or national security or to defend their tradition, culture or religion. The idea of human rights insists that nothing can justify such treatment – all individuals have a right never to be treated in those ways.

Questions for discussion

1   Are there universal equal human rights applicable (a) to all societies, (b) to all individuals?
2   What is the basis of human rights held by each individual equally?
3   Do you think that human rights are absolute, that is, should never be overridden in any circumstances? Can you think of any circumstances where it would be right to override human rights?
4   Why are moral rights, independent of the law, important?
5   Should individual rights limit what legislators may enact and so what a majority of electors may vote for?
6   Which, if any, of the criticisms of the idea of moral rights do you find convincing?

8

EQUALITY AND SOCIAL JUSTICE

Equality

It is a fundamental assumption of contemporary moral and political philosophy that every person has equal intrinsic moral value. Each person matters equally; each person's life is equally important. Each person is entitled to equal respect and concern simply by virtue of being a person, regardless of class, 'race', sex, religion, nationality, culture, ability, sexual orientation, and so on.

This fundamental moral equality of persons implies an ideal of a society of equals, a society whose members respect and treat each other as equals, and thus do not deny each other equal liberties or opportunities. The ideal of a society of equals implies the ideal of a political society of equal citizens, with equal rights, liberties and opportunities. It thus implies that government ought to ensure equality of citizens' rights, liberties and opportunities, and ought to treat each citizen with equal respect and concern. It also implies that society, through its laws and policies, ought to distribute its resources in a way that expresses the moral and social equality of its members, and so ought to limit inequality of income and wealth. Arguably, it implies ensuring that 'no one is less well off than anyone needs to be'.[1]

Equality is a modern idea, proclaimed in the eighteenth-century Enlightenment and American and French Revolutions. It is opposed to the idea of a fundamental moral inequality, such as aristocratic, racist or sexist ideas of superiority, founded on discredited ideas of natural, hereditary hierarchies of class, caste, sex or 'race'. Residues of these ideas persist, of course, and with significant effects. However, equality has become the political and moral orthodoxy in liberal-democratic societies.

113

In such societies, the kinds of discrimination and inequality of opportunity that are generally recognized as unjust have continually expanded to include discrimination on the grounds of religion, class, colour, ethnicity, sex, disability and sexual orientation. Since the Second World War, and especially since the radicalism of the 1960s and 1970s, anti-Semitism, class snobbery, racism, sexism, homophobia and Islamophobia have become increasingly widely recognized as unjust and unacceptable. Each persists, but no longer as prevailing, accepted, common-sense assumptions.

It is often argued that the reason discrimination on the basis of characteristics such as colour, sex or sexual orientation is wrong is that these characteristics are unchosen. However, this would imply that discrimination on the basis of a chosen religion or chosen sexual orientation would not also be wrong. Rather, each of those bases of discrimination is wrong when and because it is irrelevant. When it is relevant, it is not wrong. (There are some situations in which colour, sex, religion or sexual orientation is a relevant consideration.) To deny someone an opportunity or to treat someone less favourably without a relevant reason is to wrong them by treating them unfairly.

What is the basis of equality of persons? Each person is a sentient being, with the capacity for pleasure and pain, happiness and unhappiness, satisfaction and frustration of their wants and interests. This gives each person the same basic needs and interests in physical security, economic welfare and freedom. This is the basis for equality in utilitarianism. Each person is also a rational being, capable of choosing their ends and their means to them. This rationality gives them a moral capacity to know what is right and wrong and to choose moral ends and moral means. This is the basis for equality in Kantianism.

John Rawls elaborates the Kantian view. The basis of equality, he says, is that each human being is a moral person, characterized by two features. Each is capable of forming, revising and rationally pursuing a conception of the good, that is, a conception of what is valuable in human life, which determines their specific interests. And each is capable of having, at least to a minimum degree, a sense of justice, that is, a skill in judging things to be just or unjust, supporting those judgements with reasons, and having a desire to act justly. These are natural attributes.[2]

It has been argued that contemporary moral and political theories are all based on equality of persons. They do not appeal to conflicting ultimate values, such as freedom versus equality, as their foundation. Counterposing freedom and equality is a mistake because they are not alternatives. Freedom is one of the things to which equality applies and equality is one of the ways in which freedoms can be distributed.[3] Rather than appealing to conflicting ultimate values, every plausible moral or political theory has the same ultimate value of equality in the sense of treating people as equals, who are entitled to equal respect and concern.[4] All enduring approaches to the ethics of social arrangements advocate equality of something.[5] Utilitarianism treats equally the interests of all sentient beings in calculating what will maximize overall happiness or welfare. Kantian moral philosophy regards persons as having 'innate equality' by virtue of their humanity or reason,[6] which gives each person a moral capacity in virtue of which each person is equally owed respect. Rawls's theory of justice explicates this Kantian idea. It gives each citizen an equal say in the choice of principles of justice. Those principles require equal basic liberties, political equality, equal opportunities and income and wealth to be as equal as is rational and reasonable, which, he argues, is to maximize the lifetime prospects for resources for the worst-off group. Libertarianism claims that extreme inequality of wealth and income is just if it is the result of voluntary transactions, but its fundamental principle is equality of rights (against force, theft and fraud). Justifications of inequality in one dimension (for example, income or wealth) typically appeal to equality in another dimension (for example, equal right to one's labour and its products, or equal income for equal productive contributions). Any plausible moral or political theory must be committed to equality at a fundamental level, otherwise it is based on arbitrary discrimination and lacks the impartiality required of any moral or political theory.[7]

Social justice

Social justice may be defined as the right distribution of the benefits and burdens of society. Benefits include rights, liberties, opportunities (for example, in education and employment), wealth and income, including publicly provided services. Burdens include duties, prohibitions, work (its amount and kind), and taxation. The idea of a right distribution of burdens and benefits raises the questions of which burdens and benefits ought to be distributed equally and which unequally, what justifies inequalities and how much inequality is justified. Social justice is thus a complex and controversial concept, of which there are various conceptions of the right distribution, especially of economic benefits and burdens.

Aristotle stated a formal principle of justice, namely that it requires treating equals equally and unequals unequally, in proportion to their inequality. (If different treatment is inconsistent with this principle, it amounts to arbitrary discrimination.) However, this principle is only formal because it immediately raises the question of the respects in which people are equals and ought to be treated equally, and the respects in which people are unequals and ought to be treated unequally. The fact that everyone has the same basic needs, interests and capacities makes them equals who, in many situations, ought to be treated equally. A person's colour, sex, religion, ethnicity and sexual orientation are differences that, in most situations, are irrelevant such that unequal treatment on these grounds is unjust. Differences that may justify unequal treatment in situations where they are relevant include a person's special needs, such as those arising from disability, illness or pregnancy, and a person's deeds. What people do, what choices they make, may establish unequal desert. In criminal justice, the guilty deserve punishment, the innocent do not, and the seriousness of their crime determines the amount of punishment deserved. In the economic aspect of social justice, other things being equal, someone who works deserves more income than someone who chooses not to work; someone who saves deserves more wealth than someone who chooses not to save; someone who bears additional burdens (for example, takes on extra responsibilities, works longer hours or does a particularly stressful or dangerous job) deserves more benefits (for example, more pay) than someone who does not. A just economic distribution must be sensitive to those deeds for which individuals are responsible.

Which kinds of equality does social justice require?

Which inequalities are just and which are unjust? Which things does social justice require to be equally distributed? This question is open to a series of answers that are increasingly inclusive and egalitarian. Increasingly egalitarian implications have been drawn from the concepts of equality and social justice. We shall consider equality of civil rights, equality of democratic political rights, formal equality of opportunity, fair equality of opportunity and equality of condition as kinds of equality that social justice requires.[8]

A minimal conception of social justice would require each individual to have equal civil rights to security and liberty. Security rights include rights to the protection of the law, against arbitrary arrest, to a fair trial and against torture. Liberty rights include rights to the freedoms of speech, religion, expression, association and occupation. These rights protect morally important interests that each person has. Social justice requires that each citizen has these rights equally. This implies that social justice requires the *liberal* state – that is, a state that respects and protects individuals' security and liberty rights. This is now uncontroversial. More controversially, right-wing libertarians think that equality of civil rights, based on fundamental natural rights against force, theft and fraud, is the *only* kind of equality that social justice requires. This implies that social justice requires a free market and minimal state, that is, a state that protects individuals' security, property and liberty rights, but does nothing else.[9] However, such a social system would produce massive inequalities of income, wealth, welfare, opportunity, economic and political power, accumulating in families over generations, which, non-libertarians argue, would be unjust.

As well as equal civil rights to security and liberty, it is widely accepted that social justice also requires equality of democratic political rights. Each adult should have equal rights to vote and to stand for political office, as well as rights to the freedoms of political expression, association and assembly. The Universal Declaration of Human Rights includes 'the right to take part in the government of the country, directly or through freely chosen representatives' (article 21). Various arguments support the idea that social justice requires democracy. First, if adult individuals have a right to self-determination, then they have equal *rights* to participate in the collective decisions about the laws and policies to which they are subject. Second, since each person is affected by such collective decisions, fairness demands *equal* rights to participate in the process of decision-making. Third, government ought to treat each citizen equally, and equality of democratic political rights is most likely to promote this. Fourth, democratic government is the most reliable way to ensure respect and protection for citizens' equal security and liberty rights, and other human rights. Fifth, democratic government is responsive to its citizens' interests and so is most likely to adopt economic and social policies that are just. So, for various reasons, social justice requires not only the liberal state but also the *democratic* state. (Right-wing libertarians tend to be lukewarm about democracy, seeing it not as unjust in itself, but as potentially unjust because the majority may vote for policies that redistribute income from the rich minority, which, libertarians think, violates their property rights.)

Joshua Cohen observes that the connections between a democratic *society* – that is, a society of equals, entitled to equal respect and equal rights – and democratic *government* run in both directions. Once members of society are regarded as equals, rather than located in a natural hierarchy of unequal worth and entitlement, it is natural to express the respect owed to persons as equals in equal political liberties and democratic government. Conversely, once there is political democracy, in which all sections of society are entitled to bring their interests and judgements to bear in political discourse and voting, it is natural to regard all members of society as equals, with a claim to equal concern and respect.[10]

In liberal-democratic societies it is widely accepted that social justice requires not only equality of security, liberty and democratic political rights but also equality of opportunity, particularly in education and employment. If an individual is denied an equal opportunity in education or employment for no relevant reason, they are treated unfairly. Unequal opportunities also waste talent and thus harm society as a whole, but are wrong independently of that consequence. *Formal* equality of opportunity requires non-discrimination on irrelevant grounds such as colour, sex, religion, ethnicity, sexual orientation or disability. This implies that social justice may require not the free market but state intervention in the form of anti-discrimination legislation, outlawing discrimination on irrelevant grounds. That social justice requires this is slightly more controversial because such legislation limits property rights, for example, a business owner's and others' freedom to practise discrimination. Because of its restriction of property rights, libertarians oppose anti-discrimination legislation, not because they favour discrimination but because they oppose the state *enforcing* non-discrimination. However, in liberal-democratic societies, such legislation is now widely accepted as necessary for social justice.

Formal equality of opportunity requires equal opportunities for people who are equally qualified. However, opportunities to become qualified may be unequal, varying with parental income, education and attitudes, such that competitors have unequal starting places. This leads to the idea that social justice requires not merely formal but also *fair* equality of opportunity, that is, equal opportunities to become qualified, or equal starts for competitors, so that competition is fair.[11] The ideal is that there should be equal opportunities for equal talent: children should not be advantaged or disadvantaged by their parents' wealth, occupation or connections. If someone is denied an equal opportunity on these irrelevant bases, it is as unjustified and unfair as racial or sexual inequality of opportunity. The ideal of fair equality of opportunity requires government action to equalize opportunities, such as state provision of access to education, social security benefits, housing and health care. Thus, social justice requires not only the liberal-democratic state but also the *welfare* state, in order to equalize opportunities. Equalizing opportunities may also require affirmative action policies to counteract obstacles of prejudice or poverty; for example, targeting educational resources at the poor. This is perhaps the prevailing conception of social justice in liberal-democratic societies. However, it may be criticized as insufficient for social justice for several reasons.

First, the ideal of fair equality of opportunity is unattainable. Whatever government does, the more affluent will secure advantages for their children – better education, employment and health care. Private education is an important means by which the wealthy buy advantages for their children. In Britain at least, the privately educated, especially those educated in the most prestigious private schools, are over-represented in higher education, especially the most prestigious universities, and in the most powerful and lucrative jobs (in finance, government, civil service, media, judiciary). Even in state education, attainment correlates strongly with parental social class. A recurrent theme in British education policy since 1944 has been attempts to equalize educational opportunity among social classes (for example, by comprehensivization and the expansion of higher education). Such measures have improved overall educational standards, but wide class inequalities remain. More could be done to equalize opportunity, for example, legally limiting expenditure per pupil in private schools to the average in state schools, and requiring each university's admissions to reflect the proportions of privately and publicly educated. Such measures would maintain affluent parents' liberty to buy private education but block them from buying unequal opportunity. But unequal opportunities would remain. The basic cause of rich children having better opportunities than poor children is the economic inequality between their families. Economic inequalities cause unequal opportunities from conception: the less affluent their parents, the worse the child's chances with respect to health, abilities and education; and these inequalities of opportunity cumulate.[12] Thus, the basic cause of inequality of opportunity is inequality of condition. Therefore, to further equalize opportunities, as social justice requires, demands limiting inequality of condition (discussed below).

A second criticism of fair equality of opportunity as insufficient for social justice is that its ideal of equal opportunity for equal talent entails unequal opportunity for unequal talent. Even if the ideal of fair equality of opportunity could be achieved, it would mean better life prospects for those born more talented than for those born less talented. Talent (that is, in this context, whichever qualities enable acquisition of high income and wealth) is the result of luck, not choice, and therefore is not deserved. Good or bad luck in genes or upbringing does not justify the lucky receiving the further advantages of high income and wealth and the unlucky receiving additional disadvantages. This implies that social justice ought to be concerned not only with equal opportunity for equal talent but also with the condition of the less talented. (Efficiency may provide a reason to provide incentives for the talented to use their talents productively, but efficiency is not justice.)

A third criticism of fair equality of opportunity as insufficient for social justice is that it is concerned with how individuals get their places within the structure of unequal social positions, not with that structure of unequal positions, that is, with the inequality of income, wealth, power and status. The ideal of fair equality of opportunity would be a meritocracy, or perfect social mobility, where an adult's social position depends only on their talent and effort, uninfluenced by their parents' social position. An objection to this ideal as insufficient for social justice is that what ought to be of fundamental concern is the inequality of income and wealth between rich and poor, not only *who* becomes rich or poor. A society in which talented people from poor backgrounds rose to become very rich while untalented people from rich backgrounds fell into relative poverty would realize the ideal of fair equality of opportunity (for one generation at least) but would not be a just society because people are not responsible for their talents. If some individuals from poor backgrounds rise up the income scale, this does not alter the situation of the class of poor people. This implies that social justice ought to be concerned not only with the opportunity to attain unequally rewarded positions, but also with the extent of inequality of reward. These three criticisms of fair equality of opportunity as insufficient for social justice lead to concern with inequality of condition.

Inequality of condition refers to the inequalities of income, wealth, work and leisure time, and the resulting inequalities of living standards and welfare (that is, satisfaction of needs and wants). Does social justice require equality of condition as a political goal? (If it does, it would have to be balanced against other values, such as freedom and efficiency.) If social justice includes equality of condition, means to that end would include full-employment economic policies, minimum wage legislation, setting the minimum wage at the highest level consistent with full employment, and high-quality public education, health and social security systems financed by progressive taxation. Whether social justice requires equality of condition is the most controversial aspect of social justice, because inequality of condition has several justifications as well as many objectionable consequences (and because material interests are at stake).

There are several distinct justifications of inequality of condition. First, there is an argument from freedom. People ought to be free to do what they choose with their abilities and money (provided they do not violate the rights of others). People make different choices about education and training, occupation, starting a business, saving, investment, and so on. Their choices result in wide inequality of income and wealth. So, one argument in support of wide inequality of condition is that it is the outcome of freedom, which government ought to accept rather than try to counteract by redistribution from rich to poor. An objection to this argument is that the appeal to freedom provides a reason only against egalitarian policies that would restrict freedom of choice with respect to education, occupation, enterprise, and so on. However, those freedoms are compatible with other policies to reduce inequality of condition, such as progressive taxation of the income and wealth that results from those choices, full-employment economic policies, optimizing the minimum wage and high-quality public services.

A second argument for inequality of condition is that some people's scarce skills contribute more to production so they *deserve* more income than others. It may be objected that having skills that are currently scarce relative to effective demand for them is a questionable conception of desert. An individual is not responsible for society's level of supply of, or demand for, their skills. It may also be objected that people deserve income proportionate to their productive contributions only to the extent that they are responsible for their productive abilities and contributions. To a large extent, these are due to factors for which the individual is not responsible.

A third argument for economic inequality is that unequal incomes may *compensate* unequal burdens. Jobs that are dangerous, unhealthy, stressful, boring or otherwise unpleasant deserve more pay than jobs that are safe, healthy, interesting or comfortable. This basis of desert is independent of productivity. However, the idea of compensation justifies unequal pay in order to *equalize* the package of burdens and benefits of different jobs, so the underlying idea is equality, not inequality, of condition. Consequently, this argument does not oppose policies in pursuit of equality of condition. (Market incomes often do not compensate unequal burdens – pleasant, interesting, comfortable, healthy jobs tend to be well-paid, while unpleasant, boring, dangerous and unhealthy jobs tend to be low-paid.)

A fourth argument for inequality of condition appeals to its good consequences for society as a whole (not only for the relatively advantaged). It is argued that inequality of income and wealth benefits everyone by providing incentives for work, education, training, saving, investment and enterprise, which increase production. This may be true, but it may be observed that incentives do not require the degree of inequality of income often wrongly described as 'incentives'. Competitive and innovative capitalist economies differ markedly in their degree of income inequality. For example, the ratio of the average pay of chief executive officers to that of the average employee is 10:1 in Japan, 11:1 in Germany, 16:1 in France, 25:1 in Britain and 531:1 in the United States.[13] So, even if incentives justify income inequality, they justify a much narrower range of inequality than often supposed. Nevertheless, if and insofar as incentives really are necessary for efficiency, this provides a powerful justification for inequality of condition.

There are many objections to wide inequality of condition, especially to disadvantages for which the individual is not responsible (and, conversely, many reasons to limit economic inequality). Thomas Scanlon observes that the diverse objections to inequality of condition are based on values other than equality of condition. The moral equality of persons leads to the political goal of equality of condition not because that is itself a fundamental moral value but via other values.[14]

The idea that equality of condition is *intrinsically* valuable is vulnerable to Derek Parfit's levelling-down objection, that it implies that there is something good about reducing inequality in a way that benefits no one.[15] Larry Temkin replies that undeserved inequality is unfair and unfairness is bad, so there is at least one respect in which levelling down is good, even if there is no one for whom it is good.[16] However, the following arguments are for the *instrumental* value of equality of condition and so are not vulnerable to the levelling-down objection.

One objection to inequality of condition is that it causes preventable deprivation, hardship and suffering, which redistribution from the rich to the poor can relieve.[17] However, here the reason for reducing inequality is the urgency of the needs and wants of the badly off, not the inequality between them and the better-off.[18] That is, the objection is really to poverty, not to inequality.

A common view is that poverty, but not inequality, is objectionable. That is, it is claimed that what matters is the absolute position of the badly off, not their position relative to the better-off. The political implication of this view is that, provided the welfare state ensures everyone can meet their basic needs so no one falls below a minimum level, it does not matter about inequality above that level. Harry Frankfurt argues for this kind of view. He argues for a principle of sufficiency: everyone should have enough to meet their needs for a decent life, which may be broadly conceived, but above that level, inequality does not matter. On this view, what is morally important 'is not that everyone should have *the same* but that each should have *enough*. If everyone had enough, it would be of no moral consequence whether some had more than others.'[19]

Frankfurt argues that preoccupation with economic equality diverts people's attention from what would be a satisfactory income for their own purposes. It may be objected that any definition of sufficiency will be arbitrary and implausibly imply that redistribution from the rich to those just below the sufficiency line is morally important, but redistribution to those just above it is not. However, the main weakness of the sufficiency principle is that there are many objections not just to poverty but to *inequality* of condition, including that above the sufficiency level.

First, wide inequalities of income and wealth cause inequalities of social status and esteem. Income, wealth and lifestyle are indicators of status and esteem. This stigmatizes the relatively poor and may cause them to be viewed, and to view themselves, as inferior, thus undermining their self-esteem. The lifestyle of the affluent sets the norm for society as a whole and those who are much worse off are made to feel inferior.[20] Wide economic and social inequalities may generate objectionable attitudes of snobbery, arrogance and contempt among the rich and deference and servility among the relatively poor, undermining their self-esteem.[21] These effects of economic inequality occur even among people whose absolute standard of living is well above sufficiency. The democratic 'ideal of a society in which people all regard one another as equals'[22] is incompatible with wide inequality of condition. A more equal society would promote the mutual respect and self-esteem of all its members.

Second, economic and social inequality causes inequality of physical and mental health and life expectancy across the socio-economic scale. The worse-off have poorer diets and housing, live in more polluted environments, have less autonomy at work and experience more stress than the better-off, with the result that their physical and mental health is worse and they have a shorter life expectancy. Even in rich countries with welfare states, inequality of condition results in many preventable deaths. Reducing inequality of condition could reduce inequality of health, preventable ill-health and premature deaths.[23]

A third objection to inequality of condition is that large economic inequalities give some people power over the lives of others. The rich have the economic power to determine what is produced and what employment is available.[24] Scarce productive resources are devoted to producing luxuries for the rich while others' needs are unmet. The rich may be able to dictate terms of employment to the relatively poor. The affluent buy private health care, taking scarce medical resources from less affluent people in greater medical need. The affluent drive up property prices, making home ownership unaffordable for people on moderate incomes. Again, these are effects of inequality, not poverty, and occur even among people who are above a sufficiency line.

Fourth, economic inequality gives unequal political power and influence, which is another way it gives some people power over the lives of others. The rich and the companies they control have great political power. This occurs through their financing of political parties, candidates and campaigns, through their ownership and control of most communications media, which set the political agenda, and through their control of investment. Governments compete to offer the policies most attractive to investors (low taxation of the rich and lax regulation of business). Governments avoid antagonizing large companies and owners of mass media. The poor have relatively little political power. As a result, government policies tend predominantly to serve the interests of the rich and their companies. Limiting economic inequality promotes genuine democracy, which social justice requires.

A fifth objection to wide inequality of condition is that, as already explained, it causes unequal starting points and thus unequal opportunities and unfair competition, particularly in education and economic activities. If competition is unfair, the resulting distribution of income and wealth is unjust. Social justice requires fair equality of opportunity, which requires limiting inequality of condition to give roughly equal starts and to ensure that competition is as fair as possible.

Sixth, it may be argued that society's wealth is produced by the combined and complementary efforts of the workforce as a whole and so should be distributed as equally as would be rational and reasonable. In objection to this, it may be claimed that individuals with scarce skills contribute more and so should receive larger shares of the social product. In reply, it may be observed that entrepreneurs and others with scarce marketable skills could produce little without the contributions of every member of their organization, or without the contributions of health, education, transport and utilities workers, or without the science, technology, infrastructure and social organization that enable them to be highly productive. In short, the wealth of society is produced by the combined efforts of the workforce as a whole and it is impossible to disentangle individual contributions. This argument supports a more equal distribution of the social product.

Seventh, another argument for limiting economic inequality is from the fact that money and most goods have a diminishing marginal value, that is, the more you have, the less valuable any extra is; conversely, the less you have, the more valuable any extra is. Therefore, if money is redistributed from the rich to the poor, the poor gain more welfare (satisfaction of needs and wants) than the rich lose. Therefore, such redistribution increases the overall level of welfare. (This redistribution must be balanced against the need for incentives to increase production.) Frankfurt objects that individuals differ in the satisfaction they can derive from money, so money is not equally valuable to everyone.[25] However, these individual differences occur among the rich and among the poor rather than between the rich and the poor. Redistribution from rich to poor would produce a net increase in satisfaction even though it would disbenefit rich individuals unequally and benefit poor individuals unequally.

An eighth objection to wide inequality of condition is that it has bad consequences for society as a whole (not only for the disadvantaged) in at least three ways. First, Richard Wilkinson establishes the effect of a society's degree of inequality on the health and life expectancy of its population as a whole. Comparing rich societies, the more unequal a society, the worse is its overall health and life expectancy. It is not only that, within societies, poorer people have worse health than richer people do. It is also the case that, among rich societies, the more unequal societies have worse overall health and life expectancy than the more equal ones. And if we compare one society in different periods, more equality improves overall health and life expectancy. Government action that reduces income inequality improves the health and life expectancy not only of the poor but also of society as a whole. (Although the link between equality and health is well established, it is not certain why it exists. It is thought that wide inequality leads to a more competitive society with more economic insecurity and status anxiety, each of which causes stress, which is known to harm health.)[26] A second way that wide inequality harms society as a whole is that, again comparing rich societies, the more unequal a society, the higher its rate of violent crime. Homicide rates correlate strongly with income inequality.[27] A third way that wide economic inequality harms society as a whole is that it damages society's sense of solidarity or community, it reduces trust and creates a more divided, indifferent society, which harms everyone.[28]

So, to sum up, wide economic inequality causes inequalities of social status and esteem, health, life expectancy, economic power, political power, opportunities and shares in the collective product of society. Each of these inequalities may be regarded as unjust, because they make the worse-off people worse off than they need be. What is objectionable is not merely that some people are worse off than others, but that they are worse off than they need be. Wide economic inequality also harms society as a whole by producing suboptimal overall levels of welfare, health, life expectancy, violent crime and solidarity. Again, these preventable deficits, being the products of social institutions and policies, are objectionable because they make people worse off than they need be. These objections to wide inequality of condition suggest that equality of condition, albeit balanced against competing values such as freedom and efficiency, is instrumentally valuable even if it is not thought to be an intrinsically valuable ideal. This suggests that social justice requires not only equality of civil and political rights and fair equality of opportunity, but also equality of condition.[29]

Questions for discussion

1 Which kinds of discrimination and unequal opportunity are unjust?
   (a) Religious or ethnic discrimination;
   (b) Class discrimination;
   (c) Racial discrimination;
   (d) Sexual discrimination;
   (e) Discrimination against people with disabilities;
   (f) Discrimination on grounds of sexual orientation.
2 Which kinds of equality does social justice require?
   (a) Security and liberty rights;
   (b) Democratic political rights;

    (c) Formal equality of opportunity;
    (d) Fair equality of opportunity;
    (e) Equality of condition.

3   Which arguments for inequality of condition are most convincing?

4   Which arguments against wide inequality of condition are most convincing?

9

MORAL RELATIVISM

Moral or ethical relativism is the idea that morality is relative to each culture. It claims that moral judgements are, and can only be, based on a culture's beliefs, values and customs; there are no universal moral principles. Moral or ethical subjectivism, which is a more extreme version of relativism, asserts that morality is relative to each individual. It claims that moral judgements are, and can only be, based on (report or express) an individual's feelings; there are no objective moral principles. Relativist and subjectivist views of morality are quite common in liberal-democratic societies, and many students initially express them. It is often said that moral beliefs are merely opinions, whether of cultures or of individuals, which are equally 'valid'; there is no one right answer to moral questions. Moral relativism is implicitly appealed to by conservatives, to claim that traditional cultural practices are immune to moral criticism because they are 'our tradition' or 'our culture', as well as by would-be radicals, to claim that freedom, democracy and human rights are merely 'Western' values, whose absence from a society is merely a cultural difference, which ought to be tolerated, and whose promotion is 'moral imperialism'. However, few philosophers defend moral relativism or subjectivism. One who does, Gilbert Harman, says:

> Moral relativism denies that there are universal basic moral demands and says different people are subject to different basic moral demands depending on the social customs, practices, conventions, values, and principles that they accept.[1]

The fact of moral diversity

Moral relativism starts from the familiar fact that different cultures, both present and past, have different moral beliefs – both general

moral principles and particular moral judgements. Practices that
are or were believed to be morally permissible by one culture are or
were believed to be morally wrong by another. Examples include
abortion, infanticide, euthanasia, homosexuality, promiscuity,
paedophilia, polygamy, genital mutilation of children, slavery,
oppression of women, torture, capital punishment, meat-eating,
cannibalism, military aggression and conquest, consumption of
alcohol, cannabis or hallucinogens, racial, ethnic or religious discrimination and segregation, and honour killing. This diversity
of moral beliefs gives plausibility to the moral relativist claims
that there are no universal or objective moral standards and that
morality is relative to culture.

However, there is less moral diversity than there appears to be,
for three reasons.[2] First, different customs may reflect different
circumstances, not different values. For example, practices such
as child labour or toleration of hazardous working conditions
may reflect poverty, not disvaluation of education or of health and
safety. Second, different practices may reflect different factual
beliefs, not different moral values. The same values, when combined with different factual beliefs, generate different customs.
For example, respect for women may be expressed in different
dress codes, respect for the dead may be expressed in different
funerary practices, and respect for life may be expressed in opposing views on capital punishment for murder. Third, some values
and norms are necessary for the survival of any society, and so are
universal. For example, care of infants, prohibition of gratuitous
violence, truth-telling, promise-keeping, reciprocity and respect
for personal property. The details vary, but any society must have
such basic moral rules, so some moral rules are universal. This
limits diversity among cultures. So, moral diversity can be exag-
gerated, but it does exist.

Varieties of moral relativism

Moral relativism may refer to at least three distinct ideas: descrip-
tive ethical relativism, which is a factual claim about moral principles, meta-ethical relativism, which is a theory about moral
principles, and normative relativism, which is itself a moral
principle.[3]

Descriptive ethical relativism

This is the claim that the moral principles of cultures or individuals conflict fundamentally, that is, the disagreement would persist even if there were perfect agreement about all the relevant facts. This is a factual claim about the diversity of moral principles. Opponents of moral relativism can accept this factual claim. What they reject are the following claims, which moral relativists infer from the fact.

Meta-ethical relativism

This is the claim that there are no universal or objective moral principles, which could be used to assess the moral beliefs of cultures or of individuals. Different moral beliefs, it implies, are equally valid, sound or true. It denies that there is one correct moral evaluation of any moral issue and that moral principles can be universally or objectively correct (or true or most reasonable). This is a theory about moral principles and judgements.

Normative relativism

This is the claim that if a culture believes something is right or wrong, then it *is* right or wrong in that culture. It claims that the moral beliefs of a culture determine right and wrong in that culture; so what is right in one culture may be wrong in another. Polygamy, meat-eating, consuming alcohol or child labour are examples. Normative relativism implies that individuals ought to conform to the moral principles of their culture. This is itself a moral principle.

Universalism

Universalism is opposed to both meta-ethical and norma-tive relativism. It claims that there are some moral principles that are universal and are objective or impartial in that they are the most reasonable moral principles for all cultures and all individuals. It holds that the moral beliefs and practices of cultures, including one's own, and of individuals, including oneself, can be rationally and critically assessed. Universalism need not claim to know which are the most reasonable universal moral principles, only that we can work towards them through moral argument, which moral philosophy aims to do.[4] Utilitarian and Kantian moral theories and human rights provide examples of moral principles that are claimed to be universal and objective. Universalism can accept that some matters, such as funerary practices, standards of public decency, dress codes and etiquette, are merely matters of cultural convention or custom; there is no universal or objective rule. It denies the moral relativist claim that *all* moral issues are like this because there are no universal moral principles.

Arguments for moral relativism

The main argument for meta-ethical relativism is from the fact of fundamental moral diversity. From the fact that different cultures (and individuals) have different moral beliefs, meta-ethical relativism infers that there are no universal or objective moral standards. Morality is, and can only be, relative to each culture (or individual).

It may be objected that the fact that different cultures and individuals have different fundamental moral beliefs does not support the meta-ethical relativist conclusion that there are no universal or objective moral standards. The fact that beliefs conflict does not entail that there is no universal or objective answer to be had. The fact that cultures or individuals have *factual* beliefs that conflict obviously does not entail that there is no universal and objective answer to be found. Similarly, it is objected, the fact that cultures or individuals have *moral* beliefs that conflict does not entail that there is no universal and objective answer to be sought. Some cultures believe that slavery or torture is morally permissible, others believe that they are wrong. Meta-ethical relativism infers that there is no universal or objective moral standard with which to judge slavery or torture. Normative relativism infers that these practices are right in some societies and wrong in others. In contrast, universalist moral views can argue that slavery and torture are universally and objectively wrong, and that cultures or individuals that believe otherwise are mistaken.

The fact that conflict of beliefs does not entail that there is no universal or objective answer is harder to see in relation to moral beliefs than it is in relation to factual beliefs because many moral questions, such as those concerned with abortion, euthanasia or drug laws, remain controversial, whereas slavery and torture are now uncontroversial. In relation to controversial moral questions, we may not know the right answer, but it does not follow that there is no right answer. (We can work towards it through critical examination of the arguments on each side.) Similarly, there are factual questions to which the right answer is unknown, or even unknowable, but it does not follow that there is no right answer. So, the fact of moral diversity does not entail meta-ethical relativism.

In reply, the moral relativist can challenge the analogy between factual beliefs and moral beliefs. There are objective facts to which factual beliefs purport to correspond. But there are no objective morals to which moral beliefs can correspond. The dichotomy between facts and values undermines the analogy. The universalist can respond that, nonetheless, the reasons that can be given to support particular moral beliefs can be critically examined and thus some beliefs can be shown to be more or less reasonable than their rivals. Through this process, we can work towards the moral beliefs that are supported by the best reasons.

There is also an argument from moral diversity to normative relativism. Some practices are believed to be right in one culture but believed to be wrong in another. From this observation, normative relativism infers that the practice is right in one culture and wrong in another. It may be objected that this argument is invalid because it goes from facts (about beliefs) to values. It goes from *beliefs* about what is right or wrong to a conclusion about what *is* right or wrong. However, what people believe to be right or wrong does not establish what is right or wrong.

Another argument for meta-ethical and for normative relativism is from the value of toleration. Moral relativism, both meta-ethical and normative, rightly denies that the moral beliefs of one's own culture are special. That is to say, it denies ethnocentrism, the assumption of one's own culture as the norm, as universally right. Moral relativism may seem attractive because it seems to be opposed to the arrogant, ethnocentric assumption that one's own culture is superior to others. Such claims were used to try to justify imperialism and colonialism, and moral relativism may seem to be opposed to such practices and to their ethnocentric justification. Relativism, in contrast to ethnocentrism, regards each culture's moral beliefs and practices as equally correct. So, relativism may seem to support toleration of different cultures' moral beliefs and practices.

It may be objected that the argument from toleration to moral relativism is incoherent. Meta-ethical relativism says that one moral belief or custom is not morally better than another. So, meta-ethical relativism entails that tolerance is not better than intolerance. Normative relativism says that toleration is right in tolerant cultures but wrong in intolerant ones. So, for relativists to appeal to toleration as a universal value is self-contradictory.

Conversely, moral relativism cannot coherently criticize ethno-centric, imperialistic or intolerant beliefs and practices. Meta-ethical relativism denies that one moral belief or custom is inferior to another. So, if a culture believes that its religion or way of life or economic system is superior to those of other societies and ought to be imposed on those other societies, by force if necessary, meta-ethical relativism denies that such ethnocentric or imperialistic moral beliefs or practices can be judged to be wrong. Normative relativism implies that people in an imperialist or intolerant (racist, anti-Semitic or homophobic) culture ought to comply with its imperialism or its intolerance. So, both meta-ethical and normative relativism are no more associated with tolerance than they are with intolerance.

Moral relativism may seem to express a liberal, egalitarian, democratic, tolerant outlook in regarding the moral beliefs of each culture (or individual) as equally valid. However, it would be incoherent for relativism to appeal to the values of freedom, equal-ity, democracy or tolerance as if they were universal, superior to their opposites, because both meta-ethical and normative relativism deny that there are any such universal values. For the same reason, both meta-ethical and normative relativism must be uncritical of illiberal, oppressive, hierarchical, undemocratic or intolerant cultures. Indeed, normative relativism implies that members of such cultures ought to comply with such beliefs.

Moral relativism gains its appeal from the false assumption that the alternative to it is ethnocentrism. Ethnocentrism and moral relativism may seem to be opposites, but this is mistaken. Ethnocentrism is uncritical of the moral beliefs and practices of one's own culture. Moral relativism (both meta-ethical and normative) is uncritical of the moral beliefs and practices of every culture. Moral relativism is generalized ethnocentrism.

In contrast, universalism holds that there are universal and objective moral principles, which can be used to examine critically the moral beliefs and practices of all cultures, including one's own. Universalism is opposed to both ethnocentrism and moral relativism. An egalitarian-liberal universalism can argue that freedom, equality, democracy and toleration are morally better than their opposites, universally and objectively. It can argue that ethnocentric beliefs and practices, and the imperialism and colonialism they have been used to justify, are universally and objectively wrong. And it can criticize liberal-democratic societies and cultures for their illiberal, undemocratic, inegalitarian and intolerant features.

The objections to the arguments for moral relativism from the fact of moral diversity and from the value of toleration question the two main reasons given in support of moral relativism, but they do not refute relativism. Let us turn to some objections to moral relativism.

Objections to moral relativism

One objection to moral relativism is that it is incoherent, because it undermines itself. The relativist denial of universality or objectivity applies to that claim itself. Relativism implies that relativism itself is merely culturally relative or subjective, not universally or objectively true.

However, the distinction between meta-ethical and normative relativism enables avoidance of this quick dismissal of moral relativism as incoherent. Meta-ethical relativism can coherently claim both that (i) moral principles and judgements are culturally relative or subjective, not universal or objective, and that (ii) that meta-ethical relativist claim (i), which is not itself a moral principle or judgement, is universally and objectively true.[5] So, meta-ethical relativism is not incoherent.

Normative relativism, since it is a moral principle, may still appear to be incoherent. It claims that the moral beliefs of a culture determine right and wrong in that culture, and claims that individuals ought to conform to the moral beliefs of their culture. Yet it proposes this second claim as a *universal* moral principle, true for all cultures. So, normative relativism seems vulnerable to the objection of incoherence.

However, normative relativism can avoid the charge of incoherence by distinguishing between first-order moral principles, which it claims are culturally relative, and normative relativism itself, which is a second-order moral principle, a principle about first-order principles, which it claims is universal. Analogously, the first-order rule about driving on the left or the right is relative to society – there is no universally or objectively right rule – but it is a universal second-order rule that one ought to comply with whichever first-order rule obtains in the society in which one is driving. Normative relativism can regard all first-order moral standards similarly, as merely cultural conventions, and assert its own universal second-order principle of an obligation to conform to the local conventions. So, normative relativism is not incoherent.

It may seem that meta-ethical and normative relativism could not be coherently combined. Meta-ethical relativism denies that there can be universal moral principles but normative relativism asserts a universal moral principle. However, the normative relativist could say that meta-ethical relativism is true of first-order moral principles but not of normative relativism's second-order principle. Thus, normative relativism could be combined coherently with a modified meta-ethical relativism. So, neither meta-ethical relativism nor normative relativism, nor their combination, can be quickly dismissed as incoherent.

Normative relativism has some internal problems. One is how to distinguish cultures from each other. Societal cultures are not separate or discrete; they influence, overlap with and merge into each other. In addition, societies are multicultural and include diverse religious, ethnic, class, gender, generational and regional cultures. Sub-cultures proliferate. These sub-societal cultures interact. A problem for the normative-relativist claim that individuals ought to conform to their culture's moral rules is that any individual is in several such cultures, which may conflict. A second internal problem is this: however cultures are distinguished, how do we determine the moral beliefs of a culture, since any culture is internally diverse? Are they those of its authorities? If so, which ones? Political, religious, judicial, philosophical and other authorities may disagree. Or are they those of the majority of all its members? If so, how are members defined (are dissidents or here- tics members?) and how big and how stable a majority does it need to be? The moral beliefs that legitimize controversial practices – such as religious, racial, ethnic or sexual discrimination, genital mutilation, slavery or torture – may not be shared by the victims of such practices. Why should their beliefs be discounted in deter- mining the moral beliefs of a culture? So, the normative relativist idea of the moral beliefs of a culture is variously problematic.

The main objection to meta-ethical and normative relativism and subjectivism is that they are inconsistent with some of our fundamental assumptions about morality. They are inconsistent with the ideas of moral disagreement, moral argument, moral deliberation, moral criticism, moral progress, moral knowledge, and universal human rights, interests and values.

Moral disagreement

People have different moral beliefs about, for example, abortion, euthanasia, capital punishment, homosexuality and drug laws. Whichever our beliefs, we regard them as correct (true or the most reasonable) and the opposite beliefs as mistaken. We do not think that our beliefs are merely different, merely cultural conventions (like etiquette) or subjective (like tastes). We *disagree*. We do not regard our moral beliefs in the ways that moral relativism and subjectivism regard moral beliefs, as merely matters of cultural custom or subjective feelings, which cannot be correct or mistaken. To view moral convictions in that way is to fail to understand what a moral conviction is.

Moral argument

When confronted with someone with moral beliefs opposed to our own, we give reasons for our beliefs and reasons against theirs. They do the same. We reply to each other's reasons. We try to convince each other. We engage in *moral argument*. Through consideration of competing moral judgements and moral principles, the reasons given in their support, objections to those arguments, replies to those objections, rejoinders to those replies, and so on and so forth, we can get closer to, and perhaps arrive at, the moral judgements and principles that are the most reasonable. If moral beliefs were merely matters of cultural custom or subjective feelings, moral argument would be pointless.

Moral deliberation

When we reflect on a controversial moral issue (say, abortion, euthanasia, the justification of punishment, civil disobedience, drug laws) about which we do not have a settled belief, we consider the reasons that can be given on each side. We try to decide which view is supported by the most convincing reasons. We do not think each view is equally correct. If moral beliefs were merely cultural customs or based on subjective feelings, moral deliberation would be pointless.

These familiar facts about moral disagreement, moral argument and moral deliberation would make no sense if moral relativism or subjectivism were true. If morality were merely a matter of cultural custom or subjective feelings, so that no one moral judgement is better than another, there would be no moral disagreement, merely difference, and so moral argument and deliberation would be pointless. Moral argument and deliberation presuppose that there is a right answer to be sought.

Moral criticism

Moral relativism, both meta-ethical and normative, rightly denies the ethnocentric idea that the moral beliefs and practices of other cultures may be criticized merely because they are different from those of one's own culture. However, it wrongly infers from this that the moral beliefs and practices of other cultures, and one's own, may not be criticized. Meta-ethical relativism denies that there are any universal moral standards with which to criticize the moral beliefs and practices of a culture. Normative relativism claims that the norms of a culture are morally right in that culture.

Moral relativism, then, is inconsistent with the idea that a culture's moral beliefs and customs, including those of one's own culture, can be criticized. If a culture believes that racial, ethnic or religious discrimination, oppression of women or homosexuals, genital mutilation, or cruel treatment of animals is morally right, moral relativism (both meta-ethical and normative) denies that we can say that those beliefs and practices are morally wrong. It regards them merely as different customs – right in that culture, even if wrong in another.

Gilbert Harman notes that the moral relativist denies that there is a basic moral prohibition against injuring others. Many groups' moral beliefs 'do not prohibit harm or injury to outsiders'. So, a member 'has no reason to avoid harm or injury to outsiders, according to the relativist'. For example, a professional criminal's code may recognize obligations to comrades but no obligation not to harm outsiders. The moral relativist denies that an obligation against harming others applies to people who do not believe in it. The criminal has no reason not to harm his victims.[6] Moral relativism (both meta-ethical and normative) denies that we can criticize such beliefs.

Moral relativism also implies uncritical acceptance of the moral beliefs and practices of one's own culture. So, if our culture's customs include cruelty to animals, indifference to desperate poverty abroad or environmental damage, meta-ethical relativism denies that they can be criticized and normative relativism says that they are right for us. However, no belief or practice is justified merely because it is part of a culture or tradition.

Societal moral progress

Practices that were once regarded as morally acceptable are now regarded as morally wrong. They may persist, but are no longer accepted as morally justifiable. Examples include domestic violence, marital rape, slavery, torture, imperialism, military aggression and racial, religious and sexual prejudice and discrimination. Non-relativists can think of these social changes as moral *progress* – that is, our current beliefs and practices are not merely different from, but are morally better than, the former beliefs and practices. However, according to moral relativism (both meta-ethical and normative), the old cultural beliefs and practices were merely different, not inferior. According to normative relativism, the old practices were right when they were the accepted norm. Moral relativism denies that these cultural and social changes, or any others, constitute moral progress. It denies the concept of moral progress (and regress), because it denies that one cultural moral belief or practice can be judged to be better than another.

Individual moral progress

As a result of argument and reflection about moral questions, sometimes individuals revise their moral beliefs. For example, some people who grew up in a culture in which racism, sexism, homophobia, and indifference to distant poverty, cruelty to animals and environmental destruction prevailed, become convinced that these things are wrong. They regard their revision as moral progress – their old beliefs were wrong and the revised ones are better. You may disagree with these examples but still recognize the process of revising one's moral beliefs as a result of critical reflection. Meta-ethical relativism and subjectivism deny that change in moral beliefs can be regarded as progress (or regress), because they deny that the new beliefs can be judged to be better (or worse) than the old ones; they are merely different.

Moral knowledge

For moral relativism, there are only diverse moral beliefs, each equally 'valid' in its culture. There can be no universal or objective moral knowledge. We simply learn the moral beliefs of our culture. For universalism, in contrast, we can critically assess, revise and reject the moral beliefs of our culture. Through moral argument, deliberation and criticism we can come to know that certain moral beliefs, including some prevalent in our culture, are false, as they are based on false factual claims or faulty reasoning. We can acquire moral knowledge, which enables moral progress. For example, racist, sexist, homophobic and speciesist beliefs, although widely held, turn out, on critical examination, to be groundless (that is, supported by no good reasons).[7]

Universal human rights, interests and values

Moral relativism denies the universality of human rights, and that of the values and interests they protect. The idea of universal human rights insists, against moral relativism, that all human beings, whatever their culture, have morally important interests in security, freedom and welfare. That people in all cultures value these things, at least for themselves,[8] is shown by the practical choices they make.[9] The universality of the interests and values that human rights protect challenges the relativist claim that all values are relative to particular cultures.

* * *

A resolute moral relativist or subjectivist could accept that moral relativism is inconsistent with the ideas of moral disagreement, moral argument, moral deliberation, moral criticism, moral progress, moral knowledge, and universal human rights, interests and values. They could reply that those ideas are delusions, resulting from failure to recognize the culturally relative or subjective nature of all values and moral judgements. The objections to moral relativism may not amount to a refutation – this may not be possible – but they perhaps indicate that belief in moral relativism incurs costs that few would accept. Perhaps the best response to moral relativism and subjectivism is to consider attempts to provide moral principles that are universal and objective, the two most influential of which are utilitarian and Kantian moral theories.

Questions for discussion

1 Does the fact of moral diversity among cultures and individuals establish the meta-ethical relativist claim that there are no universal or objective moral principles?

2   Does the fact of moral diversity establish the normative
    relativist claim that what is right in one culture is wrong in
    another?
3   Does the value of toleration support either meta-ethical or
    normative relativism?
4   Is moral relativism compatible with the idea of:
    (a) Moral disagreement?
    (b) Moral argument?
    (c) Moral deliberation?
    (d) Moral criticism?
    (e) Moral progress?
    (f) Moral knowledge?
    (g) Universal human rights, interests and values?

10

UTILITARIANISM

Utilitarianism has been an influential, widely held and challenging moral and political theory over at least the last two centuries. Utilitarianism claims, first, that what is good is utility, which utilitarians variously define as pleasure or happiness or the satisfaction of desires or of interests. It then claims, second, that morality is concerned with maximizing utility, that is, happiness or welfare. Whichever way the good is defined, utilitarianism holds that it is rational to maximize it. Utilitarianism claims that the fundamental principle of morality is that the right action or rule is the one that would maximize utility. In calculating which actions or rules would maximize utility, the utility of everyone affected must be taken into account and treated equally. Benefits to some may outweigh harms to others. For utilitarianism, then, whether an action, policy, rule or institution is right or wrong depends on whether its overall consequences are good or bad for all affected. That which has the best consequences is right.

Utilitarianism is a teleological (goal-based) theory in that it judges the morality of actions or rules according to the extent to which they serve the goal of maximizing utility. It is a consequentialist theory in that it judges the morality of actions or rules only by their consequences, by their net effects on utility (that is, the sum of their good effects minus the sum of their bad effects).

Utilitarianism thus defines and relates the two basic concepts of ethics, the good (states of affairs) and the right (actions, policies, rules or institutions) in the following way. First, it defines the good independently of the right, that is, non-morally. It defines the good as utility, that is, pleasure, happiness or satisfaction of wants or interests. It then defines the right as whichever actions or rules would maximize utility for all affected. Thus in utilitarianism the good is prior to, and determines, the right.[1]

This chapter summarizes the classical utilitarianism of Jeremy Bentham and John Stuart Mill, explains the varieties of contemporary utilitarianism, identifies many attractions of utilitarianism, considers its implications for liberty, rights, equality and social justice, and discusses objections to utilitarianism and utilitarian replies.

Bentham's and Mill's utilitarianism

Jeremy Bentham (1748–1832) and John Stuart Mill (1806–73), the main founders of utilitarianism, illustrate the elements and structure of the theory identified above. Bentham[2] claimed that humans are naturally governed by pain and pleasure. These alone determine 'all we do', say and think. And these alone indicate 'what we ought to do, ... the standard of right and wrong'.

Bentham's questionable factual claim that our *own* happiness determines what we *do* and his moral claim that *everyone's* happiness determines what we *ought* to do, are in tension. If the factual claim were true, it would make utilitarian morality dependent on reward and punishment to align moral conduct with pursuit of one's own happiness. However, it is the moral claim we are concerned with, so we can set aside the factual claim.

Utility, Bentham says, means producing 'benefit, advantage, pleasure, good or happiness' or preventing 'mischief, pain, evil or unhappiness'. The value of a pleasure or pain depends on its intensity, duration and probability. It might be objected, Bentham notes, that pleasure is not the only value – the arts and sciences, for example, are valuable too. He replies that the value of all arts and sciences 'is exactly in proportion to the pleasure they yield'. If the game of pushpin gives more pleasure than music or poetry, 'it is more valuable than either'. For Bentham, then, utility (pleasure or happiness) defines what is good.

This conception of the good is then used to determine what is right. Bentham proposes the principle of utility, or the greatest happiness principle. This is the principle that 'approves or disapproves of every action' according to its tendency 'to augment or diminish' happiness. It applies to every action, not only of individuals but also of government.

This 'greatest happiness' principle is often referred to as, in Bentham's phrase, 'the greatest happiness of the greatest number',[3] but this addition is mistaken. It is redundant, because the greatest happiness already takes into account the number affected. It makes the principle indeterminate, because you cannot maximize two things that may conflict. It is also misleading, because it is often misunderstood to imply that utilitarianism requires doing what the majority wants, whereas all utilitarians agree that sufficiently intense interests of a minority outweigh weak interests of a majority.

Bentham exhibits the essential elements and structure of utilitarianism: first, a conception of the good as pleasure or happiness (utility); and second, a conception of the right as whatever maximizes that good.

Mill's utilitarianism also has this structure. He says that both utility and happiness mean 'pleasure, and the absence of pain'. Unhappiness is pain and the absence of pleasure (II, 1, 2).[4] Pleasure and freedom from pain 'are the only things desirable as ends'. All desirable things are desirable either for the pleasure inherent in them or as means to pleasure or prevention of pain (II, 2; IV, 1).

Mill remarks that ultimate ends are not amenable to direct proof, so he cannot prove the utilitarian doctrine that happiness 'is the only thing desirable, as an end' (I, 5; IV, 1, 2). He observes that the only proof that something is visible or audible is that people see or hear it. Similarly, the only possible evidence 'that anything is desirable, is that people do actually desire it' (IV, 3). However, it may be objected that Mill here conflates the ethical question of what is worthy of desire with the factual question of what is desired.

Mill considers the objection that to suppose that life has 'no higher end than pleasure' is 'a doctrine worthy only of swine' (II, 3). In reply, he observes that humans have higher mental faculties than animals and human happiness must include gratification of those faculties. The pleasures of the intellect, feelings, imagination and moral sentiments are more valuable than 'those of mere sensation'. Compared to bodily pleasures, mental pleasures are 'more desirable and more valuable' (II, 4). They are of a higher quality in that almost everyone who has experienced both kinds of pleasure prefers to use their higher faculties. No intelligent, educated, sensitive or moral person would prefer to be the opposite even if they would then be more satisfied (II, 5, 6).

Given this conception of the good as happiness, Mill, following Bentham, proposes the principle of utility, the greatest happiness principle, as 'the foundation of morals'. This principle holds that 'actions are right in proportion as they tend to promote happiness, wrong as they tend to produce [unhappiness]' (II, 2). According to Mill, 'the morality of actions depends on the consequences which they tend to produce' and, according to utilitarianism, 'the good and evil of the consequences is measured solely by pleasure or pain'.[5]

The utilitarian standard of right conduct requires one to be 'strictly impartial' between one's own happiness and that of others. 'To do as you would be done by, and to love your neighbour as yourself, constitute the ideal perfection of utilitarian morality' (II, 17).

It may be objected that it is too demanding to require that people always act to promote the interests of everyone. In reply, Mill observes that the utilitarian standard of morals is the test of the morality of actions, but need not be their motive. Almost all actions are done from other motives, and rightly so if the principle of utility permits them (II, 18). Humankind may 'obtain a greater sum of happiness when each pursues his own, under the rules and conditions required by the good of the rest, than when each makes the good of the rest his only object'.[6]

It may be objected that there is not enough time to calculate and weigh the effects of all possible actions before acting. Mill's reply is that 'there has been ample time', the past duration of humanity, during which people have learnt by experience the tendencies of actions. One does not need to work out anew whether murder or theft harms human happiness (II, 23). The traditional rules of morality are based on empirical beliefs about the effects of actions on human happiness. We do not need to test each action against the principle of utility. Customary morality provides the necessary subordinate principles that derive from and apply the fundamental principle of utility (II, 23; III, 1). Rights and justice are ultimately based on utility (V, 25, 32, 36). Happiness is generally 'more successfully pursued by acting on general rules', or rights and obligations, 'than by measuring the consequences of each act'.[7] However, we continue to learn about the effects of actions on happiness and so the received moral rules are capable of utilitarian improvement (II, 23).

The complexity of human affairs entails that exceptionless moral rules cannot be framed. Hardly any kind of action is always obligatory or always wrong. Conflicts of obligations inevitably arise. The principle of utility, as the 'ultimate source of moral obligations', decides between conflicting obligations (II, 24). For example, utilitarianism supports a general rule against lying, but also supports exceptions when lying is necessary to prevent 'great and unmerited evil' (II, 22). To save a life, utilitarianism would imply a duty to steal necessities or to coerce a medical practitioner (V, 37) – actions that in other circumstances would be wrong.

In his replies to these two objections, Mill exhibits what is now known as indirect utilitarianism. That is, although the principle of utility is the criterion of right action, it is not normally a direct guide to practical decision-making, but is the ultimate justification of subsidiary moral rules, which are. When those rules conflict, the principle of utility adjudicates.

The utilitarian theory of morality is 'grounded' on the theory that happiness is the only desirable end (II, 2). Mill's arguments from the utilitarian conception of the good (happiness) to the utilitarian principle of morality (the maximization of happiness) are unconvincing. First, he claims that happiness, being the end of human action, 'is necessarily also the standard of morality', the rules whose observance might maximize happiness for humankind and other sentient beings (II, 10). However, other moral theories could grant that happiness is the end of individual action, but deny that its maximization is the standard of morality. Second, according to Mill, 'each person's happiness is a good to that person, and the general happiness, therefore, a good to the aggregate of all persons' (IV, 3). Again, his premise may be granted, but the conclusion does not follow from it. Third, Mill claims as a psychological fact that human nature is so constituted that happiness is the 'sole end of human action, and the promotion of it the test by which to judge all human conduct; from whence it necessarily follows that it must be the criterion of morality, since a part is included in the whole' (IV, 9). Again, even if his premise is granted, his conclusion does not follow from it.

So, like Bentham, Mill exhibits the essential structure of utilitarianism, namely, a conception of the good as utility or happiness, and a conception of the right as the maximization of the good.

Varieties of contemporary utilitarianism

Bentham and Mill conceive the good (utility) as pleasure or happiness.[8] Now, 'preference utilitarians' conceive the good as satisfaction of preferences, since people may want things other than, and perhaps in conflict with, their pleasure or happiness, for example, knowledge, understanding, achievement, autonomy or to practise their religion, which might deny them pleasures. Preference utilitarianism leaves it to each individual to define their own good. 'Welfare utilitarians' conceive utility as the satisfaction of interests rather than preferences, since some preferences may be irrational, ill-informed or short-sighted, for example, for addictive or health-harming things.[9] Since interests include most preferences, which typically include happiness, which typically includes pleasure, 'welfare' will be used as a synonym for utility.

Maximizing total utility would require individuals and governments to strive to increase the population so long as the gains in utility to the extra people outweigh any losses in utility to the existing people. Maximizing total utility thus requires increasing the population indefinitely, despite falling average utility. A utilitarian response to this problem is to reformulate the principle of utility as maximizing average, rather than total, utility. (If the population is assumed to be constant, these amount to the same thing.)[10]

Utilitarianism claims that the right is whatever maximizes the good. This principle of utility can be applied to acts (act-utilitarianism) or to rules (rule-utilitarianism).

Act-utilitarianism applies the utility principle to each possible act: the right action is that which would maximize utility. In most circumstances, truth-telling, respecting property, keeping promises and not harming others have the best consequences and so maximize utility. However, in some circumstances, lying, stealing, breaking a promise, harming or even killing would have better overall consequences than any alternative and so would be the right action, according to act-utilitarianism, for which the end justifies the means.

According to act-utilitarianism, the right act is the one that will maximize utility. However, it need not claim that we always have to work out the consequences of each possible action before acting; we often lack the time to do so. Rather, certain rules, such as keeping promises, may be adopted because following them generally has good consequences. In addition, personal bias may distort utilitarian reasoning while following a rule is more likely to maximize utility. However, in act-utilitarianism, in contrast to rule-utilitarianism, rules are only rough and ready 'rules of thumb', which generally have good consequences but which ought to be broken when obeying them would have bad consequences.[11] According to Smart, the chief persuasive argument for utilitarianism is that any rule or duty will on some occasions have bad consequences that utilitarian principles could prevent. If the purpose of morality is to subserve happiness, we ought to reject any moral rule that conflicts with the utility principle.[12]

Indirect act-utilitarianism, in contrast to rule-utilitarianism, maintains that utility-maximization is the theoretical criterion for determining the morality of actions. However, in contrast to direct act-utilitarianism, it holds that it should not be the guide to everyday moral deliberation about what to do. This is because we cannot know all the consequences of each possible action and because utility calculation is too complicated, time-consuming and prone to bias and error. If everyone were to try to maximize utility with each action, as *direct* act-utilitarianism prescribes, the results would probably not maximize utility. Instead, *indirect* act-utilitarianism selects non-utilitarian moral norms (principles, rules, duties, rights, dispositions and habits) for practical decision-making that would, if generally followed, unintentionally maximize utility. The attempt to maximize utility directly would produce consequences that were less good than those that would result from accepting, inculcating and following non-utilitarian norms, such as a duty to keep promises, a habit of telling the truth, a right to personal autonomy or a disposition to favour one's family. These non-utilitarian moral norms are to be inculcated, internalized and adhered to. They are not merely rules of thumb to be broken when doing so would maximize utility. There is, then, a distinction between our everyday, practical moral thinking, which should not typically be act-utilitarian, and our critical, theoretical moral thinking about our practical moral norms, which thinking should be act-utilitarian. Act-utilitarianism selects, revises and resolves conflicts between non-utilitarian moral norms whose general acceptance will indirectly maximize utility.[13]

Rule-utilitarianism applies the utility principle not to acts but to possible moral rules, in order to work out the ideal set of rules for society to follow. The right rules are those that, if generally followed, would maximize utility. In contrast to act-utilitarianism, the principle of utility is not the criterion of the rightness of actions. Rather, right actions are those that comply with the utility-maximizing rules. Lying, stealing, breaking promises and killing generally have bad consequences, so rules prohibiting them may be justified on utilitarian grounds. Actions that comply with those utility-maximizing rules are right.

Rule-utilitarians argue, then, that the most effective way to maximize utility is to adhere to rules that are chosen to maximize utility. Rules serve to maximize utility because they are easier to communicate, inculcate, remember and apply than are act-by-act utility calculations.[14]

John Rawls contrasts act-utilitarianism's 'summary' conception of rules, as summarizing past decisions made by direct application of the principle of utility, with the 'practice' conception of rules, as defining a practice such as promising or punishment. This practice conception of rules, he argues, saves utilitarianism from traditional objections such as that it permits punishing the innocent when doing so would have good consequences, or it permits breaking a promise when doing so would have marginally better consequences than keeping it. A rule-utilitarian justification of the practice of promising does not allow the promisor discretion to use utilitarian reasoning to decide whether or not to keep the promise. The purpose of the practice of promising is to forbid such utilitarian discretion. A rule-utilitarian justification of the practice of punishment does not allow officials discretion to punish the innocent, or to punish disproportionately, on utilitarian grounds. For classical utilitarians such as Bentham and Mill, the utility principle was mainly for judging institutions, which are systems of rules, rather than actions.[15]

Rule-utilitarianism, then, justifies rules that typically maximize utility. However, there will be circumstances in which breaking the rule would maximize utility. In such circumstances, should the rule be followed? If rule-utilitarianism says that the rule should not be followed when doing so would not maximize utility, then it reverts to act-utilitarianism. If it insists that the rule should be followed even when doing so would not maximize utility, then, according to act-utilitarianism, it abandons utilitarianism for irrational 'rule worship'.[16]

Rule-utilitarianism might respond to this dilemma by including exceptions in the rules. Since following simple rules, against lying, stealing, breaking promises or harming others, would not maximize utility in some situations, rule-utilitarianism must reformulate the rules to include the exceptions, thus permitting, for example, lying or killing when necessary to prevent serious harm. However, formulating the rules that would maximize utility would require including more and more exceptions until arriving at the utility-maximizing rules, which would forbid lying, killing, and so on, except when doing so would maximize utility. Rule-utilitarianism would thus arrive back at act-utilitarianism.[17] Rule-utilitarianism may reply that rules with many exceptions may be the utility-maximizing rules in theory but would be too complicated and too unpredictable and so would not be the utility-maximizing rules in practice. Simpler rules would maximize utility. But then rule-utilitarianism again becomes vulnerable to the act-utilitarian objection that it would require acting on a rule in cases when doing so would not maximize utility.

These distinctions – pleasure/happiness/preferences/interests, total/average, act/rule and direct/indirect – are independent of each other, so together they generate many possible forms of utilitarianism. However, all forms of utilitarianism share the principle that utility-maximization is the criterion of rightness: The right act or rule is the one that would maximize total or average utility.

Attractions of utilitarianism

An attractive feature of utilitarianism is that it seems to give morality a solid foundation. That pleasure, happiness or satisfaction of wants or interests are good, and pain, unhappiness or dissatisfaction are bad, seem almost to be undeniable natural facts, not challengeable value-judgements.

Second, this feature enables utilitarianism to take into account the interests of nonhuman animals. Utilitarianism considers humans as sites of pleasure, happiness, wants or interests, so it naturally extends to nonhuman animals that are also such sites. Nonhuman mammals, at least, have the capacity to experience pleasure and pain. They thus have interests, which must be taken into account in deciding what actions or rules would be right. Peter Singer argues that animal farming and much experimentation on animals cause suffering that is greater than the benefits to humans, so maximizing utility implies that vegetarianism is morally obligatory and non-medical experimentation, at least, is morally wrong.[18]

Third, it may seem that rationality demands that we maximize the good (however it is defined). Rationality seems to demand choosing what has the best consequences; choosing a suboptimal outcome seems irrational. Utilitarianism seems to offer a rational morality.

Fourth, utilitarianism is simple. It proposes a single fundamental principle of morality: maximize utility. When subsidiary moral rules, obligations or rights conflict, this principle resolves the conflict. In any situation, there is a uniquely right action. The principle of utility seems to dispel the illusion that morality is complex.

Fifth, in moving from facts about pleasure, happiness, wants or interests to moral judgements, utilitarianism exhibits impartiality and objectivity: All interests are considered equally. No interests are privileged – not those of oneself, one's family, one's nation or one's species.

Sixth, utility provides a universal standard of morality, which is independent of the moral codes of particular cultures and with which they can be critically assessed and revised.[19]

Seventh, utilitarianism makes morality sensitive to the facts of each situation. Consequently, it denies that certain actions (for example, promise-breaking, lying, stealing or killing) are intrinsically and always wrong. They are wrong only when and because they do not maximize utility. In situations in which they are necessary to produce the best consequences, when necessary to save lives or to prevent other serious harm, for example, then they are right. This sensitivity to the facts, and the resulting flexibility, may seem attractive.

Eighth, utilitarianism seems to transform moral questions into the factual question of what will maximize utility. To some people, calculating costs and benefits seems to be an attractive way of avoiding moral judgements.

Ninth, utilitarianism challenges traditional moral beliefs, for example, on the treatment of animals, victimless crimes (such as drug use and prostitution), punishment, distant poverty, civil disobedience, abortion and euthanasia.[20]

Tenth, utilitarianism challenges the common method of using our moral intuitions to test proposed general moral principles. This method begs the question of whether our moral intuitions are correct. Our intuitions are unreliable. For they are influenced by natural selection, emotion, tradition, upbringing and self-interest. Some may not withstand critical examination. Or they may be mutually inconsistent. For example, a person may have conflicting intuitions about whether it is right to harm an innocent person in order to prevent greater harm to others.[21] One reason we have conflicting intuitions is that, as Thomas Nagel observes, every choice about how to act is two choices – about our own action and about the state of affairs that results.[22] Peter Singer argues that we should not take intuitions as data, which moral theory must fit. We should be critical towards intuitions, distinguishing between those that have a rational basis and those that do not. 'No conclusions about what we ought to do can validly be drawn from ... what most people ... think we ought to do.'[23] James Rachels observes that moral philosophy can be a subversive activity which can undermine the deepest assumptions of ordinary morality.[24]

An eleventh attractive feature of utilitarianism is its comprehensiveness. The principle of utility is proposed as the fundamental principle of morality for all topics. Contrast this with Kantian ethics, which is concerned with moral relations among persons and does not naturally extend to our duties towards animals or the natural environment. Similarly, Rawls acknowledges that social contract theory cannot address those topics. His theory of justice proposes principles of justice for social institutions, which are distinct from the principles of justice for individuals and from those for international relations. Rawls does not think the principles for those three subjects derive from more fundamental principles. Rawls's pluralism, with its different principles for different subjects of justice, is less economical than utilitarianism's monism, with its one fundamental principle for all topics (although it may be that utilitarianism is neatly wrong and Rawls is untidily right).

So, utilitarianism is a moral theory that is naturalistic, non-speciesist, rational, simple, impartial, objective, universal, fact-sensitive, subversive and comprehensive. These attractive features make it an alluring moral theory, but not necessarily the most reasonable one.

Utilitarianism, liberty, rights, equality and social justice

Liberty

Welfare is often maximized if individuals have freedoms to pursue their own preferences and interests. Basic liberties, such as the freedoms of opinion, expression, association and assembly, tend to promote utility. Conversely, denial of such freedoms causes frustration and unhappiness. Utilitarianism thus supports liberty as instrumentally valuable. Mill's *On Liberty* advocates the freedoms of thought, expression, association and action, if harmless to others. These freedoms, he argues, promote happiness by allowing individuals to pursue their own good in their own way, by developing their abilities to discern and pursue what is good and by fostering diversity, innovation and improvement in ideas and practices, which benefits society. Mill claimed that his liberalism was founded on his utilitarianism. The utilitarian view that liberty promotes welfare implies opposition to legal prohibition of victimless offences such as adult consensual homosexuality, prostitution, pornography or drug use.

However, utilitarianism can also have illiberal implications. It justifies restrictions on liberty when they would maximize utility. If a majority wants the freedom of a minority restricted, the satisfaction of the majority's preferences would, in certain circumstances, outweigh the frustration of the minority's, so doing so would maximize utility. If an oppressed group is not dissatisfied with its situation (perhaps because of a belief that it is natural, inevitable or God's will), then utilitarianism implies that there is no need to change it. (A welfare utilitarian could avoid this implication by distinguishing between the group's desires and its interests.)[25] If enough people find an opinion offensive, restricting freedom of expression may maximize utility. Maximizing welfare could justify paternalistic limitations on the freedom to engage in unhealthy or risky activities. Utilitarianism supports freedom only instrumentally, as a means to utility-maximization, so only if and when it maximizes utility. Indirect and rule-utilitarianism apply this test to moral norms and rules, not to each act, so they allow more liberty than direct act-utilitarianism does, but they still value liberty, and thus norms and rules that allow liberty, only instrumentally, and thus contingently. It may be objected that liberty is intrinsically valuable, independently of its contribution to utility, and individuals have a *right* to basic liberties, independently of whether they maximize utility, so discrimination against minorities, oppression, denial of freedom of expression, and paternalism are unjust even when they would maximize utility.

Rights

Rights protect morally important interests (for example, in security and in basic liberties) from being overridden by utility maximization. They limit what may be done to produce good consequences. Rights need not be thought of as absolute; they may be liable to be overridden when necessary to protect more important rights, but not for a larger sum of less important interests. For utilitarianism, in contrast, any interest may be overridden when doing so would have sufficiently good overall consequences, which may be merely a larger sum of lesser interests. So, utilitarianism seems unable to recognize rights, since the interests that rights would protect are, for utilitarianism, liable to be overridden when necessary to maximize utility.

However, indirect and rule-utilitarianism argue that they can accommodate legal and moral rights, as means to maximize utility. For example, rights to security and to basic liberties indirectly maximize utility. This is because attempting to maximize utility unconstrained by rights would result in uncertainty, abuse and fear, which recognizing and protecting those rights would avoid. Protecting rights will typically maximize utility. Exercising one's rights need not maximize utility in every case. John Harsanyi argues that most people would prefer to live in a society whose moral code protects individual rights and does not permit violation of them except in rare cases. This, he says, is the basic argument for rule-utilitarianism. Society would achieve more utility by following a rule-utilitarian code than an act-utilitarian code.[26]

It may be objected that the utilitarian justification of rights recognizes and protects rights for the wrong reason. It bases rights not directly on the interests of the individual right-holder, but indirectly on the interests of society as a whole. It regards violations of rights not as directly wronging the individual but as indirectly harming society as a whole. However, violations of rights wrong their victims independently of any effects, such as fear, on others.

A second objection is that, although protecting rights will typically maximize utility, there will be circumstances in which violating a right would have better consequences than respecting it would have. Since utilitarianism justifies rights only as means to maximize utility, utilitarian rights are insecure, liable to be overridden when doing so would maximize utility. Utilitarianism implies that it would be right to sacrifice individuals' rights when it would have sufficiently good consequences for society as a whole. For example:

- Secretly framing and publicly punishing an innocent person may maximize utility by satisfying a public desire for reprisal or by deterring serious crime.
- Invading the privacy of a celebrity (say, by placing a hidden television camera in her bedroom or bathroom) for the entertainment of the public would maximize utility if it was the preference of a sufficiently large number of voyeurs.
- Involuntary organ 'donation' (say, from an anaesthetized patient without family) would save several lives for each one sacrificed.
- Involuntary medical experimentation could similarly maximize utility. Since experimentation on animals can be misleading (because some things that harm test animals do not harm humans, and vice versa), breeding humans especially for medical experimentation would maximize utility. (Surrogate mothers could be deceived about the destiny of their babies, who would not otherwise be conceived, so even they would benefit from the breeding programme.)
- The secret rape of a permanently comatose patient would maximize utility.

In each of these examples, individuals' rights and utility maximization conflict. Indirect and rule-utilitarianism can justify recognition and protection of rights in many circumstances but, when rights and utility unequivocally conflict, the utilitarian must either sacrifice rights or abandon utilitarianism.

One utilitarian response to such examples is to argue that such actions would not in fact maximize utility, because they would cause anxiety and fear in the population. In reply, the examples can be modified such that they would maximize utility, say, by keeping the rights-violating action secret or by restricting potential victims to a small minority. However, this utilitarian response distracts from the issue of principle. Utilitarianism affirms the principle that it is right to sacrifice individuals' morally important interests when it would maximize utility. The anti-utilitarian insists that moral rights prohibit such sacrifice.

Another utilitarian response to the objection that utilitarianism can, in certain circumstances, justify terrible deeds is that it would do so only to avoid consequences that would be worse. For example, utilitarianism might justify torture if necessary to prevent a terrorist outrage. The non-utilitarian who would not choose the terrible deed would thereby choose consequences that would be worse.[27] However, it may be replied, utilitarianism justifies sacrificing individuals' rights not only when necessary to protect other rights (which some non-utilitarians would accept) but also to achieve a greater sum of lesser interests.

Equality and social justice

Utilitarianism treats people equally only in the procedural sense that each person's utility counts equally in calculating what would maximize utility. This utilitarian rule of equal consideration of interests does not entail any substantive equality (of rights, liberties, opportunities, resources or welfare), because it requires any inequalities that would maximize utility. Nor does it presuppose any commitment to the moral equality of persons, because unjust (racist, sexist, homophobic, sectarian) preferences or interests are counted equally in a utility calculation. It may be objected that preferences or interests should not be regarded as non-moral facts to be counted equally. Those that are morally wrong should not be counted at all in determining what is right.

Justice is not a fundamental concept for utilitarianism. Utilitarianism is concerned with maximizing welfare and indifferent to its distribution. It does not matter how welfare is distributed, provided its total or average is maximized. However, maximizing welfare requires that the means to welfare (rights, liberties, opportunities, money, goods) are distributed in the way that maximizes welfare.[28] Whichever distribution of the means to utility is the one that maximizes utility is deemed the right one, no matter how unequal it may be.

Utilitarianism implies that inequality of rights, liberties or opportunities would be right if it would maximize utility. For example, if a racial, religious or ethnic majority had a preference for, or interest in, lesser rights, liberties or opportunities for a minority, discriminatory policies could maximize utility. It may be objected that such inequalities are unjust even if they would maximize utility. Utilitarians may reply that the minority's interest in equal rights, liberties or opportunities is more intense than the majority's interest in discrimination, so the former would outweigh the latter, and so utilitarianism would not justify discrimination. One rejoinder to this is that a sufficiently large number of people's sufficiently intense desires for discrimination against a sufficiently small minority would maximize utility, and so be justified according to utilitarianism. Another, more fundamental, rejoinder is that individuals' rights, liberties and opportunities ought not to depend on such utility calculations, that justice requires equal rights, liberties and opportunities irrespective of utility calculations.

For utilitarians since Bentham, the aim of government ought to be to promote the welfare of the whole population, which implies support for democratic equality of political rights, because governments that face elections tend to be sensitive to their electorate's preferences whereas those that don't tend to be indifferent to them.[29] Democracy thus tends to produce policies that promote utility. However, utilitarianism supports democracy only as a means to promoting utility. If a benevolent dictatorship could be shown to promote utility more effectively, utilitarianism would support it. (This is improbable but not impossible. For example, an undemocratic government that favoured the poor might promote utility more effectively than an elected government influenced by the rich, or an anti-corruption military regime might promote utility better than a corrupt elected government.) It may be objected that citizens have an equal *right* to participate in the political process, so social justice requires democracy independently of whether it promotes utility.

Henry Sidgwick drew some implications from utilitarianism that suggest it is inconsistent with the ethos of a democratic society. Utilitarianism accepts that utility is generally produced by rules such as truthfulness, keeping promises and obeying the law. According to Sidgwick, common-sense morality imposes such simple rules, but utilitarianism would, in theory, advocate more complex rules that include exceptions that maximize utility. However, in practice, such complex rules might have worse consequences than the simple rules of common-sense morality. Utilitarian advice permitting utility-maximizing lying, promise- or law-breaking may be dangerous if made public.

> Thus, on Utilitarian principles, it may be right to do and privately recommend, under certain circumstances, what it would not be right to advocate openly; it may be right to teach openly to one set of persons what it would be wrong to teach to others.

Some actions, such as lying or law-breaking, may have good consequences if done covertly but bad consequences if done openly. So, for utilitarianism, it may be right to do secretly what it would be wrong to do openly. In contrast to utilitarianism, common-sense morality holds that an action that 'would be bad if done openly is not rendered good by secrecy'. However, 'there are strong utilitarian reasons for maintaining' this common, but false, opinion. So, utilitarianism implies 'that the opinion that secrecy may render an action right which would not otherwise be should itself be kept comparatively secret'. Utilitarianism thus implies 'an esoteric morality, differing from that popularly taught'. But its 'doctrine that esoteric morality is expedient should itself be kept esoteric'. So, utilitarianism may imply that it is expedient to confine utilitarianism 'to an enlightened few', leaving 'mankind generally' believing in simple, absolute moral rules, which are false but popular belief in which has good consequences.[30] Utilitarianism's (especially indirect utilitarianism's) implication that the public should be taught false but useful non-utilitarian moral beliefs, while utilitarianism's own principles should be kept esoteric, conflicts with the democratic idea of a society of equals, who share certain basic moral and political principles. When political and other authorities act on covert utilitarian grounds while publicly proclaiming non-utilitarian principles, they act against the idea of democratic, open and accountable government.

For utilitarianism, economic or social equality is not intrinsically valuable. The utility-maximizing distribution of resources must balance egalitarian and inegalitarian considerations. However, there is general agreement that utilitarianism has broadly egalitarian implications.

The main utilitarian argument for economic equality is from the diminishing marginal utility of money and most goods. That is, the more one has, the less valuable any extra is. Conversely, the less one has, the more valuable an increase is. The utility of money or goods to an individual varies inversely with the amount they already have. Any given sum of money is likely to give more welfare to a poor person than to a rich one. So redistribution of resources from the rich to the poor increases total utility. This implies utilitarian support for egalitarian policies.[31] For example, state provision of social security, education, health care and housing, financed by progressive taxation, increases expected utility because the gains in welfare for the beneficiaries probably exceed the losses to taxpayers. It may be objected that individuals have a right to such resources as a matter of social justice, independently of whether it maximizes overall utility. In addition, it may be objected that egalitarian redistribution to maximize utility need take no account of personal responsibility, so would permit taxing savers or the frugal to help the prodigal or the lavish. Responsibility-insensitive redistribution may be unavoidable in practice, but should not enter into the definition of the right distribution, as maximizing utility permits.

A second utilitarian argument for equality is that inequality tends to produce envy, which is 'disagreeable'. To the utilitarian, it 'makes no difference ... whether it is justified or unjustified'. If the disadvantaged feel no envy, even of 'outrageous' privileges, this source of disutility does not exist so the argument from envy does not apply.[32] It may be objected that envy is no objection to an inequality that is just and that lack of envy is no justification of an inequality that is unjust.

The main utilitarian argument for economic inequality is that it provides incentives to increase productivity, which increases the total wealth available for distribution and thus tends to increase welfare. If egalitarian redistribution reduces economic growth, it may make the poor worse off in the longer term and so may not maximize welfare.[33]

A second utilitarian argument for economic inequality is that high taxation may antagonize affluent taxpayers or increase emigration. As with envy, it makes no difference whether these reactions are justified. 'These states of mind are facts, and moral judgements have to be made in the light of the facts as they are.'[34] It may be objected that envy and hostility to taxation should not be regarded as non-moral facts. They may be justified or unjustified. Unjustified attitudes should not enter into determining what is right (although they may influence what is expedient).

For utilitarianism, the right distribution of income and wealth is the utility-maximizing one, which requires taking into account these conflicting considerations. The act-utilitarian Smart, the rule-utilitarian Harsanyi and the indirect-utilitarian Hare agree that, balancing the need for incentives to increase productivity against the diminishing marginal utility of resources, utilitarianism implies support for the moderately egalitarian policies of the welfare state.[35] Other policies proposed to maximize utility include guaranteed employment for everyone willing and able to work,[36] a guaranteed minimum income,[37] inheritance and wealth taxes to equalize wealth in order to equalize opportunity, income and welfare,[38] and workers' collective ownership and democratic control of firms.[39]

The practical political implications of utilitarianism are always uncertain because they depend on numerous, complicated and disputed facts about the effects of social institutions and policies on the multiple interests of millions of people. It is not committed to any particular institutions or policies as a matter of fundamental principle, such as moral rights. Some utilitarians support laissez-faire capitalism, as a means to maximize production and thus maximize welfare, while others support socialism, as the means to equalize distribution and thus maximize welfare. However, given those competing considerations, a plausible interpretation of the political implications of utilitarianism is that it implies that liberal-democratic welfare-state capitalism, perhaps with some more radically egalitarian policies, is the system most likely to maximize utility.

Objections to utilitarianism

The priority of right

A fundamental objection to utilitarianism is to its non-moral conception of the good (whether it is defined as pleasure, happiness, preference satisfaction or welfare). The objection is that pleasure, happiness, preferences or interests are not non-moral facts. Some are morally impermissible and should not be taken into account in determining what is right. Rather than the utilitarian equal consideration of interests, impermissible interests should not be taken into consideration at all. For example, a preference for, or an interest in, racial, religious, ethnic or sexual discrimination is unjust and ought not to be taken into consideration in determining what is right. The same is true with an interest in exploitation of the weak or in an unjust share of resources. Not all preference-satisfaction or happiness is good, only that which is morally permissible. The right is prior to the good.[40]

Goods other than utility

Another objection to the utilitarian conception of the good as utility (pleasure, happiness or the satisfaction of preferences or interests) is that some things are good not because they produce utility, but they produce utility because they are good (for example, knowledge, understanding, achievement, autonomy, beauty and friendship). These things are valuable independently of utility, not merely as means to it, and so are valuable even when they reduce utility. Any theory that conceives the right as maximizing the good cannot recognize the plurality of intrinsic goods.[41] However, even if the utilitarian conception of the good is granted, the idea that maximizing the good determines the right actions or rules is open to various objections.

Impracticability

A common objection to utilitarianism is that it is impracticable because of epistemic difficulties: we cannot know all the consequences of each possible action or set of rules; we cannot measure happiness or the intensity of wants; we cannot compare the utility of heterogeneous things; we cannot compare the happiness of different people. However, this objection is not decisive. If utilitarianism correctly identifies the fundamental principle of morality, we ought to implement it as best we can, despite all those practical difficulties. In addition, indirect and rule-utilitarianism do not regard utility-maximization as the guide to everyday practical decision-making, but select moral norms or rules that generally maximize utility, and so are less vulnerable to this objection.

Exploitability

The epistemic difficulties in applying utilitarianism make its practical implications highly uncertain, given that they often depend on complicated and uncertain facts, about multiple consequences for multiple interests. This uncertainty makes utilitarianism readily exploitable by people with decision-making power in government or business. They can claim that, in making their decision about an act or rule, all interests have been taken into account and their decision is justified as having the best overall consequences for everyone affected. Again, indirect utilitarianism is less vulnerable to this objection. Utilitarians can also reply that a moral theory should not be criticized for its *mis*use, and that alternative theories are also liable to misuse. Nevertheless, the criticism remains that utilitarianism is especially prone to such misuse because whether or not it *is* misuse is so uncertain.

Too strict

According to act-utilitarianism, the right action is the one that would have the best consequences. This implies that, in any situation, of all the courses of action open, only one, the utility-maximizing one, is right. One has discretion only if there are two or more actions that have equally good consequences. In contrast, in ordinary moral thinking (as in Kantian moral theory) some actions are morally obligatory, others are prohibited and many are permissible – neither obligatory nor prohibited. So, in many situations, more than one action is permissible. Utilitarianism, in contrast, lacks latitude in that only the utility-maximizing action is right. Again, indirect and rule-utilitarianism are less vulnerable to this objection because they may argue that the liberty not to maximize utility at all times may indirectly maximize utility.

Too demanding

Another objection is that utilitarianism is too demanding because it requires us to be impartial, to treat our own interests in the same way as all other interests. This implies that continual self-sacrifice is obligatory (for example, giving one's time and money to help the needy). Consequently, utilitarianism has no place for supererogation, that is, action above and beyond duty. For example, many non-utilitarians agree that there is a moral duty to help people in absolute poverty, but think that giving to the extent that utility maximization would require would be supererogatory. However, utilitarianism can reply that this objection appeals to our natural inclination to prefer our own interests, which is morally misleading, and we ought to strive to overcome our natural resistance to the demands of impartiality. It can also reply that allowing people to pursue their own interests to a limited extent is indirectly the most effective way to maximize utility.

Special obligations

A related objection is that we have special obligations to family, friends, benefactors, colleagues and others to whom we are related. We ought to give their interests priority over those of strangers, not treat them impartially. Again, this objection appeals to a natural inclination to prefer family, benefactors and friends to strangers. Utilitarianism can reply that we ought to strive, against our inclinations, for impartiality, not to discriminate against strangers. In addition, it can reply that limited preferences to help family and friends may indirectly be the most effective way to maximize utility. Peter Singer argues that intuitions about special obligations must be examined impartially, and limited preferences for family, friends, benefactors and neighbours can be justified impartially, as promoting overall happiness.[42]

There are also special obligations that arise from promises and agreements entered into. If you have promised or agreed to do something, you are under an obligation to do it. However, direct act-utilitarianism implies that whether you ought to do it depends on utility calculation, which will often require not fulfilling your obligation (for example, giving to charity rather than repaying a debt). Rule-utilitarianism would support a rule requiring fulfilment of such obligations because such a rule would promote utility. It implies that it is right to follow the rule because the rule maximizes utility, and it is wrong to break promises because doing so weakens the institution of promising. However, this rule-utilitarian account supports keeping promises for the wrong reason. Promises and agreements give rise to obligations to specific persons, not only to everyone to maintain the institutions of promising or contracting. Secretly breaking a promise or an agreement may not harm the institution, but it still wrongs an individual.[43] Furthermore, a rule permitting utility-maximizing exceptions would be superior at promoting utility than would a rule requiring fulfilment of obligations in all cases.

Desert

A related objection to consequentialist moral theories such as utilitarianism is that how people ought to be treated depends not only on consequences but also on their past actions: people *deserve* reciprocation, rewards or punishments. However, utilitarianism is concerned only with consequences, so it cannot adequately recognize desert. Utility-maximizing acts or rules may happen to treat people as they deserve, but only because doing so would have good overall consequences and not because they deserve it. Again, if utilitarianism comes to the right conclusion, it does so for the wrong reason.

*   *   *

We have seen that utilitarianism is characterized by two elements: a conception of the good as pleasure, happiness or the satisfaction of preferences or interests; and a conception of the right as whichever actions or rules maximize that good. Even if that conception of the good is granted, several objections suggest that maximizing it does not determine the right. But a fundamental objection to utilitarianism is to its non-moral conception of the good. Pleasure, happiness and the satisfaction of preferences or interests are not inherently good; they are good only if they are morally permissible. The good is not independent of, and prior to, the right. On the contrary, the right is prior to, and determines, the good. This leads us to Kantian moral theory.

Questions for discussion

1   Do you agree that happiness or preference satisfaction is the only thing that is good as an end in itself?
2   Is morality essentially about maximizing happiness?
3   Does utilitarianism have any practical implications that are morally unacceptable?
4   Which, if any, of the objections to utilitarianism are convincing?

11

KANTIAN MORAL PHILOSOPHY

According to the moral philosophy of Immanuel Kant (1724–1804), the principles of morality are found in pure reason, 'free from everything empirical' such as knowledge of human nature (G, 410).[1] Thus, morality is not founded on desires, whether one's own (ethical egoism) or everyone's (utilitarianism). Moral duties are commands of reason (G, 413). Moral laws are universal for all rational beings and so cannot be based on the particularities of human nature or its circumstances (G, 389, 408, 410n, 442). They are then applied to human nature (when knowledge of human nature and circumstances is pertinent). Since it is our own reason that tells us what we ought to do, morality is not imposed by any external authority (God, the law, custom or tradition). Rather, to be governed by morality is to be governed by reason and thus to be self-governed or autonomous.

Since morality is founded on reason, everyone, except the very young and the severely mentally ill or disabled, has the ability to *know*, to work out, what is right and wrong. We do not need moral philosophy to tell us this, but we may need it to achieve clarity and consistency, and to address new problems.[2] Everyone also has the capacity to *do* the right thing, for the right reason, namely, because it is right. We may fail to do so, but we *can* do so. This common moral capacity, founded on reason, confers *dignity* on each person, equally, irrespective of social position.

Kantian ethics and utilitarianism relate the concepts of the good and the right in opposite ways. Utilitarianism starts from a conception of the good (pleasure, happiness or preference- or interest-satisfaction), given independently of morality, and uses it to try to work out the right (actions, rules, policies and institutions). Kantianism, in contrast, starts from a conception of the right, of morality, which enables us to identify which ends and means are permissible, prohibited or obligatory.[3] It denies that the good can be conceived independently of the right (CP, 65). Pleasure, happiness or the satisfaction of preferences or interests may seem to be good independently of morality. But some pleasure, happiness or satisfaction (for example, that of the rapist, the torturer or the thief) is immoral and therefore bad. Suffering or unhappiness may appear to be bad independently of morality, but the unhappiness suffered in just punishment is right and therefore good. Kant's moral philosophy is concerned not with happiness – either one's own (egoism) or everyone's (utilitarianism) – but with how we can be *worthy* of happiness (G, 393; CP, 136; PW, 64).

According to Kant, a human being can be viewed as having two contrasting aspects. A human being is a *natural* being, a rational animal. As a rational animal, we have theoretical reason, which enables us to know the world as it *is*, and empirical practical reason, by means of which we can set ourselves ends and can know effective means to our ends. A human being is also a *moral* being, with morally practical reason, or pure practical reason (MM, 151, 173–4, 183, 186f). Our moral reason enables us to know what we *ought* to do; it thus enables us to choose moral ends and moral means. Our moral reason can restrain, resist and overcome the powerful opposing forces of our inclinations (MM, 145f, 221, 224).[4] To bring all one's capacities and inclinations under the control of one's reason is to rule oneself; unless reason governs, feelings and inclinations control one (MM, 166). To be governed by morality is to be governed by a law that, through our reason, we give to ourselves, and thus to be self-governing, autonomous. Because we are both natural and moral beings, whose inclinations often oppose morality, we experience morality as a constraint, as duty (MM, 14, 145).

Moral duties are categorical imperatives

Moral duties are *imperatives* – morality commands or prohibits what we morally *must* do or not do. Morality is not just one consideration to be weighed against others – it overrides all other considerations. Moral imperatives are *categorical*, unconditional, in that they do not depend on one's desires. They declare an

action or omission to be objectively necessary without reference
to any purpose (G, 414f). Morality does not say 'if you want a good
reputation, you must not lie'; it says 'you must not lie' (G, 441).
Moral duties thus contrast with prudential rules, which are hypothetical imperatives: *If* you want X, then you must do Y. For example, if you do not want to be punished, you must not steal. These
imperatives do depend on your desires. They advise necessary
means to ends. But morality commands certain conduct unconditionally, not as a means to some end (G, 414, 416; CP, 31, 37).[5] So,
moral duties take the form of categorical imperatives – actions
you must do or not do whatever your desires may be. Categorical
imperatives forbid or oblige certain actions and permit others
(MM, 14–15).

Moral duties may be perfect or imperfect. Perfect duties allow no
discretion; for example, the duty not to defraud. Imperfect duties
allow latitude over how, but not whether, to comply. For example,
the duty to help others allows discretion over whom, when, where
and how, but not whether, to help; the putative duty to develop
our talents allows discretion over which, when and how, but not
whether, to develop. Consequences are pertinent to judgements
about how to carry out imperfect duties. For example, in deciding
how to exercise the duty to help others, pertinent facts are where
need is greatest and help would be most effective.

Moral duties need not be simple commands, such as 'you must
not kill'. Like legislation, moral duties may need to be more complicated. For example, the duty against killing prohibits only
intentional killing of harmless persons, because it must permit
killing in self-defence and, in war, killing legitimate targets and
unintentionally killing non-combatants. Similarly, the duty not to
lie must, despite Kant, include exceptions that allow lying when
necessary to prevent serious wrongdoing. But complicated moral
duties, like legislation, remain imperative and categorical.

Moral duties identify not only permissible and impermissible
means to our ends but also identify obligatory ends (in addition to
our various permissible personal ends). What ends are duties, ends
that we ought to set ourselves? First, it is a duty to pursue one's own
perfection, which means, first, cultivating one's talents, knowledge
and understanding and, second, cultivating one's disposition to
act from duty. Second, it is a duty to promote the happiness of
others. Duties of right, which identify permissible means to our

ends, are perfect duties. Duties of virtue, which identify ends that
we ought to pursue, are imperfect, allowing latitude over how and
how much one perfects oneself and helps others (MM, 147, 150–1,
153, 155f, 194–6). This latitude means that Kantian ethics is not as
strict or as demanding as utility maximization.

The Categorical Imperative

In the *Grounding for the Metaphysics of Morals*, Kant aimed to
identify and establish 'the supreme principle' of morality, which
is the foundation for specific moral duties and our ordinary moral
judgements. His method was initially to 'proceed analytically
from ordinary knowledge to ... the supreme principle' (G, 392). We
already know that, for example, deception, theft and coercion are
wrong (in most circumstances), but why are they wrong? What
principle founds and explains these judgements?

Kant names this fundamental principle the Categorical
Imperative (CI). Moral duties are categorical imperatives. The
supreme principle of morality, from which they derive, is the
Categorical Imperative. The CI is implicitly presupposed in our
moral judgements. Kant aimed to give this implicit principle an
explicit and precise formulation.

Kant gives various formulations of the CI. The two main ones are
the Formula of Universal Law and the Formula of Humanity. He
explains each using four examples that illustrate the four types of
duty that result from combining the distinction between duties to
others and duties to oneself and that between perfect and imperfect duties. His examples are the perfect duty to others not to make
false promises, the perfect duty to oneself not to commit suicide, the
imperfect duty to others to help people in need, and the imperfect
duty to oneself to develop one's talents. He argues that each of these
duties derives from each of the two main formulations of the CI.

The Formula of Universal Law

The Formula of Universal Law states: 'Act only according to that
maxim whereby you can at the same time will that it should
become a universal law' (G, 421).[6] The CI is a test of the morality of

an action. To test the morality of a prospective action, first identify the maxim on which you would be acting, that is, identify your end and means (sincerely, avoiding self-deception about your true intention): 'I will do X in order to Y (in circumstances Z)'. It is important to formulate maxims in this form, including circumstances that are part of the reason for the prospective action, otherwise morality is conceived as consisting of excessively simple rules, such as deception, coercion and killing are always wrong, regardless of circumstances. (Kant's arguments that lying and suicide are always wrong fail to take account of circumstances.) The maxim of an act is the principle on which the subject acts, and may be influenced by the subject's ignorance or inclinations (G, 421n).

Having identified your maxim, ask yourself whether you could will the maxim of your proposed action to be universal, as if it were a natural law that everyone in those circumstances acted in the proposed way. In everyday moral argument, we ask: 'What if everyone did that?' (CP, 72). This is a test of the morality of an action. If you could will your maxim to be universal, it is morally permissible. If a maxim could not be willed to be universal, it is immoral. The sense in which a maxim could not be willed to be universal, without contradiction, is this: if the maxim were universal, it would be inefficacious. As Christine Korsgaard puts it, the test question is 'could this action be the universal method of achieving this purpose?'[7] Actions that are efficacious by being the exception to the norm are immoral. In wrongdoing, we 'do not will that our maxim should become a universal law' but that its opposite should prevail; we make an exception of ourselves (G, 424). The wrongdoer wills inconsistency. The wrongdoer needs most others to act in the opposite way to his proposed maxim (for example, to promise truthfully, not to lie, steal or cheat). For Kant, immorality consists in such inconsistency, in willing one thing for oneself and the opposite for everyone else. It is independent of consequences for welfare. Kant's universalizability test is thus quite distinct from the indirect or rule-utilitarian argument that lying, cheating, stealing or promise-breaking are wrong because they harm welfare. For Kant, they are wrong because they could not be willed to be universal.[8]

The universalizability test is well illustrated by Kant's example of a maxim of obtaining money by falsely promising to repay a loan knowing that you never can (or, more generally, extricating oneself from difficulty by means of a false promise) (G, 422, 403).

Could you will a maxim of false promising to be universal? If it were, promises would be incredible and false ones would be inefficacious. So, one could not will such a maxim to be universal, because it would then be inefficacious. Kant's argument applies to lying, deception and cheating generally. If they were universal, they would not work. They work only if they are the exception. They rely on trust, which depends on most others *not* acting in those ways. It is impossible even to conceive a world in which deception is a universal law. Similarly, a maxim of theft could not be conceived as a universal law because, if everyone stole, there would be no property.

Kant argues that a maxim of never helping others in need could be conceived as a universal law but could not be willed to be universal because one may need others' help in the future (G, 423). This argument is not entirely convincing because one can imagine a rich person being indifferent to the needy and who could will universal indifference, confident that they could buy any help they might need. Kant's argument can be strengthened by considering maxims impartially, from everyone's viewpoint, not only one's own, in which case one could not will universal indifference. Following John Rawls, a way of doing this is to imagine testing a maxim of indifference in ignorance of whether one will be rich or poor, in which case it could not be willed to be universal.[9]

Kant's arguments from non-universalizability to his examples of duties to oneself are less convincing. He argues that a maxim of suicide to escape despair could not be conceived as universal, because suicide 'from self-love' contradicts self-preservation from self-love (G, 422). However, there is no contradiction in thinking that in most circumstances self-love perpetuates life but in some circumstances it ends life. So, a maxim of suicide in certain circumstances (when it is a fully voluntary decision and would not harm others) is universalizable. This illustrates the importance of including circumstances in the maxim.

Kant's fourth example is a maxim of neglecting one's talents to indulge in pleasure. One could conceive a world in which this would be universal, but Kant asserts that as a rational being one 'necessarily wills' development of one's faculties since they are multi-purpose (G, 423). Here Kant argues that one could not will indulgence merely by asserting that one must will non-indulgence. A more convincing argument might be that one could not will everyone to neglect their talents because one needs others to develop theirs, but this would support a duty to others to develop one's talents in order to contribute reciprocally, not a duty to oneself to do so.

The universalizability test identifies non-universalizable maxims as morally impermissible. So, we have negative duties not to lie, deceive, cheat, steal or never help.[10] It implies that, conversely, we have positive duties to tell the truth, respect property and help others.

Kant claims that many duties can be derived from the principle that a maxim must be universalizable. Some maxims cannot even be *thought* of as a universal law without self-contradiction, and these conflict with perfect duties. Other maxims are not impossible to conceive as universal, but could not be *willed* to be universal, and these conflict with imperfect duties (G, 424). One could not conceive a world of universal deceit. One could not will a world of universal indifference.

Allen Wood questions Kant's 'correspondence thesis' that the distinction between maxims that could not be conceived as universal and those that could not be willed as universal corresponds to the distinction between perfect and imperfect duties. Some maxims that could be conceived as universal would lead to violations of perfect duties. For example, a maxim of assaulting or killing people to promote one's self-interest could be conceived (but could not be willed) as universal, but acting on such a maxim violates a perfect, not an imperfect, duty not to assault or murder.[11]

A problem with Kant's universalizability test is that it can be morally permissible to act in ways that one could not will to be universal. Consider the following maxims: 'I will leave early in order to avoid the traffic'; 'I will book my flight early to get a lower fare'; 'I will do this to gain a (fair) competitive advantage in order to win' (in sport, employment or business). Each maxim is non-universalizable, because it would be inefficacious if everyone did it, but each is morally permissible, because it mistreats no one. This problem indicates that the Formula of Universal Law alone cannot identify moral duties and needs to be supplemented with the Formula of Humanity, to identify mistreatment.

The Formula of Humanity

The Formula of Humanity states: 'Act in such a way that you treat humanity, whether in your own person or in the person of another, always at the same time as an end and never simply as a means' (G, 429). What does Kant mean by 'humanity' in persons? 'The capacity to set oneself an end – any end whatsoever – is what characterizes humanity' (MM, 154). Our rational capacity enables us to choose our ends. The basis of the Formula of Humanity is Kant's claim that non-rational beings, or things, have value only as means, but rational beings, or persons, are ends in themselves and are not to be used merely as means (G, 428; CP, 91).

Kant's dichotomy between rational persons and non-rational things regrettably implies that non-rational human beings (infants, the unconscious, the severely mentally ill or disabled) are things, which may be used as mere means. This dichotomy also leads Kant to consign nonhuman animals, supposing them to be non-rational beings, to the category of things, asserting that 'all animals exist only as means…whereas man is the end'.[12] These implications can be avoided if Kant's category of 'things' is understood as inanimate, not non-rational, things, thus excluding non-rational human and nonhuman animals (thus allowing that they too may have intrinsic value and be ends in themselves, not merely means, and so owed treatment respectful of their intrinsic value).

Inanimate things have extrinsic value – they have value only if, because and insofar as persons (or other animals) value them, for example, as useful or beautiful. Persons confer value on things. A person, as a rational being, has intrinsic value, independently of their value to others. Persons, Kant claims, are 'above all price', irreplaceable, have no equivalent, have 'an intrinsic worth, that is, dignity' (G, 434–5).

What gives persons such supreme value according to Kant? In some places (G, 434–5), he says it is our rationality. However, rationality can merely serve self-interest or serve evil, so is not unconditionally valuable. Elsewhere, he is more specific that it is our *moral* capacity, founded on pure practical reason, which confers unconditional value on persons. What elevates humanity is our moral capacity (CP, 90). Morality is the condition of any worth of a person (CP, 76, 82). The capacity for morality confers dignity on humanity (G, 435). The resulting 'autonomy is the ground of human dignity' (G, 436, 440). Respect for persons is really respect for morality (CP, 80f, 85n). The rational capacity to 'set himself ends' gives a human being only 'extrinsic value', but it is as a moral subject that a person is above price, 'an end in himself', possessing dignity and commanding respect; this founds equality of persons (MM, 186–7). Every human being is due respect, even the worst behaved, because they remain moral beings with the capacity to improve (MM, 209f). The following passage eloquently expresses the unique worth conferred on humans by our moral capacity, which enables us to be autonomous:

> Two things fill the mind with ever new and increasing wonder and awe, the oftener and the more steadily we reflect on them: the starry heavens above me and the moral law within me. ... The former view of a countless multitude of worlds annihilates... my importance as an *animal creature*, which must give back to the planet (a mere speck in the universe) the matter from which it came. ... The latter, on the contrary, infinitely raises my worth as that of an *intelligence* by my personality, in which the moral law reveals a life independent of all animality... (CP, 169)

The Formula of Humanity requires that we always act in ways that respect the nature of persons as rational choosers of their own ends, and thus capable of morality and thus of autonomy.

So, the basis of the Formula of Humanity is the contrast between inanimate things, which have value only as means, and persons, who, as rational and moral beings, are uniquely and supremely valuable as ends in themselves, and must not be used merely as means. What does it mean to treat a person 'as an end and never simply as a means'? A person is treated merely 'as a means' when made to serve an end they do not share, as if they were merely a thing, merely useful. Actions that treat persons as mere means, without their own purposes, include coercion, through force or its threat (for example, robbery or rape), deception (for example, fraud or plagiarism) and manipulation (for example, withholding crucial information or exploiting someone's emotions). Coercion, deception and manipulation force people to serve ends they do not share, and thus use them as mere means to another's ends. To treat someone as a mere means is to treat them as if they were a thing, without its own purposes, not as a rational being with their own ends. To treat a person 'as an end', in contrast, is to allow them, as a rational being, to decide for themselves what ends their actions are to serve. We may try to influence them through their reason, by trying to convince them to act in a particular way, but should allow them to decide, not coerce, deceive or manipulate

them, even for their own good – paternalism is a form of disrespect
for a person's rationality.

It is not merely that a person does not in fact consent to coercion
or deception; these are forms of treatment that it is impossible
to consent to. Someone who consents is not being coerced or
deceived. Coercion or deception denies its victim the opportunity
to consent or dissent. It might be objected that there are situations
in which people do consent to being deceived – for example, by
fellow poker players or by a conjuror. However, because the
deceived knows that deception is occurring, and consents to it,
they are not fundamentally deceived.

Treating someone as a *mere* means must not be confused with
treating someone as a means. The latter is morally permissible
and commonplace. In any market exchange, each party treats
the other as a means to their end, namely the money or the good/
service exchanged. But they are not treated as a *mere* means if it
is genuinely voluntary, if the other party also achieves what they
want from the exchange. (In some market exchanges, particularly
in the labour market, voluntariness is reduced or even eliminated
by lack of a reasonable alternative, in which case one party to the
transaction is exploited, unfairly taken advantage of, treated as a
mere means to the other's end.)

Not treating a person as a mere means, not coercing or deceiving
them, is morally necessary but insufficient, because it is compatible with indifference to them (MM, 157). We must also treat a person 'as an end' by helping them to achieve their own permissible
ends. There is a duty of beneficence, that is, doing good for others,
making others' happiness one's own end. One can benefit someone
only according to their own ideas of happiness, not one's own, so
beneficence does not allow paternalism (MM, 161f, 199, 201, 202–3).
The fact that someone consents to treatment is insufficient to establish that she is treated as an end, because someone may consent to
mistreatment, due to misinformation or lack of a reasonable alternative. Practices that fail to treat persons as ends include indifference to their needs – for example, a business that treats customers
as merely a source of money, indifferent to whether or not they are
satisfied, as in cases of mis-selling financial products by exploiting
customers' ignorance, or an employer that treats employees as if
they were inanimate resources, to be used to extract as much work
as possible at the least cost possible, indifferent to their health,

safety or work satisfaction. Even if customers and employees consent to such treatment, they are not treated as ends.

Kant illustrates the Formula of Humanity with his same four examples (G, 429f). First, the false promisor deceives the promisee, thus using them as a mere means to an end they cannot possibly share. (In contrast, asking for their help would allow them to decide and so would treat them as an end.) Second, never helping others in need fails to respect them as ends in themselves. Third, suicide, Kant claims, uses one's person merely as a means to avoid an intolerable condition. This debases one's humanity (MM, 177). (It may be objected that, on the contrary, suicide may end or avoid a dehumanizing, debilitating condition and thus respect one's humanity, dignity and rationality.) Fourth, neglecting to develop one's capacities might be consistent with humanity as an end in itself, Kant grants, but not with the advancement of nature's 'end' for humanity, which includes capacities for greater perfection. It may be objected that nature has no ends. Even if it did, that supposed fact would not establish a duty to adopt any of nature's ends (as Kant observes elsewhere). On the contrary, our moral duties often oppose our natural inclinations. Again, Kant's arguments for the duties to oneself are unconvincing.

Kant says that the Formula of Universal Law and the Formula of Humanity are ultimately different formulations of the same law. The first concerns the form of maxims, that they must be universalizable. The second concerns their content, that a rational being is an end in itself, which limits all other ends. A third formulation, the Realm of Ends, combines the other two (G, 436). The two main formulations are complementary also in the following way. The Formula of Universal Law considers whether a maxim could be adopted by all rational beings as *agents* of the maxim (whether they could all act on the maxim). The Formula of Humanity considers whether a maxim could be shared by rational beings as *recipients* of the enacted maxim (whether they could consent to the maxim). Although Kant says that the two Formulas are 'basically the same' principle (G, 438), they seem quite different. However, maxims that are non-universalizable (for example, deception or coercion) treat other people as mere means to one's ends. And treating another person as a mere means (by deceiving, manipulating or coercing them) is non-universalizable, because one could not will to be so treated. So, the two main formulations of the CI concur.

Kant says that the Formula of Universal Law is the 'rigorous method', which is better for moral judgement (G, 436–7). However, when he later derives particular duties, in the *Metaphysics of Morals*, he refers to the Formula of Humanity much more often than to the Formula of Universal Law and never uses the third formulation, the Formula of the Realm of Ends.[13]

Kant and ordinary moral judgements

Kant's method in the *Groundwork* was to identify and formulate precisely the fundamental moral principle (the CI) presupposed or implicit in ordinary moral judgements. In response to a critic who said that there was no new principle of morality in the *Groundwork*, Kant replied that there was no need for a new principle of morality, as if the world had hitherto been ignorant of it or wrong about it (CP, 8n). The fundamental principle of morality did not need to be discovered or invented because it had long been in the reason of all (CP, 110).

Even if the CI is implicit in ordinary moral judgements, it may be used to critically assess ordinary moral judgements and revise them where they are inconsistent with the fundamental principle of morality. However, on several topics, Kant seems to uncritically accept traditional views. He regarded sex as demeaning, as 'merely animal' and as treating one's partner and oneself as a 'thing'. Although Kant said that all human ends are chosen, none is determined by nature, he thought that the supposed natural purpose of sex, namely reproduction, entailed that this is its only morally permissible purpose, which is to fallaciously think that a fact can entail a value. Homosexuality and masturbation were lumped with bestiality as 'unnatural' (MM, 62, 127, 149, 178–9). The only sex that was morally permissible was that within life-long marriage. The obedience of a wife to her husband is based on his 'natural superiority' (MM, 63). Society may ignore the killing of a child born outside marriage (MM, 109). Kant's moral theory is critical of such views. Prejudices against non-reproductive sex, non-marital sex, women, and children born outside marriage fail to respect persons as ends. Discriminatory actions based on such prejudices disrespect persons and are not universalizable, because the discriminator could not will being discriminated against. Kant's traditional views that are inconsistent with his moral theory are pre-, or non-, Kantian.

Kant on lying

Kant's stance on lying is another that does not follow from his theory (and so is misleading if taken as exemplifying his theory). Kant claimed that it is always wrong to lie, even to thwart a prospective murderer who is asking the location of an intended victim. 'Truthfulness in statements that one cannot avoid is a human being's duty to everyone, however great the disadvantage to him or another that may result from it.' To lie would be to undermine trust, and thus contracts, and thus to wrong not the murderer but humanity generally. Someone who seeks permission for possible exceptions to truthfulness 'does not recognize truthfulness as a duty in itself but reserves for himself exceptions to a rule'.[14]

The claim that it is always wrong to lie does not follow from Kant's moral theory, for several reasons. First, a maxim of informing a prospective murderer of their victim's location would exemplify indifference to the victim and so could not be willed to be universal. In contrast, a maxim of lying to prevent murder (or another serious harm) could be universalized. It would not, as Kant claims, undermine trust generally. Moral duties do not have to be simple, such as 'do not lie', but can have exceptions built in, to take account of different circumstances. The circumstances included in the maxim must be part of the agent's reason for the action, not irrelevant details (inclusion of which would enable immoral maxims to be universalizable). Circumstances are not part of the reason for the action, but irrelevant details, if the maxim would have been proposed in their absence. Second, lying to thwart murder would treat the prospective victim as an end, by helping them, whereas informing the murderer of their location would exemplify indifference, which fails to treat persons as ends. True, for Kant, the perfect duty not to lie constrains performance of the imperfect duty to help.[15] However, the first argument that a maxim of lying to prevent murder is universalizable, so is not a violation of a perfect negative duty, makes possible the second argument that it is a permissible way of performing the imperfect positive duty of giving someone life-saving help. Third, Kant's objection to making an exception to allow lying to thwart murder conflates making an exception for particular circumstances with making an exception for oneself. However, the claim to which Kant objects is not that oneself, but not others, should be allowed to lie to thwart murder, but that anyone in specific circumstances (for example, where it would thwart murder) should be allowed to lie. Fourth, Kant recognizes that the grounds of obligations may conflict and that, when they do, 'the stronger ground of obligation prevails' (MM, 16–17). In the imagined situation, in which not lying conflicts with preventing murder, it is clear which is stronger and should prevail.[16] Fifth, Kant identified the similarity between coercion and deception in their non-universalizability and in their mistreatment of persons as mere means. Kant recognizes that wrongdoing necessitates coercion in the forms of self-defence, law enforcement and punishment, to thwart, prevent or punish wrongdoing. Similarly, wrongdoing may necessitate deception to thwart it (for example, to deceive prospective murderers).[17] In cases of deception or coercion that is necessary to prevent crime or to arrest criminals, the criminal deceived or coerced could not consent to the particular act of deception or coercion, but they could consent to the general policy under which the particular act is carried out. Since they are treated according to a policy to which they could consent, they are not mistreated as mere means. Sixth, as Roger Sullivan notes,[18] Kant thought that a test of a moral theory is whether it fits the moral judgements of ordinary people, and almost everyone thinks Kant was wrong to think that it can never be right to lie.

Moral motivation as crucial, powerful, and inspiring

Kant is concerned with the morality not only of actions but also of motives. (Utilitarianism's concern only with consequences makes it indifferent about motives.) Often, right action will be in our own interest – we avoid punishment, we enhance our reputation and become trusted. For Kantian ethics, it is not enough that we do the right thing. We must do the right thing for the right reason, namely, because it is right, not out of self-interest. In Kant's terms, we must act *from* duty, not merely *in accordance with* duty; our action must not merely *conform* to the moral law but must be done *for the sake of* the moral law (G, 390; CP, 75n, 84).

Kant notes that some people are constituted so sympathetically that they find 'pleasure in spreading joy', but he says that such action has no moral worth because it is done from inclination. It accords with duty and so 'deserves praise and encouragement, but not esteem' because 'its maxim lacks the moral content of an action done not from inclination but from duty' (G, 398). Allen Wood comments that, when Kant (G, 398) regards the cold person who helps others from duty, rather than the sympathetic person who helps others because he enjoys spreading joy, as deserving esteem, he is not saying that it is better to follow abstract moral rules than to care about people. Rather, 'he is saying that it is better to care about people because we value and respect them as beings with worth and dignity' than because we happen to like them or because helping them makes us feel good.[19] Moral value is concerned not with actions but with their unseen inner principles (G, 407). The moral worth of an action consists not in its beneficial effects but in its maxim (G, 399–400, 435). Merit lies not in right action but in doing it *because* it is right (MM, 153). To do good because of love or sympathy is not a *moral* maxim (CP, 86). So, an act has moral worth only when it is done for a moral reason. This does not mean that an act done out of self-interest or inclination is immoral. Rather, if the act is morally permissible, the non-moral motive makes the act morally neutral, neither meritorious nor culpable. For example, if a businessperson treats customers fairly in order to cultivate their own reputation and thus their custom, their action lacks moral worth because of its non-moral motive, but if they act fairly because it is right, their action is morally worthy (even if unintentionally it is also profitable).

It might be objected that what matters is what people do, not why they do it. Why does it matter *why* someone does the right thing? If someone does the right action not because it is right but from self-interest, then they may act wrongly when they can get away with it. Their non-moral motive will produce moral actions only in certain circumstances and not in others. But the disposition to do the right thing because it is right motivates independently of circumstances. So, moral motivation is crucial.

Kant concedes that no certain example of the disposition to act purely from duty can be cited. One can never be certain whether one, or anyone, acts purely from duty without any admixture of self-interest. Consequently, many philosophers have denied the reality of this disposition and ascribed everything to self-interest (G, 406; MM, 155, 196). But, Kant insists, moral motivation is most powerful. The 'pure thought of duty … has by way of reason alone … an influence on the human heart so much more powerful than all other incentives' (G, 410–11). Kant observes that 'the exhibition of pure virtue can have more power over the human mind … than all allurements arising from enjoyment and … happiness or from all threats of pain and harm'. Our 'receptivity to a pure moral interest and the moving force in the pure thought of virtue … is the strongest drive to the good' and the only one capable of 'continuous and meticulous obedience to moral maxims'. If human nature were not so constituted, no way of presenting the moral law indirectly, that is, through rewards and punishments, could ever produce morality of dispositions, but only following morality for one's own advantage. The moral law would be hated or despised. It would police our actions but not our motives (CP, 157–8).

Moral motivation is also inspiring. A righteous act done with no view to any advantage 'far surpasses and eclipses any similar action that was … affected by any extraneous incentive'. It 'inspires the wish to be able to act in this way' (G, 411n, 454). 'No idea can so greatly elevate the human mind and inspire it with such enthusiasm as that of a pure moral conviction', overcoming all temptations (PW, 71).

The sufficiency of moral motivation: ought implies can

The phrase 'ought implies can' is often cited in ethics but is almost always used to mean almost its opposite, not ought implies can but ought presupposes can, that is, moral requirements must not be beyond the capability of their bearers, which is the banality 'don't demand the impossible'. However, for Kant, ought implies can, that is, if we are morally obliged to do something, then we can do it. We can do it simply because we ought to, independently of any other motivation. When we fail to do what we ought, we know that we could have done it, if we so chose.

Kant (CP, 30) argues as follows. Suppose someone claims that a desire (lust, addiction, avarice) is irresistible, that they could not resist acting on it. However, if they knew that acting on it would lead straight to their death, they would find that they could resist. This shows that love of life is more powerful than any supposedly irresistible desire. Now imagine being ordered to commit an evil deed (falsely testify to condemn an innocent person, massacre innocents) or be killed. Forced to choose between committing evil and death, you ought to choose death. And you know that you could (but not whether you would) choose death. You can over-come love of life in order to avoid doing evil. You *can* do something simply because you *ought*.[20] Kant's argument shows that purely moral motivation, the desire to act from duty, is more powerful than the love of life, is the most powerful motive, can be sufficient motivation, and thus shows that ought implies can.[21]

Moral motivation and freedom of the will

Whenever we deliberate about how to act, we must presuppose that our decision, and thus our action, is not predetermined. However, this idea of 'free will', although inescapable, could be an illusion, itself merely an effect of ignorance of the causes of our decisions. Kant notes that we cannot infer knowledge of freedom of the will from experience, which exhibits only determinism. He claims that the concept of freedom is founded on the moral use of reason (CP, 5). Kant claims that the recognition that one can do something purely because one ought to do it enables recognition that one is free – 'a fact which, without the moral law, would have remained unknown' (CP, 29f).[22] Without the capacity to act from duty, Kant argues, free-dom of the will would be merely an assumption, which could be illusory. However, his argument showing the power and sufficiency of moral motivation demonstrates not freedom of the will but the causal power of moral belief. A false moral belief (for example, that of a self-sacrificing fanatical terrorist or Nazi, or a criminal who, loyal to an oath, chooses death rather than give testimony against associates) can be as powerful and sufficient a motive as a true one. And moral beliefs are liable to causal explanation, as the product of upbringing, education and so on, so Kant's argument does not establish freedom of the will. The human capacity to act purely from moral belief, and capacity for this motive to overpower all others, does not show that there is not a causal explanation of the belief, and thus of the resulting action.

Kant claimed that the concepts of God and immortality too, as well as freedom, are founded on the moral use of reason (CP, 5). He observes that no necessary connection between happiness and virtue can be expected in this world (CP, 120). Happiness 'in exact proportion to morality', which constitutes the highest good (CP, 117), 'is practically possible only on the supposition of the immortality of the soul' (CP, 129) and on the supposition of the existence of God (CP, 131). It is necessary, he dubiously claims, 'to presuppose the possibility of this highest good', therefore it is 'morally necessary to assume the existence of God' (CP, 132). Thus, the moral law, which is independent of the postulates of God, freedom and immortality (CP, 150), leads to religion, not vice versa (CP, 136). Happiness in exact proportion to virtue may be possible only if there is a God to ensure it in an afterlife, but, *pace* Kant, this gives no reason for supposing that either God or an afterlife exists.

Questions for discussion

1   Is the Formula of Universal Law a convincing test of the moral permissibility of maxims of actions?
2   Is the Formula of Humanity a convincing test of the moral permissibility of actions?
3   Is Kant right that doing the right thing *because* it is right is
    (a) crucial to the moral worth of an action?
    (b) a powerful motive?
    (c) inspires the wish to act similarly?
4   Is Kant right that the desire to act from duty, to do the right thing purely because it is right, is sufficient, without any admixture of self-interest, to motivate action?
5   How convincing is Kant's argument that the knowledge that one can do something purely because one ought to do it enables knowledge of freedom of the will?

12

JOHN RAWLS'S THEORY OF JUSTICE

John Rawls's theory of justice, which he calls 'justice as fairness', is perhaps the most influential work in moral and political philosophy produced in the twentieth century. It has stimulated an enormous interest in political philosophy, particularly in the theory of social justice. Rawls aimed to develop social contract theory to offer a systematic account of justice as a superior alternative to utilitarianism.[1] That is, he asks which principles of justice would rational people agree to, for their own advantage, from a position of equality?

In any society, there are two kinds of conflict that make principles of justice necessary. First, in any society, but especially in a liberal democracy, people have diverse and conflicting religious, philosophical, moral and ethical beliefs. Consequently, they have diverse 'conceptions of the good', that is, conceptions of what is valuable in life. This diversity is reasonable, inevitable and permanent. Consensus on such beliefs and values cannot be expected.[2] Despite this diversity, are there principles of justice on which all reasonable citizens could agree? Since a society's political institutions and laws are coercively imposed on all its citizens, in order to be legitimate they must be based on principles that all reasonable citizens could endorse, whatever their beliefs and values.[3]

Second, income and wealth are scarce relative to people's needs and wants, so members of any society also have conflicting interests over economic distribution. Are there principles of justice to determine the right distribution on which all citizens could agree? Rawls proposes his principles of justice as the most reasonable answer to these questions.

To anticipate briefly, Rawls proposes two principles of justice: first, reasonable people with conflicting beliefs and values could nevertheless agree on the principle that each citizen ought to have equal basic rights and liberties; second, inequalities of income and wealth can be acceptable as just to all reasonable citizens if there is genuine equality of opportunity and if the social system makes the worst-off group as well off as possible. A society founded on these principles would be one without oppression or exploitation.

This chapter first explains some fundamental ideas on which Rawls's theory is based. It then explains the meaning of his principles of justice. This is followed by exposition of Rawls's main arguments for each of his principles. Some implications of the principles for social institutions and policies are given. We then consider criticisms of Rawls's contractual argument for his principles, Nozick's libertarian alternative to and critique of Rawls's theory, and Cohen's egalitarian critique of Rawls.

Fundamental ideas

The fundamental ideal of a fair society
of free and equal persons

Rawls says that his theory of justice is ideal-based[4] (in contrast to goal-, duty- and rights-based moral theories such as, respectively, utilitarianism, Kantianism and libertarianism). The ideal it is based on is that of society as a *fair* system of co-operation among *free* and *equal* citizens. This ideal is the 'most fundamental', 'central', 'organizing' idea of the theory. Rawls claims that this ideal, with its component ideals of fairness, freedom and equality, is implicit in the public political culture of a democratic society. Justice as fairness tries to formulate principles of justice whose realization in social institutions would make a reality of this ideal of a society that is fair to all its citizens, who are free and equal. The principles of justice specify the fair terms of co-operation among free and equal citizens, which is 'the fundamental question of political philosophy'.[5]

Justice as fairness regards citizens as free and equal. They are equal in that each has 'the two moral powers': a capacity for a sense of justice, that is, a capacity to understand, apply and act from principles of justice; and a capacity for a conception of the good, that is, a capacity to form, revise and rationally pursue a conception of what is valuable in life. They are free in that they are not identified with any particular conception of the good, such as a religion.[6]

The principles of justice and the institutions they imply characterize an ideally just, but practicable, society, a 'realistic utopia'. They thus clarify the goal to guide reform and identify the worst injustices, which are priorities for reform.[7]

A political conception of justice, not a comprehensive moral theory

In his later writings, Rawls re-presents justice as fairness as a specifically *political* conception of justice, rather than as a part of a comprehensive moral theory. A political conception is characterized by three features. First, it applies primarily to the 'basic structure', or main institutions, of society and not to every aspect of life. Second, it does not presuppose any comprehensive religious, philosophical or moral doctrine. Third, its fundamental ideas are implicit in the public political culture of a democratic society.

These three features allow citizens with diverse religious and philosophical views to endorse it, because it is independent of, and impartial between, reasonable comprehensive doctrines. Individuals with diverse and conflicting religious and philosophical views can affirm the same political conception of justice, which they relate in their own way to their wider views.[8]

The basic structure of society as the primary subject of justice

The principles of justice, which define the ideal of society as a fair system of co-operation among free and equal persons, apply to the 'basic structure' of society, that is, to the way its main institutions distribute rights, liberties, opportunities, income and wealth. These institutions include the political constitution, legal rights, the economic system, the system of ownership of natural resources and means of production, the family,[9] social, economic and tax policies, and thus the education, social security and health care systems.

The basic structure is the 'primary subject of justice'. This is because its effects on individuals are profound, pervasive and present from birth. What are these effects?

First, the basic structure strongly affects individuals' life chances or *life prospects*. It contains unequal positions, and the socio-economic position a person is born into strongly affects their life chances with respect to education, occupation, income, wealth, health and life expectancy. A person's life prospects are also deeply affected by their native talents and their lifetime luck in relation to illness, accident, involuntary unemployment and economic conditions. So, in any society, individuals' lifetime prospects are deeply affected by the social position they are born into, the talents they are born with, their lifetime luck and how the basic structure treats these three kinds of contingencies.[10]

Second, the way the basic structure treats those three kinds of contingencies, and thus determines individuals' life chances, affects their realistic expectations and thus their *aims* and *aspirations*, and 'the vigor and confidence with which they pursue them'. Society's institutions can foster optimism and self-confidence or resignation and apathy. The social system shapes individuals' wants and aspirations and partly determines the kinds of people they are and want to be.

Third, the basic structure determines individuals' educational opportunities and thus their educated and trained *abilities*.

So, the basic structure has profound effects on individuals' life prospects, their aims and aspirations, and their educated abilities.[11]

People's unequal life prospects are unchosen, hence undeserved, and so from a moral point of view are arbitrary.[12] They are matters of 'brute luck', which is unchosen, as opposed to 'option luck', which obtains when a person chooses to gamble.[13] What principles of justice to regulate the basic structure could make unequal life prospects legitimate and consistent with the freedom and equality of citizens?[14]

Justification of principles: the original position, the veil of ignorance, and considered convictions

The ideal of society as a fair system of co-operation among free and equal citizens raises the question of how principles of justice, to specify fair terms of co-operation, are to be determined. They are to be given by an *agreement* among free and equal citizens. To be valid, an agreement must be reached under conditions that are *fair* to all. The conditions in which principles of justice are agreed must be fair and not permit unequal bargaining power, because agreement between the powerful and the powerless does not define justice. 'The main idea of justice as fairness' is that the principles of justice for the basic structure of society are those that would be agreed by rational persons, concerned to further their own interests, 'in an initial position of *equality*'. A society based on principles that free and equal persons would agree to under fair circumstances 'comes as close as a society can to being a voluntary scheme', whose members are autonomous in that their obligations are self-imposed.[15]

To equalize the parties to the contract, Rawls asks us to imagine representatives of citizens agreeing principles of justice to regulate their society in an 'original position' in which they are behind a 'veil of ignorance'. That is, the parties to the agreement, while they know general facts about human psychology and society, do not know particular facts about the citizens that they represent. They do not know their social positions (their economic class, social status, abilities, sex, and so on), their beliefs and values (for example, their religious beliefs or their conception of the good, or whether they are in a majority or minority) or their personal psychology (for example, their risk aversion).[16]

The original position with its veil of ignorance is a 'thought-experiment' that is designed to do two things. First, it eliminates bargaining advantages and disadvantages, equalizes bargaining power, and thus models fair conditions under which representatives of citizens are viewed solely as free and equal persons. The parties are equalized to represent citizens as equal persons. Second, it models restrictions on proper reasons for and against principles of justice. It is not a good reason for a principle that it favours the interests of a particular social group, such as the rich or the poor, or the interests of the holders of particular beliefs and values. The veil of ignorance excludes knowledge of social position and conception of the good and thus knowledge of particular interests. The original position precludes arguing for principles that serve particular interests by this device of excluding knowledge of particular interests. It gathers and makes 'vivid' reasonable restrictions on arguments for principles. The veil of ignorance forces us to look at society not from our own position, but objectively or impartially. The parties must choose principles whose consequences would be acceptable to *all* social positions – majorities and minorities, the most well off and the least well off. The idea of a contract models the idea that a just society is acceptable as just to all its members, whatever their position within it.[17] We can enter the original position simply by reasoning in accordance with those reasonable restrictions on arguments for principles,[18] that is, by reasoning impartially. Rawls's original position is an easily misunderstood device, but it is simply a way of thinking about moral principles impartially.

We have various considered convictions about justice, for example, that slavery, tyranny, racial discrimination, religious intolerance or persecution, and exploitation are unjust. We need principles of justice to connect coherently and organize these various judgements. The principles agreed in the original position must match our considered convictions. Principles and considered judgements have to be mutually adjusted until they are mutually coherent. The most reasonable conception of justice 'is the one that best fits all our considered convictions on reflection and organizes them into a coherent view'.[19]

Arguments from our considered convictions about justice and arguments from the original position converge on the same principles of justice. Rawls downplays non-contractual arguments for his principles, from our considered judgements about justice, because in a contract theory all arguments are made from the original position.[20] However, since the original position with its veil of ignorance is designed so that it results in principles that match our considered convictions about justice,[21] arguments directly from those convictions are at least as important as the indirect arguments via the original position.

The principles of justice

Rawls argues that the ideal of society as a fair system of co-operation among free and equal citizens is defined by the two principles of justice he proposes:

> Each person has an equal claim to a fully adequate scheme of equal basic rights and liberties, which scheme is compatible with the

same scheme for all; and in this scheme the equal political liberties, and only those liberties, are to be guaranteed their fair value.

Social and economic inequalities are to satisfy two conditions: first, they are to be attached to positions and offices open to all under conditions of fair equality of opportunity; and second, they are to be to the greatest benefit of the least advantaged members of society.[22]

The meaning of those principles needs some explanation. The first principle is, in short, the principle of equal basic liberties. Basic liberties are these: political liberty (the right to vote, participate in politics, hold public office), the freedoms of thought, conscience, speech, association, assembly, movement and occupation; the freedoms from physical assault, psychological oppression, and arbitrary arrest and seizure; and the right to hold personal property. These liberties and rights are found in various bills and declarations of rights. The basic liberties can conflict and so must be mutually adjusted into a coherent 'scheme', but they must be the same for all citizens.[23]

The 'fair value of the political liberties' means that, ideally, the chances of political influence and power should be equal for all citizens with similar abilities and motivation, regardless of their economic class or social status. Those active in politics should be drawn proportionately from all sectors of society.[24]

The first part of the second principle is the principle of fair equality of opportunity. This means not only that positions are formally open to all (that is, non-discrimination on irrelevant grounds), but also that all have a 'fair chance' to attain them, that is, people with the same ability and effort have equal life prospects regardless of their class of origin.[25]

The second part of the second principle is called the difference principle because justice requires that the basic liberties, rights and opportunities are the same for all citizens, but allows differences of income, wealth and authority. The difference principle permits only inequalities that most benefit the least advantaged. It requires social policies that maximize the lifetime prospects of the least advantaged.[26]

Who are the least advantaged? To answer this, Rawls uses the idea of 'primary goods' – things all citizens need, as free and equal persons, whatever their beliefs and values; more of each is better than less. They include rights, liberties, opportunities, authority, income, wealth, leisure time and the 'social bases of self-respect', which are aspects of institutions that foster citizens' sense of self-worth and self-confidence.[27] Social institutions can promote or undermine individuals' self-respect. For example, self-respect is undermined by racial discrimination, preventable poverty or long-term unemployment. Conversely, equality of rights, liberties and opportunities, and making the worst-off as well off as possible, are social bases of self-respect for all citizens.

Given that justice requires equal rights, liberties and opportunities, the least advantaged are the group with the lowest lifetime prospects of income, wealth and authority, those with, say, less than half the median income and wealth. They are likely to include people born into relatively poor families, people with least natural talent and people with the worst lifetime luck.[28] Rawls does not say how money and authority are to be weighted in the index of primary goods because income and authority tend to correlate. So he focuses on the distribution of income and wealth.[29]

If the principles of justice conflict, they are not to be balanced against one another. Rather, the first principle has strict priority over the second (and fair equality of opportunity has priority over the difference principle, although Rawls is less certain of this priority rule). The priority of the first principle rules out exchanging basic rights or liberties for economic advantages. A basic liberty may be limited only for the sake of another basic liberty. Each person's basic rights and liberties are inviolable. The loss of freedom for some is not made right by greater good for others.[30] The priority of the first principle means that the second principle is always to be applied within institutions that satisfy the first principle.[31]

The priority of the principle of equal basic liberties obtains once a society has reached a level of economic and social development sufficient to allow their effective exercise. It presupposes that all citizens can exercise them, so it presupposes an implicit prior principle requiring that citizens' basic needs (which include education) be met.[32]

Rawls's principles exemplify a *liberal* conception of justice in that they identify certain basic rights and liberties to protect, they give priority to individuals' rights, liberties and opportunities over claims of the general good, and they ensure all citizens adequate resources to be able to make effective use of their rights, liberties and opportunities.[33] The principles also exemplify an *egalitarian* liberalism in that they require equal basic liberties, the fair value of the political liberties, fair equality of opportunity, and limit social and economic inequalities to those that most benefit the least advantaged. The principles thus define and reconcile freedom and equality. They also explain what the Kantian idea of treating one another not as mere means but as ends implies for the basic structure of society: equality of basic liberties and opportunities and refusal to impose lower prospects on the least advantaged to further benefit the more advantaged.[34]

Arguments for the principles of justice

Rawls's argument for the principle of equal basic liberties and its priority is that it securely protects the fundamental interests of all citizens in those liberties and avoids intolerable possibilities. In contrast, the principle of utility makes the basic liberties insecure and uncertain because it would allow the basic liberties of some to be restricted or denied for the sake of benefits for others. This outcome would be unacceptable, so the risk of it could not be agreed to in good faith. Rawls claims that free and equal persons have a fundamental, non-negotiable interest in the basic liberties. This is because they provide the social conditions essential for the adequate development and the full and informed exercise of the two moral powers of free and equal persons, that is, their capacities for a sense of justice and for a conception of the good. The first principle protects this fundamental interest. In addition, putting individuals' equal basic liberties beyond political bargaining and the calculation of collective interests secures social co-operation on the basis of mutual respect.[35]

Rawls's argument for the fair value of the political liberties starts from a left-wing criticism of liberal democracy. It is argued that equality of legal rights and liberties is merely formal because large economic and social inequalities make them unequal in reality. The wealthy control political life and obtain laws and policies that serve their interests. Rawls observes that corporate interests finance political campaigns and thus distort public discussion, and that when the wealthy control public debate and influence legislation in their interests, the political liberties lose much of their value.[36]

In response to this criticism of liberal democracy, Rawls distinguishes between the basic liberties, which justice requires being the same for all citizens, and their worth or usefulness, which varies with the individual's income, wealth, authority and status. The difference principle maximizes the worth of the basic liberties to the least advantaged (which, Rawls says, 'defines the end of social justice'). Under any other principle, including more egalitarian ones, the worth of their liberties would be less. This response defeats an argument from the basic liberties in general to the conclusion that the difference principle is insufficiently egalitarian. However, it does not answer the objection that equality of political liberties may be merely formal, because the difference principle could be insufficient to prevent the wealthy from controlling politics. To answer this objection, Rawls's first principle includes a guarantee of the fair value of the political liberties.[37]

The reason for singling out the political liberties is that there is a limited amount of political influence and power, and hence competition for it. This contrasts with other basic liberties, of which there is not a fixed amount, so their use is not competitive. Consequently, the usefulness of the political liberties depends on citizens' *relative* income and wealth, whereas that of other basic liberties depends on their absolute level of resources. The first principle of justice does not guarantee the fair worth of *all* the basic liberties because that would imply equality of income and wealth, which would, compared with the difference principle, make everyone (including the worst-off) worse off, and thus make their liberties worth less, which would be irrational.[38]

The argument for equality of opportunity is simply that if positions are not open to all, those excluded are unjustly treated. Formal equality of opportunity requires all positions are open to all on the basis of ability and effort, without discrimination on irrelevant grounds. This is necessary for a just distribution of income and wealth but it is insufficient because it permits distribution to be strongly influenced by the cumulative effects of previous generations' talents, education and lifetime luck, which are morally arbitrary. *Fair* equality of opportunity requires not only that positions are formally open to all, but also that all have a fair chance to attain them. Those with the same talents and willingness to develop them 'should have the same prospects of success', regardless of their parents' income.[39]

The ideal of fair equality of opportunity is necessary but insufficient for justice, for two reasons. First, it is unattainable, because the development of talents is affected by family circumstances. In any society, a child's opportunities depend on the family's income, wealth, education and attitudes. Second, even if fair equality of opportunity were attained, it permits the distribution of income to be determined by the distribution of natural talents, which is as morally arbitrary as class of origin. Treating 'everyone equally as a moral person' requires not allowing the distribution of income according to individuals' brute luck in their parents or their talents. So, justice requires a principle that 'mitigates the arbitrary effects of the natural lottery' that distributes talents. This leads us to the difference principle.[40]

The difference principle is the most controversial of Rawls's principles of justice. He accepts that the case for it is less conclusive than that for the first principle. The 'strongest rival' to the difference principle is a conception of justice in which the principle of average utility, which requires the maximization of average welfare, replaces the difference principle in the context of the principles of equal basic liberties, fair equality of opportunity and a guaranteed minimum income.[41] In order to maximize average welfare, this rival would permit greater economic inequality than the difference principle would permit. Arguments for the difference principle must be for its superiority over this rival. Rawls gives both non-contractual and contractual arguments for the difference principle.

Rawls's first argument is in terms of reciprocity. No one deserves their brute luck in their talents or their parents. The character to develop one's abilities also largely depends on fortunate circumstances. If we wish to set up a social system in which no one further gains or loses from their good or bad brute luck in their talents or upbringing without giving or receiving compensation, we are led to the difference principle.[42]

The intuitive idea behind it is that the better prospects of those with good brute luck are just if and only if they improve the prospects of those less fortunate, particularly the least advantaged members of society.[43] Even in a just society, the child of affluent parents will have better prospects than the child of less affluent parents. This inequality in life prospects from birth is justifiable only if it benefits the least advantaged, that is, only if reducing the inequality would make the least advantaged worse off. For example, *if* higher incomes are necessary as incentives to innovate and increase efficiency, and the increased productivity benefits the least advantaged, then those inequalities are just, according to the difference principle.[44] The difference principle requires that everyone benefit from inequalities; they are not justified on the ground that advantages to some outweigh disadvantages to others (which the principle of average utility would permit). Under the difference principle, the better-off do not gain at the expense of the less fortunate, since only reciprocal advantages are allowed.[45]

A second argument for the difference principle is from self-respect. The principle expresses respect for all members of society. Rival principles, such as maximizing average utility, would make the least advantaged worse off than anyone need be and thus disrespect them. The difference principle treats no one as a mere means, but each person as an end in him- or herself. It thus supports the self-respect of all members of society. It requires that social institutions foster 'the confident sense of their own worth' among the least favoured. This limits the permissible degree of inequality of income, wealth and authority. Wide inequalities may reduce self-esteem and 'wound' self-respect. Any alternative principle (such as the utility principle) that requires some to accept lesser prospects for the benefit of those more advantaged would harm their self-respect.[46] Under the difference principle, each person is 'treated with respect as an equal, one whose life matters as much as anyone's', which fosters self-respect.[47]

The arguments from reciprocity and from self-respect lead to the argument from stability. To be stable for the right reasons a conception of justice must, when realized in the basic structure of society, generate support from the members of society, including the least advantaged. In contrast to the principle of utility, the difference principle avoids asking the less advantaged to accept lower lifetime prospects for the sake of greater advantages for the more advantaged, which is an 'extreme demand'.[48] The least advantaged could not support a social system based on this demand, but can affirm the difference principle and support a social system based on it. A social system based on the difference principle would benefit each income class and so could be justified to all its members, including the worst-off.[49] The difference principle leaves 'no one less well off than anyone needs to be'.[50]

Inequalities under the difference principle could be justified to the worst-off group because they contribute to making them as well off as possible. Any other distributive principle, including a more egalitarian one, would make the worst-off group worse off than anyone need be, that is, worse off than they would be under the difference principle. Consequently, any other principle could be reasonably rejected by them. If a social system is justified to its least advantaged members, those lucky to be better off have no legitimate grounds for complaint.[51]

True, the better-off would have less income and wealth than they would in some alternative systems. However, they have no legitimate ground for complaint because they are lucky in their talents or parents, which they cannot claim to have deserved, they enjoy the benefits of their good brute luck and they are economically better off than others. So, the difference principle is, on reflection, acceptable as just to the better-off too. The difference principle requires a distribution of income and wealth that all sectors of society can accept as just. It thus fosters the willing co-operation of all sectors of society for mutual benefit.[52]

Thus, considerations of reciprocity, self-respect and stability support the difference principle. Rawls appeals to these same considerations in arguments from the original position.

In the original position, the contracting parties seek to maximize their share of primary goods. To agree to less than an equal share would be irrational. To expect more than an equal share would be unreasonable, expecting others to be irrational. So, the parties would initially agree to equal division of all primary goods. However, if an inequality benefits everyone compared to equality, it is rational to permit it. Inequalities of income, wealth and authority can increase the total income and wealth to be distributed.[53] So, taking account of the requirements of social organization and economic efficiency, the parties would accept inequalities of income, wealth and authority that benefit everyone compared to equal division. Taking 'equal division as the benchmark, those who gain more are to do so on terms acceptable to those who gain ... the least'.[54] Persons who view themselves as equals would not agree to rival principles that require lesser life prospects for some for the sake of greater advantages for others.[55] Since the parties represent equal citizens and so start from equal division, they would agree on the difference principle, which expresses the idea that the more advantaged are not to be better off to the detriment of the less well off.[56]

The parties in the original position would seek to avoid social conditions that undermine self-respect. Without self-respect, 'nothing may seem worth doing' or one may 'lack the will to strive', so the social basis of self-respect is arguably the most important primary good. The two principles, including the difference principle, give more support to self-respect than other principles do, so this is a strong reason to adopt them.[57] The parties in the original position would also seek principles that would be stable in that they would generate support for them, and this too would support the difference principle.

Rawls does not think that any single argument establishes the difference principle, but claims that, on balance, it is the most convincing principle to regulate the distribution of income, wealth and authority.

Institutional and policy implications
of the principles of justice

The first principle applies primarily to the constitution and political system; the second applies to social and economic policies and to the design of organizations with unequal authority.[58]

The principle of equal basic liberties requires a democratic political system in which a constitution or bill of rights guarantees equal basic rights and liberties and thus limits legislation.[59] For example, it forbids legislation that would restrict the liberties of a religious or ethnic minority. Political liberty is thus limited by equality of the other basic liberties.

The fair value of the political liberties requires enabling political parties and legislators to be independent of concentrated economic power. Since the main reason the wealthy have disproportionate political influence and power is that they have great wealth, Rawls proposes distributing wealth more evenly, since in existing democracies inequalities of wealth 'far exceed what is compatible with political equality'. He also proposes reforms to insulate politics from wealth. These include public funding of political parties and restrictions on private contributions, so parties are not dependent on rich donors, the assurance of access to public media and regulation of media freedom (but not restrictions on content).[60] Rawls's comments on the media are vague, but perhaps imply a legal requirement for some or all news media to be politically impartial or balanced.

Fair equality of opportunity requires limiting accumulations of wealth, maintaining equal educational opportunities for all, state provision or funding of universal education, health care and social security benefits, and anti-discrimination legislation.[61]

To prevent concentrations of wealth detrimental to the fair value of the political liberties and to fair equality of opportunity, Rawls (following Mill) proposes progressive taxation of the *receipt* of gifts and bequests in order to encourage wider dispersal of wealth.[62]

He says little about policies specifically to implement the difference principle, except that it should set the level of transfer payments that guarantee a minimum income. He observes that fair equality of opportunity would increase the supply of educated talent and decrease the supply of unskilled labour, each of which would reduce inequality of pay. He suggests that, in a perfectly competitive economy surrounded by a just basic structure, the relative attractiveness of different jobs would tend towards equality. Perhaps for these reasons, he thinks that a just society might not need a legal minimum wage or progressive income tax (although this does not imply that existing injustices do not justify steeply progressive income tax).[63] However, the distribution of natural talents ensures that competition is imperfect, so justice cannot be left to market competition.

Social and economic policies to implement the difference principle would include full-employment policies, which are important for two reasons apart from economic efficiency. First, involuntary unemployment, especially long-term unemployment, impoverishes, demoralizes, undermines self-respect, and harms the mental and physical health of those who experience it and those threatened by it. Second, large-scale unemployment forces people to accept unattractive, low-paid jobs while full employment strengthens employees' bargaining power, forcing employers to make jobs more attractive. A straightforward way of making the worst-off as well off as possible is to set the minimum wage at the highest level compatible with full employment. Another is public provision of high-quality education, health care and social security systems funded by progressive taxation.

What economic system could realize the ideal of society as a fair system of co-operation among free and equal persons? Rawls observes that welfare-state capitalism permits large inequalities in productive property such that a wealthy minority control the economy and politics, and the social system does not realize the fair value of political liberty, fair equality of opportunity or the difference principle. It permits relative poverty and social exclusion.[64] According to Rawls, the principles of justice might be satisfied by a 'property-owning democracy' or by liberal-democratic market socialism in which firms are controlled, and perhaps owned, by their workers, or a mixture of these economic systems. In a property-owning democracy, in contrast to welfare-state capitalism, institutions work to disperse capital widely to prevent a small minority from controlling the economy and politics. Rather than redistributing market incomes by redistributive taxation and transfer payments (which would still be necessary), it ensures widespread ownership of capital and skills to enable people to enter the market on a more equal basis, thus reducing inequality of market incomes. If liberal-democratic market socialism would realize the principles of justice more, by reducing the inequalities of productive wealth, income and authority, it would be more just.[65]

Criticisms of Rawls's contractual argument

Rawls says that justice as fairness is the 'hypothesis' or 'conjecture' that the principles of justice that would be chosen in the original position are the same as those that match our considered convictions about justice.[66] However, the original position is designed so that it results in principles that match our considered convictions.[67] Thus the match is engineered so as to confirm the hypothesis. Since all the major issues of justice have to be decided in advance in order to know how to describe the original position, the contract device can be regarded as a redundant detour.[68]

Thomas Pogge argues that Rawls's contractual argument considers only how people are *affected* by institutions, but not how we *treat* one another through our institutions.[69] (This is not entirely true, because the parties' concern with the social bases of self-respect leads to concern with how we treat one another.) Consequently,

Pogge argues, it leads to results that do not fit our considered moral convictions. For example, in relation to criminal justice, because we are concerned with how we treat one another, we believe it is so important to avoid convicting the innocent that we accept the risk of acquitting the guilty. Consequently, in order to prevent wrongful convictions, we regulate police interrogation of suspects, place the burden of proof on the prosecution and require proof beyond reasonable doubt, and so accept that some criminals escape punishment.[70] However, rational contractors would regard the danger resulting from false acquittals as seriously as that of false convictions. They would accept the risk of being falsely convicted if it would sufficiently reduce the risk of being a victim of crime. Consequently, in order to reduce crime, they would agree to laxer constraints on the police, a lower standard of proof and draconian punishment to deter crime. These implications result from considering only how we risk being *affected* by crime and punishment, disregarding consideration of how we *treat* people through our criminal justice system. An adequate conception of justice must consider both how institutions treat us and how we treat one another through our institutions. Rawls's contractual argument, Pogge objects, disregards the latter perspective.[71] However, Rawls's method is to mutually adjust the contractual argument and our considered convictions about justice until they fit together coherently, which prevents the contractual argument from having the counterintuitive results that Pogge shows it would have were it not so constrained. However, this means that the contractual argument cannot serve as a fully independent test of our moral convictions.

Nozick's libertarian rival to, and critique of, Rawls's theory of justice

Robert Nozick's libertarianism starts from the fundamental premise that individuals have equal natural rights against force, theft and fraud. These individual moral rights, Nozick argues, permit only a minimal state, that is, one limited to protection of those rights. A more extensive state, particularly state welfare provision, violates individuals' rights not to be forced to help others. Non-libertarians advocate a more extensive state to pursue distributive justice. In response, Nozick develops his entitlement theory of distributive justice, which requires only the minimal state.[72]

Nozick holds that people are entitled to whatever they get from voluntary transactions, such as market exchanges, gifts, bequests and gambles. Justice depends not on how much people own but on how they got it. Rival principles, such as utility-maximization or Rawls's difference principle, he argues, conflict with liberty. If income and wealth were distributed so as to satisfy such a principle, voluntary transactions would upset the pattern. For example, talented people would earn more than others. Rival principles require state interference to counteract the distributive effects of voluntary actions, to redistribute resources that were voluntarily transferred.[73]

Property rights, according to Nozick, exclude alleged rights to life, to equal opportunities or to a minimum income, because those alleged rights require resources over which others have property rights.[74] Principles of justice, such as Rawls's, that give citizens a right to resources (social security, education or health care) would misappropriate the product of other people's work, saving and enterprise. Welfare-state redistribution (from rich to poor, employed to unemployed, healthy to sick, able-bodied to disabled, producers to pensioners) violates property rights. Taxation is like theft. 'Taxation of earnings from labor is on a par with forced labor.' Taxing earnings is in effect forcing taxpayers to work unpaid. Forcing someone to do unpaid work is to decide what purposes they are to serve. It is to be a part-owner of them. The welfare state, by forcing performance of unpaid labour, makes taxpayers partly slaves of the state.[75]

It may be objected that taxation is unlike forcing taxpayers to work unpaid for the needy. Forced unpaid labour would violate the right to freedom of occupation, but taxation of earnings is compatible with that right.

Nozick's libertarian rights are inadequate to the underlying value of self-determination, to the idea that individuals have their own lives to lead.[76] Self-determination requires resources – income, housing and education. The destitute, homeless or uneducated cannot really be self-determining. So, self-determination for all, not just the affluent, requires not the minimal state but the welfare state, to enable each citizen to lead their own life.

Nozick claims that libertarian rights 'reflect the underlying Kantian principle that individuals are ends and not merely means'.[77] However, treating persons as ends requires not only not coercing or deceiving them, but also helping them achieve their ends. The Kantian principle thus supports the enabling welfare state. Incidentally, Kant thought that the state has the right to tax prosperous citizens to meet the needs of those unable to provide for themselves.[78]

Nozick claims that whatever distribution results from voluntary transactions is just, no matter how unequal it is. However, voluntary transactions over time produce inequalities that are unjust. First, wide economic inequalities produce inequalities of opportunity for children, who are not responsible for their parents' wealth or poverty, and hence for their own resulting advantages and disadvantages.

Second, inequality of opportunity in turn undermines the fairness of subsequent competition and thus the justice of the resulting distribution. The distribution resulting from market transactions, Rawls objects, is not fair unless the prior distribution of income and wealth is fair, all have fair opportunities to learn skills and to earn, and there is fair bargaining between employers and employees. The institutions and policies that implement Rawls's principles of justice are needed to maintain these conditions for fair markets.[79]

Third, wide economic inequality, especially without a welfare state, gives employers power over employees, forcing them to work on the employer's terms, so making their contract not fully voluntary. Nozick replies that whether other people's actions make one's resulting action nonvoluntary 'depends on whether these others had the right to act as they did'.[80] This stipulation implies that whenever a police officer rightfully overpowers or arrests a criminal, they go to the station voluntarily. Nozick has to resort to this stipulation in order to deny that people can be forced by their economic circumstances.

Fourth, wide economic inequality produces unequal political influence, which undermines democracy, which justice requires.

So, Nozick's libertarianism permits wide economic inequalities, which would sacrifice many people's economic and political freedom to the property rights of the rich. Freedom for all citizens requires redistribution of wealth. This limits the freedom of the rich (which libertarianism notices) to enlarge the freedom of the less affluent (which it does not).[81]

Nozick makes several objections to Rawls's theory of justice. He objects that Rawls's difference principle requires people with good

brute luck, in talents or parents, to receive less than they would
without the taxation it supports, so they do have grounds for complaint.[82] They would be taxed to limit inequalities of opportunity,
resources and political influence. Rawls's reply is that those people
are already advantaged by their talents or parents, for which they
are not responsible, so higher incomes would compound those
undeserved inequalities. Taxation of undeserved advantages is
not a ground for legitimate complaint.

Nozick objects that Rawls treats wealth as if it belongs to society,
to share out, rather than to its producers, in proportion to their productive contributions.[83] A Rawlsian reply is that distributing wealth
according to productivity is just only insofar as individuals are responsible for their productivity. Insofar as unequal productivity
reflects their genes or upbringing, for which they are not responsible, it is unjust to distribute wealth according to productivity.

Nozick observes that things that are claimed to justify inequalities, such as talents and the capacity for effort to develop them,
Rawls regards as products of factors over which the individual has
no control, and so as undeserved. He objects that this argument
blocks reference to a person's choices and actions, and is inconsistent with 'the dignity and self-respect of autonomous beings'.[84]
In reply, as Philippe Van Parijs notes, Rawls's difference principle
maximizes the lifetime *prospects* of the worst-off *group*. Among
this group, income and wealth would vary, partly as a result of
voluntary actions (hours worked, saving, debt). The difference
principle does not require equalizing those outcomes.[85] It thus
allows the distribution of income and wealth to be sensitive to
people's choices and actions. Once the difference principle is satisfied, Rawls says, inequalities are allowed to arise from voluntary
actions.[86]

Nozick claims that people are entitled to their talents, even
though they do not deserve them, and so are entitled to whatever
flows from them, including income and wealth.[87] A Rawlsian
reply is that people's entitlement to their abilities does not entail
entitlement to what they produce with them in a complex system
of social co-operation. Each individual's productivity depends
on the rest of the social system and the science, technology,
infrastructure and social organization inherited from previous
generations. The wealth produced is the product not of a collection
of individuals but of the system of social co-operation in which

they work, and so is rightly regarded as available for society to distribute justly, according to principles all could agree to.

Nozick claims that Rawls regards people's 'natural talents as a common asset', which is tantamount to treating people as resources for others.[88] However, what Rawls says is that the difference principle regards the *distribution* of talents as a common asset, and shares the benefits of this distribution.[89] He later clarifies this as sharing 'the greater social and economic benefits made possible by the complementarities of this distribution'.[90] That is, all share not in people's talents but in their diversity and complementarity, which enables the division of labour and its productivity.

Cohen's egalitarian critique of Rawls's theory of justice

Gerald Cohen argues that Rawls, particularly in his contractual argument for his principles, conflates principles of justice with principles to regulate society. Since the latter principles may necessitate compromising justice with other values, such as efficiency, they do not define justice.[91]

In a non-contractual argument for the difference principle, Rawls observes that socio-economic inequality is largely a product of brute luck in talents and upbringing, which are unchosen. Treating 'everyone equally as a moral person' prohibits brute luck in genes or upbringing from determining distribution.[92] This implies that inequality is largely undeserved and that justice requires equality (allowing only apparent inequalities that result from voluntary choices, such as work/leisure, save/spend). However, some inequalities of authority, income and wealth increase productive efficiency and so can benefit everyone, including the worst-off. So, the difference principle allows inequalities that benefit the worst-off.

In his contractual argument for the difference principle, Rawls says that the parties in the original position regard themselves as equal moral persons and so start from equality of all primary goods. But they take organizational requirements and economic efficiency into account and so do not stop at equal division but arrive at the difference principle.[93]

So, in both his non-contractual and his contractual arguments for the difference principle, Rawls apparently thinks that *equality* would be just, by eliminating the influence of brute luck on distribution, but the difference principle compromises justice with supposed practical needs for inequalities of authority, income and wealth. The difference principle may be the right compromise between justice and efficiency, and thus the right principle for the regulation of society, but, Cohen objects, it is not a fundamental principle of justice. Misconceiving a compromise between justice and efficiency as a fundamental principle of justice discourages pursuit of more justice.

Cohen also questions the coherence of Rawls's *application* of his principles, particularly the difference principle, which requires government to pursue equality but, according to Cohen, allows individuals to pursue self-interest in their economic choices. Cohen argues that principles of justice should apply not only to social institutions and public policies but also to personal conduct, such as choice of job, how hard to work and pay demands.[94] Rawls assumes that if people with scarce marketable skills are paid incentives, they choose more productive jobs and work harder – and so produce more – than they might for average pay. Taxation can redistribute some of their extra output to the worst-off group. According to Cohen, Rawls thinks that the difference principle thus justifies such incentives. However, Cohen argues that the difference principle should apply to personal conduct. The highly paid *could* work as hard for average post-tax pay, but instead choose to exercise their power to demand and get monetary incentives to do so. Their acquisitiveness thus causes unnecessary inequality, which makes the badly off worse off than they need be, in conflict with the difference principle. Independently of income, the highly paid are already better off than the poor, because they are lucky to have scarce talents and more satisfying jobs using their talents. So, Cohen argues, to demand high post-tax pay too is unjustifiable to the poor, who are worse off in talents, job satisfaction and now income.[95] Reducing post-tax income inequality could enable the poor to be better off. If people with scarce skills demand high post-tax pay, conceding to their demand may be expedient, as a principle for the regulation of society, but it is not just.[96]

People committed to the difference principle, Cohen argues, would not demand high post-tax pay. (Pre-tax pay differentials reflecting productivity may be necessary to inform people where they can be most productive.)[97] In a society whose members are committed to the difference principle, material incentives would be unnecessary. In such a society, Cohen argues, the difference principle would mandate equality of burdens and benefits. That is, pay differentials would only compensate for the extra burdens of particular jobs (for example, danger, stress or discomfort), but the overall package of burdens and benefits of different jobs would be roughly equal. Cohen allows 'a right to pursue self-interest to some reasonable extent', which might allow modest incentive inequality but not the large inequalities that result from unrestrained exercise of market power.[98] So, Cohen argues, a just society requires not only laws and policies that are just but also an *ethos* of justice, which informs personal choices and restrains self-interest.[99]

One possible Rawlsian objection to Cohen's criticism of Rawls's application of his principles would be to say that they apply only to the basic structure, that is, the main institutions, of society, not to personal choices. The difference principle thus allows individuals to act acquisitively.[100] Rawls identifies the basic structure as the primary subject of justice because of its profound effects, particularly on people's life-chances. Cohen's main reply to this 'basic structure objection' is that chosen conduct too has profound effects on others' life-chances. An acquisitive ethos produces unnecessary and unjust inequality and relative poverty, which an egalitarian ethos would reduce. The distribution of burdens and benefits is the result of both rules and choices, so the principles of justice should apply to both. Rawls's reason for their regulation of the basic structure is also a reason for their regulation of personal conduct. Social justice requires both just policies and an ethos of justice restraining self-interest.[101]

A Rawlsian rejoinder from Andrew Williams accepts that self-interested choices affect others' life-chances but objects that Rawls's principles are inapplicable to individuals' economic choices because those choices cannot be governed by public rules. Cohen's proposed egalitarian ethos to govern choice of job, effort in work and pay negotiations could not be embodied in public rules because individuals' productive potential, effort and job satisfaction are not publicly knowable. Consequently, individuals cannot know whether others are complying with the demands of the egalitarian ethos. So, Rawls is right to limit application of the difference principle to institutions.[102] In reply, it may be accepted that equality of burdens and benefits cannot be defined by *precise* rules but an egalitarian ethos governing work and pay is capable of imprecise formulation, like some other moral duties (such as the duty to help people in need). It is better for a society to be imprecisely just than precisely unjust.

Another Rawlsian response to Cohen is to accept his argument that disequalizing incentives are incompatible with the difference principle. It is not clear that Rawls does endorse the disequalizing incentives to which Cohen objects (since Rawls often identifies incentives with compensation for costs, which equalizes benefits and burdens).[103] Even if he does, it is not as a matter of principle. If, as Cohen argues, 'Rawls must give up either his approval of incentives to the exercise of talent or his ideals of dignity, fraternity, and the full realization of persons' moral natures',[104] then justice as fairness must abandon Rawls's ambiguous approval of such incentives. This is possible because, contrary to the basic structure objection, Rawls agrees with Cohen that principles of justice apply both to institutions and to individuals' conduct. This remains the case after Rawls's re-presentation of justice as fairness as a political conception of justice primarily for the basic structure of society rather than as part of a comprehensive moral theory for every aspect of life. The 'initial focus' of a political conception of justice is both the basic structure and how its principles 'are to be expressed in the character and attitudes of the members of society who realize its ideals'.[105] Rawls regards the basic structure as the primary subject of justice but not, as Cohen claims,[106] its only subject. Rawls holds that any theory of justice must include, secondarily, principles for individuals. In addition, he thinks that a just social system must be designed so as to foster in its members 'the corresponding sense of justice' and to 'discourage desires and aspirations' that conflict with the principles of justice.[107] The principles of equal basic liberties and equal opportunities have practical implications not only for institutions but also for individuals in that they require the elimination of racial, sexual and religious prejudice and discrimination not only by legislation but also by individuals' conduct. Democratic political equality implies a moral 'duty of civility' for individuals, to conduct political discourse and vote in a non-sectarian way.[108] Similarly, the difference principle must, as Cohen says, inform personal economic conduct, even though, as Rawls says,[109] it is unsuitable to regulate conduct directly. So, Rawls's theory can accommodate Cohen's objection to special incentives for talent.

How might institutions be designed to foster the sense or ethos of justice 'corresponding' to the difference principle and 'discourage desires and aspirations' that conflict with it? The social, economic and tax policies necessary to implement the principle would themselves encourage a more egalitarian ethos, just as policies designed to increase inequalities have encouraged an ethos of greed and extravagance. In addition, Van Parijs suggests that institutions can foster solidarity between income classes by their desegregation; for example, by planning regulations that require mixed communities and by truly universal education and health care systems (by eliminating private education and health care). However, implementing the difference principle would also require principles of justice for individuals. What principles of justice for individuals does the difference principle imply? Van Parijs suggests that, behind the veil of ignorance, concern to maximize the prospects of the least advantaged would lead to commitments to work hard at the most productive job we can do, not to evade tax and not to emigrate for lower taxation. If these principles, rather than self-interest, governed individual conduct, the prospects of the worst-off would be better.[110] Joseph Carens thinks that a moral duty to maximize one's productive contribution is unreasonably demanding, but a duty to make good (not necessarily the best) use of one's abilities allows individuals to take account of their occupational preferences and yet allows post-tax income inequality to be greatly reduced.[111] It might be objected that, without large material incentives, people would not choose jobs in which they would make good use of their abilities. However, people generally prefer work that they are good at, and work that is interesting and satisfying, so occupational choice under an egalitarian tax regime might tend to follow productive potential even independently of an ethos of justice concerning occupational choice.

We have seen that Rawls's theory of justice has received criticism from the libertarian right and the egalitarian left. We have also seen that it can be developed in response to these criticisms, perhaps in ways unanticipated by Rawls himself. Such capacity for development suggests it will be a moral and political theory of enduring interest and fecundity.

Questions for discussion

1 How convincing are Rawls's arguments for each principle of
   justice?
   (a) The equal basic liberties;
   (b) The fair value of the political liberties;
   (c) Fair equality of opportunity;
   (d) The difference principle.
2 Is the original position, with the veil of ignorance, a helpful
   device?
3 How convincing is Nozick's libertarian alternative to, and critique of, Rawls's theory?
4 How convincing are the Rawlsian objections to Nozick's view
   of justice?
5 How convincing are the Rawlsian replies to Nozick's criticisms
   of Rawls's theory?
6 Is the difference principle a compromise between justice and
   efficiency rather than a fundamental principle of justice?
7 Should the difference principle inform personal economic
   conduct? If so, in what ways?

Concluding Remarks

It may be useful to summarize some of the general issues that the preceding chapters raise.

A recurrent theme has been the contrast in moral and political theory between teleology, represented by utilitarianism, and deontology, represented by Kant and Rawls. Rawls characterizes the contrast in terms of how a theory defines and relates the concepts of the good and the right. A teleological, or goal-based, theory defines the good independently of the right, that is, non-morally. It then defines the right as that which maximizes the good.[1] Morally right acts, rules and institutions are those that produce the most good. Samuel Freeman observes that defining the right as maximizing the good presupposes the idea of one rational good.[2] According to Rawls, a deep division in moral and political theory is whether a theory holds that there is one rational conception of the good or whether it allows for a plurality of opposing conceptions.[3]

Utilitarianism, the most influential teleological theory, exhibits these three features. It defines the good non-morally as utility, interpreted variously as pleasure, happiness, desire satisfaction or interest satisfaction. It then defines morally right acts, rules or institutions as those that maximize utility. It thus holds that utility is the one rational good. Utility differs among individuals according to their inclinations and desires. However, for all individuals, utility is the one rational good.

In contrast, a deontological theory, according to Rawls, does not specify the good independently of the right and/or does not define the right as maximizing the good.[4] It can thus allow that there is 'a plurality of intrinsic goods, and a plurality of ways of life that it is rational for individuals to pursue', which entails that morality is not definable as maximizing one rational good.[5] Kantian moral philosophy, Rawls's political philosophy and Nozick's libertarianism are each deontological in all three ways.

In teleological theories, the good is conceived non-morally, as prior to the right. In utilitarianism, the satisfaction of *any* desire or interest has value, which is taken into account in deciding what is right.[6] Desires or interests are taken as given, their satisfaction is taken as valuable and they are considered equally in deciding what is right.[7]

In deontological theories, in contrast, the right is prior to the good. That is, moral principles restrict the desires and interests that moral agents may take into account in deciding their own good. The priority of right defines morally permissible conceptions of the good.[8] Thus, in deontological theories, desires or interests are not taken as given but are morally assessed according to their compatibility with the Categorical Imperative in Kant, the principles of justice in Rawls or individuals' natural rights in Nozick. Desires or interests are immoral if they would mistreat persons as mere means, if they require unequal basic liberties, unequal opportunities or an unjust share of resources, or if they would violate natural rights against force, theft or fraud. If they are immoral, their satisfaction is valueless and is not to be taken into account in deciding what would be right.[9] And even morally permissible interests are not treated equally in such deliberation; rather, certain morally important interests are given priority as rights, which may not be overridden by a greater sum of lesser interests.

In utilitarianism, utility-maximization entails equal consideration of interests, that is, each person's and each other sentient being's interests must be considered equally in calculating what would maximize utility. Maximizing utility may often happen to require equality of rights, liberties, opportunities or resources, but this is contingent on facts about desires or interests. Desires for, or interests in, inequalities of rights, liberties, opportunities or resources (for example, racist, sexist or homophobic desires or interests) are taken as given and their satisfaction taken as valuable, so they may make such inequalities utility-maximizing and hence, according to utilitarianism, right. In utilitarianism, there is no moral principle of equality of persons.

In the deontological theories of Kant, Rawls and Nozick, in contrast, equality of persons is a fundamental moral principle. Those theories differ in how they explicate equality of persons in terms of equalities of rights, liberties, opportunities and resources. Whichever principles explicate equality of persons constrain utility-maximization; it is morally permissible, and hence good, only if it is compatible with those moral principles.

The idea of one rational good, such as utility, which morality seeks to maximize, can recognize individual autonomy, freedom and equality only as *instrumentally* valuable, as means to maximize the one rational good. Each is right only if and insofar as it promotes that goal. If and insofar as heteronomy, unfreedom or inequality promotes that goal, it is right. The value of autonomy, freedom and equality is made contingent on facts about desires or interests. In contrast, denial of one rational good, allowing for plural rational conceptions of the good, allows moral and political principles that recognize autonomy, freedom and equality as *intrinsically* valuable. Their value is not contingent on facts about desires or interests.

The teleological idea of morality as maximizing the good is aggregative rather than distributive. Teleological theories are concerned with the good of the world as a whole rather than with the rights of individuals. Thus, utilitarianism aims to maximize utility, directly or indirectly, and is concerned with the distribution of rights, liberties, opportunities and resources only as means to maximize utility. According to deontological theories, having this (or any other) aggregative aim as a fundamental principle leads to injustice. It can require mistreating persons as mere means; for example, pursuit of the societal good can, in certain circumstances, require punishing the innocent or punishing disproportionately to the crime. Utility-maximization can require unequal rights, liberties or opportunities, or unjust shares of resources. And it can require violating individuals' rights against force, theft or fraud. Any aggregative aim as a fundamental principle is liable to lead to injustice. The deontological theories provide moral principles that limit the morally permissible pursuit of aggregative goals.

The conception of morality as maximizing the aggregate good presupposes the idea that there is one rational good. In any society, but especially in a liberal democracy, people have diverse conceptions of the good, of what is valuable. These may be based on diverse religious or non-religious beliefs. Deontological theories' allowance for a plurality of rational conceptions of the good and of corresponding ways of life accords with this fact. Utilitarianism's idea of utility as the one rational good necessitates misconceiving religious commitments, for example, as pleasures, preferences or interests. The plurality of conceptions of the good is the social context in which the search for the most reasonable moral and political principles must occur. Rational persons who hold diverse conceptions of the good could not agree to a principle of promoting any single conception of the good, even the subjective one of utility. But, as Rawls argues, rational and reasonable persons who hold diverse conceptions of the good could agree to principles of equal basic liberties, mutual toleration, state neutrality among conceptions of the good, equal opportunities and just shares of resources.

This book started with arguments about drug laws and ends with contrasts between teleology and deontology. Diverse territory has been explored in between, but an abiding theme has been the search for the most reasonable moral and political principles for rational and reasonable persons with diverse conceptions of the good.

NOTES

1 Drug Laws

1 Legalization and decriminalization should be distinguished. Legalization is allowing currently illegal drugs to be legally produced, sold, possessed and consumed by adults, perhaps with regulations similar to those that many countries apply to alcohol and tobacco. Decriminalization is treating possession of small amounts of an illegal drug for personal use as a minor offence (like a parking offence), or not enforcing the law, but keeping severe penalties for dealing or importing.

2 For example, D. Richards, *Sex, Drugs, Death and the Law* (Rowman & Littlefield, 1982); D. Husak, *Drugs and Rights* (Cambridge University Press, 1992); T. Szasz, *Our Right to Drugs: The Case for a Free Market* (Syracuse University Press, 1996). See also S. Luper-Foy and C. Brown (eds.), *Drugs, Morality, and the Law* (Garland, 1994); P. De Greiff (ed.), *Drugs and the Limits of Liberalism* (Cornell University Press, 1999).

3 For example, M. Friedman, 'Prohibition and Drugs', in J. Rachels (ed.), *The Right Thing to Do*, 3rd edn. (McGraw-Hill, 2003). R. Stevenson ('Can Markets Cope with Drugs?', *The Journal of Drug Issues*, 20, 4 [1990]) argues for a free market in drugs, with no regulations governing labelling, advertising, sales to children, and so on, believing that drug firms would behave responsibly out of self-interest. However, his *Winning the War on Drugs: To Legalise or Not?* (Institute of Economic Affairs, 1994) calls for a regulated market, with regulations requiring health warnings and prohibiting sale to children, although only because it is politically more realistic.

4 An early example, *The Economist*, 2 September 1989, was the stimulant for the first version of this chapter.

5 For example, Law Enforcement Against Prohibition, http://leap.cc/

6 A reader for Palgrave Macmillan commented that a right to the freedom to use drugs could be called a right to use drugs. True, but the former term makes explicit that what is important here is not drugs but freedom. (Similarly, we speak of the rights to other freedoms, such as those of speech, religion or movement.)

7 J. S. Mill, *On Liberty*, various editions, ch. 1, paragraph 13.

215

8   Mill, *On Liberty*, ch. 1, paragraph 9.
9   I am grateful to a reader for Palgrave Macmillan for improving the analysis of this argument.
10 Mill, *On Liberty*, ch. 1, paragraphs 11, 13, ch. 3, paragraph 1.
11 B. Barry, *Justice as Impartiality* (Clarendon Press, 1995), pp. 83–4. I am grateful to a reader for Palgrave Macmillan for pressing me to improve the exposition of the contractualist argument.
12 J. Feinberg, *The Moral Limits of the Criminal Law*, 4 volumes (Oxford University Press, 1984–8): Vol. 1 *Harm to Others* (1984), Vol. 2 *Offense to Others* (1985), Vol. 3 *Harm to Self* (1986), Vol. 4 *Harmless Wrongdoing* (1988).
13 D. Nutt et al., 'Development of a Rational Scale to Assess the Harm of Drugs of Potential Misuse', *The Lancet*, 369 (2007), pp. 1047–53.
14 Office for National Statistics, *The Guardian*, 25 February 2005; Downing Street Strategy Unit Drugs Project, *Phase 1 Report: Understanding the Issues* (http://www.guardian.co.uk/drugs/Story/0,,1521501,00.html), p. 15.
15 D. Husak and P. de Marneffe, *The Legalization of Drugs: For and Against* (Cambridge University Press, 2005), p. 48.
16 Husak, *Drugs and Rights*, p. 95.
17 Husak, *Drugs and Rights*, pp. 124f.
18 Husak and de Marneffe, *The Legalization of Drugs*, pp. 120–2, 132, 135, 139, 156f.
19 Husak and de Marneffe, *The Legalization of Drugs,* pp. 114, 175–7.
20 I. Kant, *The Metaphysics of Morals* (ed. and trans. M. Gregor) (Cambridge University Press, 1996), pp. 180f.
21 I. Kant, *Critique of Practical Reason* (ed. and trans. L. Beck) (Prentice Hall, 1993), p. 30 (Book 1, Chapter 1, s. 6, Remark).
22 An example of roughly this position is J. Reiman, 'Drug Addiction, Liberal Virtue, and Moral Responsibility', in Luper-Foy and Brown (eds), *Drugs, Morality, and the Law*, revised as ch. 3 in J. Reiman, *Critical Moral Liberalism* (Rowman & Littlefield, 1997). I am grateful to a reader for Palgrave Macmillan for pressing me to clarify the argument in the text.
23 S. Freeman, 'Liberalism, Inalienability, and Rights of Drug Use', in P. De Greiff (ed.), *Drugs and the Limits of Liberalism*, pp. 112, 114, 117f, 122, 125–7.
24 Mill, *On Liberty*, ch. 1, paragraph 13.
25 Husak, *Drugs and Rights*, p. 68. I am grateful to a reader for Palgrave Macmillan for pressing me to clarify the argument in this and the next section.
26 For example, James Q. Wilson, 'Against the Legalization of Drugs', in H. LaFollette (ed.), *Ethics in Practice* (Blackwell, 1997).

27 For example, E. Nadelmann, 'The Case for Legalization', in J. Inciardi (ed.), *The Drug Legalization Debate* (Sage, 1991).
28 Husak, *Drugs and Rights*, p. 153.
29 W. Chambliss, 'Don't Confuse Me with Facts: Clinton "Just Says No" ', *New Left Review* 204 (March/April 1994), p. 116; Husak, *Drugs and Rights*, p. 154.
30 Downing Street Strategy Unit Drugs Project, *Phase 1 Report: Understanding the Issues*, pp. 80, 91, 94.
31 Downing Street Strategy Unit Drugs Project, *Phase 1 Report: Understanding the Issues*, p. 7.
32 United Nations Office on Drugs and Crime, *World Drug Report 2005*, http://www.unodc.org/en/world_drug_report_2005.html.
33 Stevenson, *Winning the War on Drugs*, p. 17.
34 R. Clutterbuck, *Drugs, Crime and Corruption* (Macmillan, 1995); Chambliss, 'Don't Confuse Me with Facts'.
35 Downing Street Strategy Unit Drugs Project, *Phase 1 Report: Understanding the Issues*, pp. 2, 22, 25.

2 Justifications of Punishment

1 This definition draws on T. Honderich, *Punishment: The Supposed Justifications Revisited* (Pluto Press, 2006), pp. 9–15; J. Rawls, 'Two Concepts of Rules', in his *Collected Papers* (Harvard University Press, 1999), p. 26; H. L. A. Hart, *Punishment and Responsibility* (Clarendon Press, 1968), pp. 4–5. I am grateful to an anonymous reader for Palgrave Macmillan for pressing me to improve an earlier definition of punishment.
2 The gravity of a crime must not be confused with the harm done. Intentional harm is morally worse than negligent harm, and planned or attempted crime is morally wrong even if no harm occurs.
3 J. Feinberg, 'The Justification of Punishment: The Classic Debate', in J. Feinberg and H. Gross (eds.), *Philosophy of Law*, 4th edn. (Wadsworth, 1991) p. 647.
4 This section summarizes Kant's ideas on punishment in *The Metaphysics of Morals* (trans. and ed. M. Gregor) (Cambridge University Press, 1996), pp. 105–7, 130, from where all the quotes are taken.
5 Honderich, *Punishment*, p. 31.
6 Kant, *Metaphysics of Morals*, p. 105. This suggestion is taken up in the final paragraph of this chapter.
7 I. Kant, *Lectures on Ethics* (ed. P. Heath and J. B. Schneewind, trans. P. Heath) (Cambridge University Press, 1997), p. 79.

8   I. Kant, *Critique of Practical Reason* (ed. and trans. Lewis White Beck) (Prentice Hall, 3rd edn., 1993), Part I, Book I, Chapter II, p. 63, also p. 39.

9   'Exaggeratedly', because, in a world without justice, there would still be non-moral value in human lives, just as there is non-moral value in nonhuman animals' lives, which Kant also failed to recognize.

10   Kant, *Metaphysics of Morals*, pp. 106, 109f.

11   J. Rachels, *The Elements of Moral Philosophy*, 5th edn. (McGraw-Hill International, 2007), ch. 9, pp. 136–40.

12   I. Kant, *Grounding for the Metaphysics of Morals* (trans. J. W. Ellington) (Hackett, 1981), second section, p. 30. The two main formulations of the Categorical Imperative are discussed in chapter 11.

13   Rachels, *The Elements of Moral Philosophy*, p. 139.

14   Kant, *The Metaphysics of Morals*, p. 130.

15   Kant, *Grounding for the Metaphysics of Morals*, second section, p. 36.

16   H. Bedau, 'Capital Punishment', in H. LaFollette (ed.), *The Oxford Handbook of Practical Ethics* (Oxford University Press, 2003), p. 706.

17   I am grateful to both readers for Palgrave Macmillan for pressing me to improve the explanation of restitution.

18   Feinberg, 'The Justification of Punishment', p. 649.

19   For example, A. Quinton, 'On Punishment', in H. B. Acton (ed.), *The Philosophy of Punishment* (Macmillan, 1969), pp. 58–9. Rawls notes that utilitarians generally have understood punishment in this way ('Two Concepts of Rules', p. 24).

20   Kant, *The Metaphysics of Morals*, p 105.

21   A. Goldman, 'The Paradox of Punishment', in A. J. Simmons et al. (eds), *Punishment* (Princeton University Press, 1995), p. 43.

22   S. Smilansky, *Ten Moral Paradoxes* (Blackwell, 2007), p. 34. Smilansky also argues that the amount of punishment deserved varies directly with a person's socio-economic position. Hence his 'paradox of punishment', which results, unparadoxically, from combining the conflicting principles of desert and deterrence.

23   Rawls, 'Two Concepts of Rules', esp. pp. 22f, 26–8, 33, 41. This distinction between principles for institutions and principles for actions within them in the early, rule-utilitarian Rawls is paralleled in the mature, Kantian Rawls's theory of justice, which requires society's basic institutions to pursue equality but perhaps allows citizens to be self-seeking, and thus to cause inequality, in their economic actions (see chapter 12, last section, on Cohen's critique of Rawls).

24 Hart, *Punishment and Responsibility*, esp. pp. 1, 9, 25. I am grateful
    to an anonymous reader for Palgrave Macmillan for pressing me to
    improve the exposition of Rawls's and Hart's views.
25 Goldman, 'The Paradox of Punishment'.
26 Kant, *The Metaphysics of Morals*, p. 105
27 Kant, *The Metaphysics of Morals*, p. 210.

3 Civil Disobedience: Is There a Duty to Obey the Law?

1 H. Bedau, 'Civil Disobedience', *Encyclopedia of Applied Ethics, Volume
    1* (Academic Press, 1998). On defining civil disobedience, Rawls and
    Feinberg, who will be discussed below, largely follow Bedau.
2 H. Bedau, 'Introduction' to H. Bedau (ed.), *Civil Disobedience in Focus*
    (Routledge, 1991), p. 7.
3 Bedau, 'Civil Disobedience'.
4 The analysis and assessment of these arguments is indebted to
    A. J. Simmons, 'Political Obligation and Authority', in R. Simon (ed.),
    The Blackwell Guide to Social and Political Philosophy (Blackwell,
    2002); A. J. Simmons, 'The Duty to Obey and Our Natural Moral
    Duties', in C. Wellman and A. J. Simmons, *Is There a Duty to Obey the
    Law?* (Cambridge University Press, 2005); M. B. E. Smith, 'Is There a
    Prima Facie Obligation to Obey the Law?', in W. A. Edmundson (ed.),
    The Duty to Obey the Law: Selected Philosophical Readings (Rowman
    & Littlefield, 1999); J. Feinberg, 'Civil Disobedience in the Modern
    World', in J. Feinberg and H. Gross (eds.), *Philosophy of Law*, 4th edn
    (Wadsworth, 1991).
5 In Plato's dialogue the *Crito*, in Bedau (ed.), *Civil Disobedience in
    Focus*, esp. pp. 21–4.
6 R. Dworkin, *Taking Rights Seriously* (Duckworth, 1978), ch. 7, esp. pp.
    188–93, 196f, 204.
7 Simmons, 'The Duty to Obey and Our Natural Moral Duties'; Smith,
    'Is There a Prima Facie Obligation to Obey the Law?'
8 Feinberg, 'Civil Disobedience in the Modern World', pp. 125–31.
9 Simmons, 'The Duty to Obey and Our Natural Moral Duties', p. 191n.
    In addition, Joseph Raz says there is an obligation to obey laws that
    set safety standards, because the law has superior knowledge to most
    individuals, and to obey laws that pursue collective goals that uncoor-
    dinated individuals cannot effectively pursue, such as environmental
    protection and welfare services. But such cases do not justify a general
    obligation to obey the law (J. Raz, 'The Obligation to Obey: Revision and
    Tradition', in Edmundson (ed.), *The Duty to Obey the Law*, pp. 166f).

10   Feinberg, 'Civil Disobedience in the Modern World', pp. 130f.
11   J. Rawls, *A Theory of Justice*, rev. edn. (Harvard University Press, 1999), p. 319.
12   Rawls, *A Theory of Justice*, pp. 308–11.
13   Rawls, *A Theory of Justice*, p. 319.
14   Rawls, *A Theory of Justice*, pp. 320–2, 335–6.
15   K. Greenawalt, 'Justifying Nonviolent Disobedience', in Bedau (ed.), *Civil Disobedience in Focus*, p. 187.
16   Rawls, *A Theory of Justice*, p. 327.
17   Rawls, *A Theory of Justice*, p. 330.
18   Rawls, *A Theory of Justice*, pp. 312, 342; J. Rawls, 'The Justification of Civil Disobedience', *Collected Papers*, p. 183.
19   Rawls, *A Theory of Justice*, p. 336.
20   N. Bowie and R. Simon, *The Individual and the Political Order*, 3rd edn (Rowman & Littlefield, 1998), pp. 195–6.
21   Rawls, *A Theory of Justice*, pp. 341f.
22   P. Singer, *Practical Ethics*, 2nd edn (Cambridge University Press, 1993), ch. 11, 'Ends and Means'.
23   Singer, *Practical Ethics*, pp. 295–7, 306.
24   Singer, *Practical Ethics*, pp. 298f.
25   Singer, *Practical Ethics*, pp. 299–305.

4   Global Poverty

1   This section largely follows P. Singer, *Practical Ethics*, pp. 218–22.
2   Singer, *Practical Ethics*, p. 220.
3   Singer, *Practical Ethics*, p. 220.
4   Singer, *Practical Ethics*, p. 221.
5   From T. Pogge, *World Poverty and Human Rights* (Polity Press, 2002), pp. 2, 98f.
6   Pogge, *World Poverty and Human Rights*, pp. 3f.
7   Rich countries' aggregate official development aid is only 0.22 per cent of their GNP. Of this, only a quarter goes to the least developed countries. Much aid is an instrument of foreign policy, given to governments with approved policies, rather than to the people in greatest need. (T. Pogge, 'The First UN Millennium Development Goal: A Cause for Celebration?', in A. Follesdal and T. Pogge [eds], *Real World Justice* [Springer, 2005], p. 331; P. Singer, *One World: The Ethics of Globalization* [Yale University Press, 2nd edn, 2004], pp. 190–1.)
8   J. Narveson, 'Feeding the Hungry', in J. Rachels (ed.), *The Right Thing to Do*, 3rd edn. (McGraw-Hill, 2003) applies contractarianism to world hunger.

9   Libertarianism's most compelling exposition is R. Nozick, *Anarchy, State, and Utopia* (Basic Books, 1974).

10 N. Dower, 'World Poverty', in P. Singer (ed.), *A Companion to Ethics* (Blackwell, 1991).

11 P. Unger, *Living High and Letting Die: Our Illusion of Innocence* (Oxford University Press, 1996), pp. 4ff. Unger exemplifies a utilitarian approach to global poverty and inequality.

12 I. Kant, *Grounding for the Metaphysics of Morals*, pp. 30, 36. For a Kantian approach to global poverty, see O. O'Neill, 'Kantian Approaches to Some Famine Problems', in J. Feinberg and R. Shafer-Landau (eds.), *Reason and Responsibility*, 11th edn. (Wadsworth, 2002).

13 T. Hill, 'Kantian Normative Ethics', in D. Copp (ed.), *The Oxford Handbook of Ethical Theory* (Oxford University Press, 2006), p. 500.

14 Singer, *Practical Ethics*, p. 229

15 Unger, *Living High and Letting Die*, p. 82.

16 J. Arthur, 'Rights and the Duty to Bring Aid', in H. LaFollette (ed.), *Ethics in Practice* (Blackwell, 1997).

17 Singer, *Practical Ethics*, pp. 231–2; and his Postscript to 'Famine, Affluence, and Morality', in H. LaFollette (ed.), *Ethics in Practice*.

18 Singer, *Practical Ethics*, pp. 232–4. Singer responds to this objection at greater length in his *One World*, ch. 5, and in 'Outsiders: Our Obligations to those Beyond our Borders', in D. Chatterjee (ed.), *The Ethics of Assistance: Morality and the Distant Needy* (Cambridge University Press, 2004).

19 In case it is thought that these obligations conflict irreconcilably, it may be observed that, among rich countries, Scandinavian societies are both among the least unequal societies and among the largest donors of development aid; the USA is among the most unequal societies and among the smallest donors (as a proportion of GNP).

20 G. Hardin, 'Living on a Lifeboat', in S. Luper and C. Brown (eds.), *The Moral Life*, 2nd edn. (Harcourt Brace, 1999).

21 Singer, *Practical Ethics*, pp. 239–41.

22 Singer, *Practical Ethics*, pp. 241–2.

23 Singer, *Practical Ethics*, p. 243.

24 Singer, *One World*, p. 160.

25 R. Arneson, 'Moral Limits on the Demands of Beneficence?' in D. Chatterjee (ed.), *The Ethics of Assistance*, p. 37.

26 Singer, *Practical Ethics*, p. 246.

27 P. Singer, 'The Singer Solution to World Poverty', in J. Rachels (ed.), *The Right Thing to Do*, 4th edn. (McGraw-Hill, 2007), p. 144.

28 Singer, *One World*, pp. 192–5.

29 Arneson, 'Moral Limits on the Demands of Beneficence?' pp. 34, 51, 53, 56. Also Singer, *Practical Ethics*, pp. 245f and *One World*, pp. 191f.

30 Available at http://www.unhchr.ch/udhr/index.htm

31   Pogge, *World Poverty and Human Rights*, pp. 199, 202f; T. Pogge, 'Real World Justice', *Journal of Ethics*, 9, 1–2 (2005), especially pp. 36–50.
32   Pogge, *World Poverty and Human Rights*, esp. pp. 22, 109, 112–17, 140–3, 161–7, 172–3, 200f, 244–7.
33   Pogge, *World Poverty and Human Rights*, pp. 112, 162.
34   Pogge, *World Poverty and Human Rights*, p. 113.
35   Pogge, *World Poverty and Human Rights*, pp. 113f.
36   Pogge, *World Poverty and Human Rights*, p. 165.
37   T. Pogge, ' "Assisting" the Global Poor', in D. Chatterjee (ed.), *The Ethics of Assistance*, pp. 268–9.
38   Pogge, *World Poverty and Human Rights*, pp. 18–20; and Pogge, ' "Assisting" the Global Poor', pp. 263–4, 275–7.
39   T. Pogge, 'Real World Justice', pp. 31, 33; T. Pogge, 'World Poverty and Human Rights', *Ethics and International Affairs*, 19, 1 (2005), p. 2; T. Pogge, 'A Cosmopolitan Perspective on the Global Economic Order', in G. Brock and H. Brighouse (eds), *The Political Philosophy of Cosmopolitanism* (Cambridge University Press, 2005), p. 93.
40   Pogge, *World Poverty and Human Rights*, pp. 117, 166. The perspective of a humanitarian duty to help people in severe need does not mention global injustice, economic exploitation or political powerlessness (R. Forst, 'Justice, Morality and Power in the Global Context', in A. Follesdal and T. Pogge [eds], *Real World Justice*, p. 29).

5   Liberty

1   T. Scanlon, *The Difficulty of Tolerance* (Cambridge University Press, 2003), pp. 190, 193.
2   A fundamental objection to utilitarianism (see chapter 10) is that the good cannot be conceived independently of the right. Thus, satisfaction of or harm to interests cannot be conceived as good or bad independently of moral obligations and rights.
3   The question of the conflict between utilitarianism and liberty is discussed at greater length in chapter 10, fourth section.
4   R. Dworkin, *A Matter of Principle* (Oxford University Press, 1986), pp. 351–2; J. Waldron, 'Introduction' to J. Waldron (ed.), *Theories of Rights* (Oxford University Press, 1984), p. 18.
5   J. Rawls, *Political Liberalism* (Columbia University Press, 1993), pp. 48–9; *Justice as Fairness* (Harvard University Press, 2001), pp. 6–7; Scanlon, *The Difficulty of Tolerance*, pp. 132–3.
6   B. Barry, *Justice as Impartiality* (Clarendon Press, 1995), pp. 83–4.
7   This argument can be extended to drug preferences (see chapter 1).

8 J. Rawls, *A Theory of Justice* (Harvard University Press, 1971; rev. edn. 1999).

9 Rawls, *Political Liberalism*, pp. 137f.

10 Scanlon, *The Difficulty of Tolerance*, p. 132.

11 C. Taylor, 'What's Wrong with Negative Liberty', in D. Miller (ed.), *The Liberty Reader* (Edinburgh University Press, 2006), pp. 149–51.

12 Rawls, *A Theory of Justice* (1971/1999), pp. 61/53; *Political Liberalism*, pp. 291–2, 335; *Justice as Fairness*, pp. 44–5, 114.

13 I. Berlin, *Four Essays on Liberty* (Oxford University Press, 1969), especially Introduction and 'Two Concepts of Liberty'.

14 See A. Swift, *Political Philosophy* (Polity Press, 2001), Part 2.

15 G. MacCallum, 'Negative and Positive Freedom', in Miller (ed.), *The Liberty Reader*.

16 Swift, *Political Philosophy*, pp. 61–4. This is one of the ideas that Berlin included in 'positive liberty'.

17 Berlin, 'Two Concepts of Liberty', pp. 148, 152.

18 J. Feinberg, *Social Philosophy* (Prentice-Hall, 1973), p. 5.

19 Berlin, *Four Essays*, pp. xxxviii–xl.

20 Unordinary, repudiated desires are arguably an exception, as discussed later in this section.

21 G. A. Cohen criticizes the moralized conception of freedom in 'Capitalism, Freedom, and the Proletariat', in Miller (ed.), *The Liberty Reader*, pp. 170–1.

22 Hillel Steiner denies that threats limit freedom, because they only make an action less desirable, not impossible ('Individual Liberty', in Miller [ed.], *The Liberty Reader*).

23 Berlin, *Four Essays on Liberty*, pp. liii–lv, lviii, 125.

24 Rawls, *A Theory of Justice* (1971/1999), p. 204/179.

25 Swift, *Political Philosophy*, pp. 60–1.

26 People who have succeeded in their pursuit of money, power or fame sometimes express regret about, for example, not having spent more time with their children or not having looked after their health, mistakes they might have avoided had they thought critically about what is valuable.

27 Taylor, 'What's Wrong with Negative Liberty', in Miller (ed.), *The Liberty Reader*, pp. 152–5, 160.

28 F. Hayek, 'Freedom and Coercion', in Miller (ed.), *The Liberty Reader*, pp. 81, 88, 95.

29 G. A. Cohen, *Self-Ownership, Freedom and Equality* (Cambridge University Press, 1995), pp. 57–9; Appendix to 'Back to Socialist Basics', in J. Franklin (ed.), *Equality* (London: Institute for Public Policy Research, 1997); and 'Freedom and Money', http://www.pem.cam.ac.uk/international-programmes/Cohen.pdf.

30 Cohen, 'Capitalism, Freedom, and the Proletariat', pp. 167–72, esp. p. 170.

6   Liberty-limiting Principles

1   This chapter draws extensively on J. Feinberg, *The Moral Limits of the Criminal Law*, 4 volumes (Oxford University Press): *Harm to Others* (1984), *Offense to Others* (1985), *Harm to Self* (1986), *Harmless Wrongdoing* (1988).

2   Feinberg, *Harm to Others*, pp. 36, 65.

3   Feinberg, *Social Philosophy*, p. 27; *Harm to Others*, pp. 87–9.

4   References to Mill's *On Liberty* will be given in the text as chapter number followed by paragraph number(s).

5   D. Lyons, 'Liberty and Harm to Others', in G. Dworkin (ed.), *Mill's On Liberty: Critical Essays* (Rowman & Littlefield, 1997).

6   Feinberg, *Harmless Wrongdoing*, p. 14 and ch. 32; *Harm to Others*, ch. 4.

7   Feinberg, *Harm to Others*, p. 11; *Harmless Wrongdoing*, pp. 33f.

8   Feinberg, *Harm to Others*, pp. 191ff.

9   *Offense to Others*, pp. 10–13.

10 Feinberg, *Social Philosophy*, p 28. In *Offense to Others*, Feinberg no longer treats offence as a kind of harm.

11 This and the next paragraph follow Feinberg, *Offense to Others*, ch. 8, esp. pp. 26–35.

12 Feinberg, *Social Philosophy*, pp. 43–5.

13 Feinberg, *Offense to Others*, p. 39.

14 Feinberg, *Harm to Self*, p. xvii.

15 D. Parfit, *Reasons and Persons* (Oxford University Press, rev. edn, 1987), pp. 318–21.

16 Feinberg, *Harm to Self*, pp. 58f, 76.

17 Feinberg, *Harm to Self*, pp. 25–6, 59, 61f.

18 Feinberg, *Harm to Self*, pp. 55, 92–3.

19 Feinberg, *Harm to Self*, p. 93.

20 Feinberg, *Harm to Self*, p. 56.

21 Feinberg, *Harm to Self*, p. 94.

22 I. Kant, *Political Writings* (Cambridge University Press, 1991), pp. 74, 83, 141; Mill, *On Liberty*, V, 10; Feinberg, *Harm to Self*, p. 23.

23 Feinberg, *Harm to Self*, p. 126.

24 Feinberg, *Harm to Self*, pp. 104–6 and chs. 20–26.

25 Feinberg, *Harm to* Self, pp. 124–5.

26 Feinberg, *Harm to Self*, pp. 14–15.

27 'Sado-masochists plead guilty after judge rules that people must be protected from themselves', *The Guardian*, 21 November 1990; *Regina v Brown and others*, Court of Appeal (Criminal Division), 19 February 1992; House of Lords, 11 March 1993; European Court of Human Rights, 19 February 1997.

28 This issue is discussed in T. Bayne and N. Levy, 'Amputees by Choice: Body Integrity Disorder and the Ethics of Amputation', *Journal of Applied Philosophy*, 22, 1 (2005).

29 'Woman set up her murder on "Net"', *The Guardian*, 31 October 1996.

30 'Victim of cannibal agreed to be eaten', *The Guardian*, 4 December 2003.

31 Feinberg, *Harm to Self*, p. 78.

32 Feinberg, *Harm to Self*, pp. 118, 332.

33 Feinberg, *Harm to Self*, pp. xviii, 69, 79; *Harmless Wrongdoing*, pp. 168–75.

34 G. A. Cohen, 'Are Disadvantaged Workers Who Take Hazardous Jobs Forced to Take Hazardous Jobs?', in his *History, Labour, Freedom* (Oxford University Press, 1988), ch. 12; the quote is from p. 241. The definition of what it is to be forced is modified following G. A. Cohen, 'Once More into the Breach of Self-Ownership', *Journal of Ethics*, 2 (1998), p. 82.

35 Feinberg, 'Freedom and Liberty'; *Routledge Encyclopedia of Philosophy* (Routledge, 1998). Being free to do something is having the option of doing it. Being compelled to do it is taking that option because of lack of a reasonably acceptable alternative. One cannot be compelled to take an option unless one has it. So, being compelled to do something presupposes being free to do it.

36 Cohen, 'Are Disadvantaged Workers who Take Hazardous Jobs Forced to Take Hazardous Jobs?'

37 Feinberg, *Harm to Self*, p. 21.

38 Feinberg, *Harmless Wrongdoing*, pp. xxviii, 26.

39 Feinberg, *Harmless Wrongdoing*, pp. 17ff, 128–33, 328–31.

40 The gladiatorial contest is from I. Kristol, 'Pornography, Obscenity, and the Case for Censorship', *New York Times Magazine*, 28 March 1971, reprinted in G. Dworkin (ed.), *Morality, Harm, and the Law* (Westview Press, 1994). The conception case is from D. Parfit, 'On Doing the Best for Our Children', in M. D. Bayles (ed.), *Ethics and Population*, (Schenkman, 1976). Feinberg discusses them in *Harmless Wrongdoing*, pp. 27–33, 128–33, 325–31.

41 Parfit, *Reasons and Persons*, pp. 361–3, 371–7. In *Reasons and Persons*, Parfit's example of a suboptimal, and thus putatively wrongful, conception that harms, and so wrongs, no one is that of a 14-year-old girl who could delay conception and thus give a better start in life to a different child. However, this example evokes thoughts and feelings not only about suboptimal conceptions but also about 14-year-old mothers, which his earlier example, discussed above, does not.

42 Parfit, *Reasons and Persons*, p. 372.

43   Feinberg, *Harmless Wrongdoing*, p. 324.
44   Feinberg, *Harm to Self*, pp. 18, 20. Mill (I, 11; IV, 3, 6) thought that
     his harm-prevention principle justifies compelling people to bear
     their fair share of collective burdens, but provision of public goods is
     perhaps better thought of as a distinct liberty-limiting principle.

7   Rights

1   P. Jones, *Rights* (Macmillan, 1994), pp. 3–4. Jeremy Waldron observes
     that this centrality of rights recurred only after the Second World
     War (J. Waldron, 'Nonsense upon Stilts? – a Reply', in J. Waldron [ed.],
     'Nonsense upon Stilts': Bentham, Burke and Marx on the Rights of Man
     [Methuen, 1987], p. 154).
2   Available at http://www.unhchr.ch/udhr/index.htm.
3   Saudi Arabia has expressed its disagreement with three points in the
     UDHR: freedom for a Muslim woman to marry a non-Muslim; free-
     dom for a Muslim to convert to another religion; legalization of trade
     unions and strikes. However, most Muslim countries approve the
     principles of human rights and most have signed the International
     Covenant on Civil and Political Rights, although some conservative
     Muslim regimes refuse to do so (L. Kropáček, 'Islam and Human
     Rights', in J. Krejčí [ed.], *Islam in Contact with Rival Civilizations*
     [Prague, Filosofia Publications of the Institute of Philosophy of the
     Academy of Sciences of the Czech Republic, 1998], p. 14).
4   Feinberg, *Social Philosophy*, p. 67; and J. Feinberg, 'The Nature and
     Value of Rights', in his *Rights, Justice, and the Bounds of Liberty*
     (Princeton University Press, 1980), p. 154.
5   J. Feinberg, 'In Defence of Moral Rights', *Oxford Journal of Legal
     Studies*, 12, 2 (1992), pp. 165–6.
6   R. Wasserstrom, 'Rights, Human Rights, and Racial Discrimination', in
     B. Boxill (ed.), *Race and Racism* (Oxford University Press, 2001), p. 182.
7   Feinberg, *Social Philosophy*, pp. 58–9.
8   Dworkin, *Taking Rights Seriously*, pp. xi, 92, 191; and R. Dworkin
     'Rights as Trumps', in Waldron (ed.), *Theories of Rights*, p. 153.
9   Feinberg, 'In Defence of Moral Rights', p. 149.
10   Feinberg, *Social Philosophy*, p. 59.
11   Feinberg, *Social Philosophy*, p. 60.
12   The characterizations of civil, political and welfare rights as, respec-
     tively, against the state, to participation in control of the state, and to
     benefits guaranteed by the state, come from C. B. McPherson, *The Rise
     and Fall of Economic Justice* (Oxford University Press, 1985), p. 22.
13   J. Raz, *The Morality of Freedom* (Oxford University Press, 1986),
     p. 166. This account of rights does not apply to some institutional

rights, namely, the powers of office holders, which may not serve
their personal interest (Jones, *Rights*, p. 31).

14 Jones, *Rights*, pp. 32, 35.

15 T. Regan, *The Case for Animal Rights* (Routledge, 1984).

16 However, it may be that, for Kant, duties have only conceptual or
definitional priority over rights, in that rights are explained in terms
of the duty to treat persons as ends, but rights have moral or foundational priority over duties in that the primary point of the duty
to treat persons as ends is to protect their rights (J. Mackie, 'Can
There Be a Rights-Based Moral Theory?', in Waldron [ed.], *Theories
of Rights*, pp. 169–70, 180; T. Pogge, *World Poverty and Human Rights*,
pp. 55, 225, Kant, *The Metaphysics of Morals*, pp. 31–2).

17 J. Waldron, 'A Right to Do Wrong', in his *Liberal Rights* (Cambridge
University Press, 1993), ch. 3.

18 Waldron, 'Nonsense upon Stilts? – a Reply', p. 194.

19 J. Raz, 'Rights-based Moralities', in Waldron (ed.), *Theories of Rights*;
also Raz, *The Morality of Freedom*, ch. 8.

20 This and the next paragraph follow Feinberg, *Social Philosophy*,
pp. 61–3.

21 Feinberg, *Social Philosophy*, pp. 66f, 94–5; 'The Nature and Value of
Rights', p. 153; and 'In Defence of Moral Rights', p. 157n.

22 Feinberg, 'In Defence of Moral Rights', p. 156; Mackie, 'Can There Be
a Right-based Moral Theory?' pp. 169–70, 180.

23 Feinberg, 'In Defence of Moral Rights', p. 155.

24 Raz, *The Morality of Freedom*, p. 180.

25 Feinberg, *Social Philosophy*, p. 85.

26 Wasserstrom, 'Rights, Human Rights, and Racial Discrimination',
p. 184.

27 C. Beitz, 'Human Rights and the Law of Peoples', in D. Chatterjee
(ed.), *The Ethics of Assistance*.

28 J. Cohen, 'Is There a Human Right to Democracy?' in C. Sypnowich
(ed.), *The Egalitarian Conscience: Essays in Honour of G. A. Cohen*
(Oxford University Press, 2006), p. 232.

29 Beitz, 'Human Rights and the Law of Peoples', pp. 196–8, 202.

30 See Jones, *Rights*, ch. 5.

31 Jones, *Rights*, p. 95.

32 Jones, *Rights*, p. 118.

33 The utilitarian Jeremy Bentham, recognizing only legal rights as real,
regarded natural rights as 'nonsense' (from *Anarchical Fallacies*, in
J. Waldron [ed.], *'Nonsense upon Stilts': Bentham, Burke and Marx on
the Rights of Man*, p. 53). The communitarian Alasdair MacIntyre
asserts that 'There are no such [natural or human] rights and belief
in them is one with belief in witches and unicorns' (*After Virtue*, 2nd
edn [University of Notre Dame Press, 1984], p. 69).

34 A. Sen, 'Elements of a Theory of Human Rights', *Philosophy and Public Affairs*, 32, 4 (2004), pp. 352–3; and *Development as Freedom* (Oxford University Press, 1999), ch. 10.
35 G. Vlastos, 'Justice and Equality', in Waldron (ed.), *Theories of Rights*, pp. 51, 55, 57.
36 Feinberg, *Social Philosophy*, p. 90.
37 Feinberg, *Social Philosophy*, pp. 87f.
38 Nozick, *Anarchy, State, and Utopia*, especially pp. 29–35.
39 L. W. Sumner, 'Rights', in H. LaFollette (ed.), *The Blackwell Guide to Ethical Theory* (Blackwell, 2000), p. 293.
40 J. Mandle, *Global Justice* (Polity Press, 2006), p. 43.
41 A. Buchanan, *Justice, Legitimacy and Self-Determination: Moral Foundations for International Law* (Oxford University Press, 2004), p. 128.
42 Wasserstrom, 'Rights, Human Rights, and Racial Discrimination', pp. 191–2.
43 Feinberg, 'The Nature and Value of Rights', pp. 151, 155, *Social Philosophy*, pp. 58–9; 'In Defence of Moral Rights', p. 155; also Raz, *The Morality of Freedom*, p. 188.
44 Dworkin, *Taking Rights Seriously*, pp. 191–2, 205; *A Matter of Principle*, pp. 190, 198.
45 T. Scanlon, 'Human Rights as a Neutral Concern', in his *The Difficulty of Tolerance: Essays in Political Philosophy*, pp. 78–81.
46 J. Rawls, *The Law of Peoples* (Harvard University Press, 1999). Rawls regards only articles 3–18 of the UDHR as 'human rights proper'. Buchanan argues for a more extensive list of human rights as a moral basis for international law, including the legitimacy of states, in *Justice, Legitimacy and Self-Determination: Moral Foundations for International Law*.
47 See C. Wellman, *The Proliferation of Rights: Moral Progress or Empty Rhetoric* (Westview Press, 1999).
48 Waldron, *Liberal Rights*, pp. 12–13.
49 Jones, *Rights*, pp. 209–10.
50 J. Feinberg, 'In Defense of Moral Rights: Their Social Importance', in his *Freedom and Fulfillment: Philosophical Essays* (Princeton University Press, 1992), p. 222.
51 Jones, *Rights*, p. 212.
52 *Anarchical Fallacies*, in Waldron (ed.), *'Nonsense upon Stilts': Bentham, Burke and Marx on the Rights of Man*, p. 53.

8   Equality and Social Justice

1 Joshua Cohen identifies this as the intuitive idea behind John Rawls's difference principle to regulate the distribution of income

and wealth (J. Cohen, 'Taking People as They Are?', *Philosophy and Public Affairs*, 30 [2002], p. 336).
2   J. Rawls, *A Theory of Justice*, rev. edn, pp. 41, 442, 444.
3   A. Sen, *Inequality Re-examined* (Oxford University Press, 1992), pp. 22–3.
4   W. Kymlicka, *Contemporary Political Philosophy*, 2nd edn, (Oxford University Press, 2002), pp. 3–4, developing R. Dworkin, *Taking Rights Seriously*, p. 180.
5   Sen, *Inequality Re-examined*, pp. ix, 12.
6   I. Kant, *The Metaphysics of Morals*, p. 30.
7   Sen, *Inequality Re-examined*, pp. 18–19.
8   The sequence of equalities follows R. Arneson, 'Equality', in R. Simon (ed.), *The Blackwell Guide to Social and Political Philosophy* (Blackwell, 2002).
9   R. Nozick, *Anarchy, State, and Utopia.*
10 J. Cohen, 'For a Democratic Society', in S. Freeman (ed.), *The Cambridge Companion to Rawls* (Cambridge University Press, 2003), pp. 96f.
11 Arneson, 'Equality', p. 89. The term 'fair equality of opportunity', and much of the objection to its insufficiency, comes from Rawls, *A Theory of Justice*, chapter II.
12 B. Barry, *Why Social Justice Matters* (Polity Press, 2005), pp. 14f, 44f, 47–50.
13 G. Morgenson, 'Explaining (or not) Why the Boss is Paid so Much', *New York Times*, 25 January 2004, section 3, p. 1, quoted in Barry, *Why Social Justice Matters*, p. 217. Barry observes that productivity (output per hour) is lower in the US than in Germany and France (p. 202).
14 T. Scanlon, 'The Diversity of Objections to Inequality', in his *The Difficulty of Toleration*, p. 202. The following series of objections to inequality of condition is based largely on Scanlon's list.
15 D. Parfit, 'Equality or Priority?' in M. Clayton and A. Williams (eds), *The Ideal of Equality* (Palgrave Macmillan, 2002), p. 98.
16 L. Temkin, 'Equality, Priority, and the Levelling Down Objection', in *The Ideal of Equality*, pp. 132, 154f.
17 For example, the UK Office for National Statistics reports 25,700 'excess winter deaths' in England and Wales in the mild 2005/6 winter (*The Guardian*, 28 October 2006). This annual occurrence is due mainly to poverty among the elderly. Societies with colder climates but less poverty have lower excess winter death rates.
18 Scanlon, 'The Diversity of Objections to Inequality', p. 203.
19 H. Frankfurt, 'Equality as a Moral Ideal', in L. Pojman and R. Westmoreland (eds), *Equality: Selected Readings* (Oxford University Press, 1996), pp. 261–2.

20 Scanlon, 'The Diversity of Objections to Inequality', p. 204.
21 Rawls, *Justice as Fairness*, p. 131.
22 Scanlon, 'The Diversity of Objections to Inequality', p. 204.
23 It has been estimated that if government reduced income inequality in Britain merely to the level of the early 1980s (when it was less than now but historically large), and if this reduced the class inequality in mortality rates to the levels experienced then, there would be 7,500 fewer premature deaths each year (R. Mitchell et al., *Inequalities in Life and Death: What if Britain were More Equal?* [The Policy Press, 2000], pp. 11–12). No doubt such estimates are imprecise, but they indicate the force of this objection to wide economic inequality and this reason to reduce it.
24 Scanlon, 'The Diversity of Objections to Inequality', p. 205.
25 Frankfurt, 'Equality as a Moral Ideal', pp. 263–4.
26 R. Wilkinson, *Unhealthy Societies: The Afflictions of Inequality* (Routledge, 1996) and R. Wilkinson, *The Impact of Inequality* (Routledge, 2005).
27 O. James, *Juvenile Violence in a Winner-Loser Culture: Socio-economic and Familial Origins of the Rise of Violence against the Person* (Free Association Books, 1995), pp. 7–8, 64–7, 106; Wilkinson, *The Impact of Inequality*, pp. 47–51, 125–6, 146–7.
28 Wilkinson, *The Impact of Inequality*, esp. ch. 2.
29 If equality of condition should be a political goal, the question arises whether it should be defined in terms of opportunities for, or outcomes of, resources (income, wealth and leisure time), the capabilities that resources enable and/or the resulting welfare. The question of how equality of condition should be defined should not be mistaken as that of the definition of, or the point of, equality.

9 Moral Relativism

1 G. Harman, 'Is There a Single True Morality?' in P. K. Moser and T. L. Carson (eds.), *Moral Relativism: A Reader* (Oxford University Press, 2001), p. 172.
2 This paragraph largely follows J. Rachels, *The Elements of Moral Philosophy*, 5th edn. (McGraw-Hill International, 2007), pp. 23–7.
3 The following characterizations of these varieties of moral relativism follow R. Brandt, 'Ethical Relativism', in Moser and Carson (eds.), *Moral Relativism*, pp. 25–8.
4 Derek Parfit observes that 'Non-Religious Ethics has been systematically studied, by many people, only since the 1960s', so is less advanced than the sciences (*Reasons and Persons*, p. 453).
5 T. L. Carson and P. K. Moser, 'Introduction' to Moser and Carson (eds), *Moral Relativism: A Reader*, p. 14.

6 Harman, 'Is There a Single True Morality?', pp. 172–3.
7 I am grateful to Palgrave Macmillan's reader for suggesting that I indicate how relativism and universalism differ over the question of moral knowledge.
8 Some religious people claim that they do not value freedom because obedience to their religion is supremely valuable. However, if the state prohibited their religion or made another religion compulsory, they would realize that they do value the freedoms of religion, speech and association.
9 B. Barry, *Culture and Equality* (Polity Press, 2001), p. 285.

10 Utilitarianism

1 J. Rawls, *A Theory of Justice* (1971/1999), pp. 24–5/21–2.
2 J. Bentham, *The Rationale of Reward* and *Introduction to the Principles of Morals and Legislation*, excerpted in P. Singer (ed.), *Ethics* (Oxford University Press, 1994), pp. 199f, 306–12.
3 Bentham wrote that 'it is the greatest happiness of the greatest number that is the measure of right and wrong' ('Fragment on Government', quoted in W. Shaw, *Contemporary Ethics: Taking Account of Utilitarianism* [Blackwell, 1999], p. 8).
4 References to J. S. Mill, *Utilitarianism*, will be given in the text as chapter number followed by paragraph number(s).
5 J. S. Mill, 'Bentham', quoted in S. Freeman, 'Utilitarianism, Deontology, and the Priority of Right', *Philosophy and Public Affairs*, 23, 4 (1994), p. 325n.
6 Mill, *Collected Works*, ed. J. Robson (Routledge, 1963–91), vol. X, p. 337, quoted in J. Skorupski, *Why Read Mill Today?* (Routledge, 2006), p. 16.
7 Mill, 'Letter to Grote', quoted in J. Riley, 'Mill on Justice', in D. Boucher and P. Kelly (eds), *Social Justice: from Hume to Walzer* (Routledge, 1998), p. 46.
8 These might have been distinguished in that pleasure and pain are products of specific experiences, while happiness and unhappiness are more general and enduring states of mind, produced by things in addition to pleasure and pain.
9 R. Goodin, 'Utility and the Good', in P. Singer (ed.), *A Companion to Ethics* (Blackwell, 1991).
10 H. Sidgwick, 'Issues for Utilitarians' (excerpt from *The Methods of Ethics*), in P. Singer, *Ethics* (Oxford University Press, 1994), pp. 314–15; Rawls, *A Theory of Justice* (1971/1999), p. 162/140.

11 J. J. C. Smart, 'An Outline of a System of Utilitarian Ethics', in
    J. J. C. Smart and B. Williams, *Utilitarianism: For and Against*
    (Cambridge University Press, 1973), pp. 42–4.

12 Smart, 'An Outline', pp. 62, 68.

13 R. Hare, 'Ethical Theory and Utilitarianism', in A. Sen and B. Williams
    (eds), *Utilitarianism and Beyond* (Cambridge University Press, 1982);
    R. Hare, *Moral Thinking: Its Levels, Methods and Point* (Clarendon
    Press, 1981); R. G. Frey, 'Act Utilitarianism' and B. Hooker, 'Rule
    Consequentialism', both in H. LaFollette (ed.), *The Blackwell Guide
    to Ethical Theory* (Blackwell, 2000).

14 R. Goodin, *Utilitarianism as a Public Philosophy* (Cambridge
    University Press, 1995), pp. 17f.

15 J. Rawls, 'Two Concepts of Rules', *Collected Papers*, pp. 27–8, 31, 33n,
    34, 36, 43.

16 Smart, 'An Outline', p. 10; D. Lyons, 'Utility and Rights', in his *Rights,
    Welfare, and Mill's Moral Theory* (Oxford University Press, 1994).

17 This argument derives from D. Lyons, *Forms and Limits of
    Utilitarianism* (Clarendon Press, 1965).

18 P. Singer, *Practical Ethics*, chs 3 and 5; and *Animal Liberation*, 2nd
    edn (Pimlico, 1995).

19 Shaw, *Contemporary Ethics: Taking Account of Utilitarianism*, p. 7.

20 See chapters 1–4 and, for example, P. Singer, *Practical Ethics* and
    Unsanctifying Human Life, ed. H. Kuhse (Blackwell, 2002).

21 P. Singer, 'Ethics and Intuitions', *Journal of Ethics*, 9, 3–4 (2005).

22 T. Nagel, *The View from Nowhere* (Oxford University Press, 1989), p. 183.

23 Singer, 'Ethics and Intuitions', pp. 346, 348, 351; Singer, *Unsanctifying
    Human Life*, p. 62.

24 J. Rachels, 'Moral Philosophy as a Subversive Activity', in E. R.
    Winkler and J. R. Coombs (eds), *Applied Ethics: A Reader* (Blackwell,
    1993), p. 115.

25 I am grateful to Palgrave Macmillan's reader for this point.

26 J. Harsanyi, 'Rule Utilitarianism, Equality, and Justice', *Social
    Philosophy and Policy*, 2, 2 (1985), pp. 117–18, 121, 127.

27 P. Pettit, 'Consequentialism', in P. Singer (ed.), *A Companion to Ethics*,
    p. 234.

28 J. J. C. Smart, 'Distributive Justice and Utilitarianism', in J. Arthur
    and W. Shaw (eds), *Justice and Economic Distribution* (Prentice-Hall,
    1978), p. 104.

29 P. Bean, 'Utilitarianism and the Welfare State', in P. Bean and S.
    MacPherson, (eds), *Approaches to Welfare* (Routledge & Kegan Paul,
    1983), p. 276.

30 H. Sidgwick, 'Issues for Utilitarians' (excerpt from *The Methods of
    Ethics*), in P. Singer (ed.), *Ethics*, pp. 315–17, from where all quotations
    in this paragraph are taken.

31   R. Hare, 'Justice and Equality', in Arthur and Shaw (eds), *Justice and Economic Distribution*, p. 125; Harsanyi, 'Rule Utilitarianism, Equality, and Justice', pp. 124–5; R. Brandt, *Facts, Values and Morality* (Cambridge University Press, 1996), pp. 206–7, 214; Smart, 'Distributive Justice and Utilitarianism', pp. 104–5.

32   Hare, 'Justice and Equality', p. 126.

33   Harsanyi, 'Rule Utilitarianism, Equality, and Justice', p. 125.

34   Hare, 'Justice and Equality', pp. 125–6.

35   Smart, 'Distributive Justice and Utilitarianism', p. 113; Harsanyi, 'Rule Utilitarianism, Equality, and Justice', p. 125; Hare, 'Justice and Equality', p. 125.

36   Brandt, *Facts, Values and Morality*, p. 218.

37   Goodin, *Utilitarianism as a Public Philosophy*, ch. 14; G. Scarre, *Utilitarianism* (Routledge, 1996), p. 142.

38   Shaw, *Contemporary Ethics: Taking Account of Utilitarianism*, p. 243.

39   J. S. Mill, *Principles of Political Economy*, quoted in W. Shaw, *Business Ethics* (Wadsworth, 4th edn, 2002), pp. 92–3; D. Haslett, *Capitalism with Morality* (Oxford University Press, 1994).

40   Rawls, *A Theory of Justice* (1971/1999), pp. 30f/27f.

41   Freeman, 'Utilitarianism, Deontology, and the Priority of Right', pp. 324, 342.

42   P. Singer, 'Outsiders: Our Obligations to those Beyond our Borders', in D. Chatterjee (ed.), *The Ethics of Assistance*.

43   J. Feinberg, *Harm to Others*, pp. 94–5.

11   Kantian Moral Philosophy

1   References to Kant's work are given as follows: G = *Grounding for the Metaphysics of Morals*, trans. J. Ellington (Hackett, 1981), with page references to the standard Prussian Academy edition of Kant's works, which are given in most translations; CP = *Critique of Practical Reason*, trans. L. Beck (Prentice Hall, 3rd edn, 1993); MM = *The Metaphysics of Morals*, trans. M. Gregor (Cambridge University Press, 1996); PW = *Political Writings*, ed. H. Reiss, trans. H. Nisbet (Cambridge University Press, 2nd edn., 1991); PP = *Perpetual Peace: A Philosophical Essay*, trans. M. Campbell Smith (Thoemmes Press, 1992).

2   R. Sullivan, *An Introduction to Kant's Ethics* (Cambridge University Press, 1994), pp. 13, 110. In contrast, Thomas Nagel remarks that 'we are at a primitive stage of moral development', with 'only a haphazard understanding of how to live, how to treat others, how to organize ... societies', so the 'idea that the basic principles of morality are *known* ... is one of the most fantastic conceits' to which humans are drawn (*The View from Nowhere* [Oxford University Press, 1989], p. 186).

3 J. Rawls, *Lectures on the History of Moral Philosophy*, ed. B. Herman (Harvard University Press, 2000), p. 227.

4 There is an undeniable evil in human nature but there is also a 'natural moral capacity', which can control it (PP, 132). Since our moral capacity is natural, 'natural' is not an ideal term for our non-moral aspect.

5 Imperatives, hypothetical or categorical, are objective practical laws, valid for every rational being (CP, 17f).

6 Similar formulations include these: 'I should never act except in such a way that I can also will that my maxim should become a universal law' (G, 402). 'Act as if the maxim of your action were to become through your will a universal law of nature' (G, 421). 'We must be able to will that a maxim of our action become a universal law' (G, 424). '[M]axims must be so chosen as if they were to hold as universal laws of nature' (G, 436). 'Act according to that maxim which can at the same time make itself a universal law' (G, 436–7). 'Act always according to that maxim whose universality as a law you can at the same time will' (G, 437). 'So act as if your maxims were to serve at the same time as a universal law (for all rational beings)' (G, 438). 'So act that the maxim of your will could always hold at the same time as the principle giving universal law' (CP, 30). '[A]ct upon a maxim that can also hold as a universal law' (MM, 17f). 'So act that the maxim of your action could become a universal *law*' (MM, 152)

7 C. Korsgaard, *Creating the Kingdom of Ends* (Cambridge University Press, 1996), p. 135.

8 I am grateful to Palgrave Macmillan's reader for pressing me to clarify this point.

9 Rawls, *Lectures on the History of Moral Philosophy*, pp. 175f; and 'Themes in Kant's Moral Philosophy', *Collected Papers*, p. 502.

10 Kant says that the common principle 'Do not do to others what you do not want done to yourself', although it appears to be similar to the CI, is a derivative of it. It has several limitations: It does not contain the ground of duties to oneself, or of positive duties to help others (because someone may agree to forgo help if he is excused helping others), or of strict duties to others, for the criminal would be able to dispute with the judge who punishes (that is, harms) him (G, 430n). Thus, the CI is consistent with, but more precise than, ordinary moral thought.

11 A. Wood, *Kant's Ethical Thought* (Cambridge University Press, 1999), pp. 99–100, following B. Herman, *The Practice of Moral Judgement* (Harvard University Press, 1993), pp. 116–19. Wood also argues (pp. 98–9) that there are some maxims (for example, for revenge) that would lead to violations of *both* perfect and imperfect duties. However, this argument relies on misformulating a maxim, not specifying both the end and the means (that is, what one will do to get revenge).

12 I. Kant *Lectures on Ethics*, trans. P. Heath (Cambridge University Press, 1997) p. 212. Kant claims that only persons, who have reason and thus autonomy, have inherent value. But if non-rational humans (infants, and so on) have inherent value, and the right to be treated with respect, then personhood is not the correct criterion of inherent value. Tom Regan argues that what has inherent value is a subject of a life, a being with consciousness, feelings, desires and thus welfare. All subjects of a life, not only persons, have inherent value, are ends, may not be used as mere means, are owed treatment respectful of their inherent value, and have a corresponding right to be treated respectfully. This includes non-rational humans and nonhuman mammals (Regan, in C. Cohen and T. Regan, *The Animal Rights Debate* [Rowman and Littlefield, 2001], pp. 199–204; T. Regan, *The Case for Animal Rights* [Routledge, 1984]). The Formula of Humanity's statement of a duty to treat persons only in ways that respect their nature as rational beings might be paralleled by a duty to treat nonhuman animals only in ways that respect their nature as sentient beings.

13 Wood, *Kant's Ethical Thought*, pp. 139–41, 167.

14 I. Kant, 'On a Supposed Right to Lie from Philanthropy', in S. Darwall (ed.), *Deontology* (Blackwell, 2003), pp. 29, 32.

15 I am grateful to Palgrave Macmillan's reader for raising this objection.

16 I am grateful to Palgrave Macmillan's reader for pressing me to clarify this argument.

17 The comparison between lying and self-defence as ways to thwart wrongdoing is suggested in C. Korsgaard, 'The Right to Lie: Kant on Dealing with Evil', in *Creating the Kingdom of Ends*, p. 144.

18 Sullivan, *An Introduction to Kant's Ethics*, pp. 103, 110.

19 Wood, *Kant's Ethical Thought*, p. 363, n.7.

20 'He … can do something because he knows that he ought' (CP, 30). 'It is always in everyone's power to satisfy the commands of the categorical command of morality' (CP, 38). We 'know that we *can* do it because … we *ought* to do it' (CP, 165). Respecting duty above all else, overcoming the most seductive temptations – 'man … can do this just because he ought' (PW, 71). A person '*can* do what … he *ought* to do' (MM, 146).

21 Kant's insistence that purely moral motivation is crucial, powerful, sufficient and inspiring informs his suggestions about moral education (CP, 159–66).

22 Moral self-constraint makes known the inexplicable property of freedom. The more one is constrained morally, by the idea of duty, the freer one is. One proves one's freedom 'by being unable to resist the call of duty' (MM, 17, 42, 145n, 147n).

12   John Rawls's Theory of Justice

1   TJ, viii, 22. In this chapter, the following abbreviations will be used for page references to Rawls's work: TJ = *A Theory of Justice* (Harvard University Press, 1971); TJ rev. edn. = *A Theory of Justice: Revised Edition* (Harvard University Press, 1999); PL = *Political Liberalism* (Columbia University Press, 1993); LP = *The Law of Peoples* (Harvard University Press, 1999); JF = *Justice as Fairness: A Restatement* (Harvard University Press, 2001).

2   TJ, 127, 447–8; JF, 3, 34, 36, 84.

3   PL, 137f, 217; JF, 41, 84, 89–91.

4   'Justice as Fairness: Political not Metaphysical', in *Collected Papers*, pp. 400–1n.

5   PL, 3, 9, 14f, 20, 34–5; JF, 4f, 6–8, 14, 27, 39, 56, 79, 136, 140, 176n; LP, 143.

6   PL, 19; JF, 18–19, 21.

7   TJ, 8–9, 13, 245f; JF, 13.

8   PL, xv, xviii, xix, 9, 11–14, 38, 223; JF, 26–7, 32f; LP, 143.

9   TJ, 7.

10 TJ, 7, 96; JF, 10, 55, 65.

11 TJ, 259; PL, 68, 269f; JF, 56f.

12 TJ, 7, 15, 74–5, 101–2, 311.

13 The idea of brute luck, which is implicit in Rawls, comes from Ronald Dworkin, *Sovereign Virtue: The Theory and Practice of Equality* (Harvard University Press, 2000), p. 73. Susan Hurley questions the idea of luck in genes or parents because there is no one for whom these are good or bad luck; someone with different genes or parents would be a different person (S. L. Hurley, *Justice, Luck, and Knowledge* [Harvard University Press, 2003], pp. 117ff). Nevertheless, a person is not responsible for either.

14 JF, 40, 56.

15 TJ, 11–13, 438, emphasis added; PL, 22f; JF, 14–15, 79.

16 TJ, 12, 136f; PL, 23; JF, 15, 82.

17 TJ, 18f, 21, 82, 516; PL, 23–5, 275; JF, 16–19, 80, 82, 87.

18 TJ, 19, 138; PL, 27, 274; JF, 86.

19 TJ, 19–21; PL, 8, 124; JF, 31.

20 TJ, 75, 104.

21 TJ, 120, 446–7.

22 PL, 5–6. I use this formulation because Rawls's statements of the two principles in *Theory* (TJ, 60, 302; TJ rev. edn, 53, 266) put the two parts of the second principle in the wrong order and his statement of them in *Justice as Fairness* (JF, 42) omits the second part of the first principle.

23 TJ, 61; TJ rev. edn. 53; PL 291f, 295, 335; JF, 44f, 114.

24 TJ, 225, 228; PL, 327, 358; JF, 46, 149.
25 TJ, 301; JF, 43f.
26 JF, 64, 129.
27 TJ, 62, 92f, 396; TJ rev. edn., xiii; PL, 180f; JF, 57–60, 88.
28 TJ, 98; JF, 59.
29 TJ, 94, 96f.
30 TJ, 28, 61, 63, 151; PL, 295; JF, 46–7, 111.
31 JF, 46, 61.
32 PL, 7; JF, 44n.
33 PL, 6, 156–7.
34 TJ, 179f.
35 TJ, 28, 156n, 160f, 169, 175f, 206f, 211, 543, 563, 573; TJ, rev. edn., xii; JF, 45f, 100, 102f, 104f, 110, 112, 115.
36 TJ, 225; JF, 148; LP, 139.
37 TJ, 204f; PL, 325–8; JF, 149f.
38 PL, 328–9; JF, 150f.
39 TJ, 72f, 84.
40 TJ, 73–5.
41 JF, 95, 120.
42 TJ, 101f, 104.
43 TJ, 15, 75.
44 TJ, 78.
45 TJ, 64–5, 104; JF, 124.
46 TJ, 107, 178–81, 534.
47 J. Cohen, 'Taking People as They Are?' *Philosophy and Public Affairs*, 30 (2002), p. 366.
48 TJ, 178; JF, 127.
49 TJ, 102–3, 250; JF, 128.
50 Cohen, 'Taking People as They Are?' p. 366.
51 J. Cohen, 'Democratic Equality', *Ethics*, 99 (1989), p. 729.
52 TJ, 102–4; JF, 126.
53 TJ, 150f, 543.
54 PL, 282; JF, 123.
55 TJ, 14.
56 JF, 124.
57 TJ, 440, 534, 536.
58 TJ, 61, 199.
59 JF, 145.
60 TJ, 225f; PL, lviii, 235n, 328 357f; JF, 51, 149f.
61 TJ, 73, 275; PL, 363; JF, 44, 174.
62 TJ, 277–9; JF, 161.
63 TJ, 87, 158, 277–9, 305, 307.
64 TJ rev. edn., xv; JF, 137–8, 140.
65 TJ 274, 280; TJ rev. edn., xiv, xv; JF, 135, 139f, 178.

66 TJ, 48; JF, 82.
67 TJ, 120, 446–7.
68 Kymlicka, *Contemporary Political Philosophy*, pp. 61, 68; Dworkin, *Taking Rights Seriously*, ch. 6.
69 T. Pogge, 'The Incoherence between Rawls's Theories of Justice', *Fordham Law Review*, 72 (2004), pp. 1742f.
70 T. Pogge, 'Equal Liberty for All?', *Midwest Studies in Philosophy*, XXVIII (2004), pp. 272–4, 280.
71 Pogge, 'Equal Liberty', pp. 273f, 280.
72 Nozick, *Anarchy, State, and Utopia*, pp. ix, xi, 230.
73 Nozick, pp. 151, 160–3.
74 Nozick, pp. 179n, 235, 238.
75 Nozick, pp. 168f, 171f.
76 Nozick, p. 34. This criticism is made by Kymlicka, *Contemporary Political Philosophy*, pp. 122–7.
77 Nozick, pp. 30–1.
78 Kant, *The Metaphysics of Morals*, pp. 101, 149.
79 PL, 266–7.
80 Nozick, p. 262.
81 G. A. Cohen, 'Capitalism, Freedom, and the Proletariat'.
82 Nozick, p. 197.
83 Nozick, p. 199.
84 Nozick, p. 214.
85 P. Van Parijs, 'Difference Principles', in S. Freeman (ed.), *The Cambridge Companion to Rawls* (Cambridge University Press, 2003), pp. 213–16.
86 TJ, 96.
87 Nozick, pp. 225–6.
88 Nozick, p. 228.
89 TJ, 101, quoted Nozick, p. 228.
90 TJ, rev. edn., 87; JF, 75–6.
91 G. A. Cohen, 'Facts and Principles', *Philosophy and Public Affairs*, 31 (2003), pp. 241f, 244f.
92 TJ, 75.
93 PL, 281–2; JF, 123.
94 G. A. Cohen, 'Incentives, Inequality, and Community', in G. Peterson (ed.), *The Tanner Lectures on Human Values*, vol. 13 (University of Utah Press, 1992), 'The Pareto Argument for Inequality', *Social Philosophy and Policy*, 12, 1 (1995), 'Where the Action is: On the Site of Distributive Justice', *Philosophy and Public Affairs*, 26 (1997), and *If You're an Egalitarian, How Come You're so Rich?*, (Harvard University Press, 2000), ch. 8 and 9, especially pp. 140–1. A similar critical revision of Rawls was developed independently by Joseph

Carens and recapitulated in his 'An Interpretation and Defense of the Socialist Principle of Distribution', *Social Philosophy and Policy*, 20, 1 (2003).

95   Cohen, 'Incentives', pp. 280, 286f, 295–7, 300f.
96   Cohen, 'Incentives', pp. 326, 328.
97   Carens, 'An Interpretation and Defense', p. 150.
98   Cohen, 'Incentives', p. 302; S. Scheffler, 'Is the Basic Structure Basic?' in C. Sypnowich (ed.), *The Egalitarian Conscience: Essays in Honour of G. A. Cohen* (Oxford University Press, 2006), pp. 119f.
99   Cohen, 'Incentives', pp. 296, 310, 312f, 315–19, 327–8; 'Where the Action Is', pp. 6, 13–15, 18.
100 Scheffler doubts that Rawls would make this objection ('Is the Basic Structure Basic?' p. 112).
101 Cohen, 'Where the Action is', pp. 17–24.
102 A. Williams, 'Incentives, Inequality, and Publicity', *Philosophy and Public Affairs*, 27 (1998), pp. 234, 237.
103 P. Smith, 'Incentives and Justice: G. A. Cohen's Egalitarian Critique of Rawls', *Social Theory and Practice*, 24, 2 (1998), pp. 211–16; Scheffler, 'Is the Basic Structure Basic?' p. 114.
104 Cohen, 'Incentives', p. 322; 'Where the Action is', pp. 15–17.
105 PL, 11–12; also JF, 26.
106 Cohen, 'Where the Action is', pp. 4, 15, 18, 21f. Rawls does say, inconsistently, that a political conception of justice applies 'solely' to the basic structure (PL, 223, for example).
107 TJ, 108, 261; TJ rev. edn., 93, 230f.
108 PL, 217–19, 242, 252f; JF, 90, 92, 117.
109 PL, 266f.
110 Van Parijs, 'Difference Principles', pp. 227, 230–1. Formulating principles of justice for individuals does not mean, as Van Parijs suggests (p. 228), reverting from Rawls's specifically political conception of justice to a comprehensive moral theory.
111 Carens, 'An Interpretation and Defense', pp. 150, 154f, 163, 168, 172.

Concluding Remarks

1   J. Rawls, *A Theory of Justice* (1971/1999), pp. 24/21–2.
2   S. Freeman, 'Utilitarianism, Deontology, and the Priority of Right', p. 324.
3   J. Rawls, 'Social Unity and Primary Goods', *Collected Papers*, p. 360.
4   Rawls, *A Theory of Justice*, pp. 30/26.
5   Freeman, 'Utilitarianism, Deontology, and the Priority of Right', p. 342.

6 Rawls, *A Theory of Justice*, pp. 30/27.
7 Freeman, 'Utilitarianism, Deontology, and the Priority of Right', p. 339.
8 Freeman, pp. 335f; Rawls, *Theory*, pp. 31/27–8.
9 Freeman, p. 339.

REFERENCES

Arneson, R. 'Equality', in R. Simon (ed.), *The Blackwell Guide to Social and Political Philosophy* (Blackwell, 2002).

Arneson, R. 'Moral Limits on the Demands of Beneficence?' in D. Chatterjee (ed.), *The Ethics of Assistance* (Cambridge University Press, 2004).

Arthur, J. 'Rights and the Duty to Bring Aid', in H. LaFollette (ed.), *Ethics in Practice* (Blackwell, 1997).

Barry, B. *Justice as Impartiality* (Clarendon Press, 1995).

Barry, B. *Why Social Justice Matters* (Polity Press, 2005).

Bayne, T. and Levy, N. 'Amputees by Choice: Body Integrity Disorder and the Ethics of Amputation', *Journal of Applied Philosophy*, 22, 1 (2005).

Bean, P. 'Utilitarianism and the Welfare State', in P. Bean and S. MacPherson, (eds), *Approaches to Welfare* (Routledge & Kegan Paul, 1983).

Bedau, H. (ed.), *Civil Disobedience in Focus* (Routledge, 1991).

Bedau, H. 'Civil Disobedience', *Encyclopedia of Applied Ethics, Volume 1*, (Academic Press, 1998).

Bedau, H. 'Capital Punishment', in H. LaFollette (ed.), *The Oxford Handbook of Practical Ethics* (Oxford University Press, 2003).

Beitz, C. 'Human Rights and the Law of Peoples', in D. Chatterjee (ed.), *The Ethics of Assistance* (Cambridge University Press, 2004).

Bentham, J. *Anarchical Fallacies* (excerpt), in J. Waldron (ed.), *'Nonsense upon Stilts': Bentham, Burke and Marx on the Rights of Man* (Methuen, 1987).

Bentham, J. *The Rationale of Reward* and *Introduction to the Principles of Morals and Legislation*, excerpted in Peter Singer (ed.), *Ethics* (Oxford University Press, 1994).

Berlin, I. 'Two Concepts of Liberty', in *Four Essays on Liberty* (Oxford University Press, 1969).

Berlin, I. *Four Essays on Liberty* (Oxford University Press, 1969).

Bowie, N. and Simon, R. *The Individual and the Political Order*, 3rd edn. (Rowman & Littlefield, 1998).

Brandt, R. *Facts, Values and Morality* (Cambridge University Press, 1996).

Brandt, R. 'Ethical Relativism', in T. L. Moser and P. K. Carson (eds), *Moral Relativism: A Reader* (Oxford University Press, 2001).

Buchanan, A. *Justice, Legitimacy and Self-Determination: Moral Foundations for International Law* (Oxford University Press, 2004).

Carens J. 'An Interpretation and Defense of the Socialist Principle of Distribution', *Social Philosophy and Policy*, 20, 1 (2003).

Carson, T. L. and Moser, P. K. 'Introduction' to P. K. Moser and T. L. Carson (eds), *Moral Relativism: A Reader* (Oxford University Press, 2001).

Carter, I. et al. (eds), *Freedom: A Philosophical Anthology* (Blackwell, 2007).

Chambliss, W. 'Don't Confuse Me with Facts: Clinton "Just Says No" ' *New Left Review*, 204 (1994).

Chatterjee, D. (ed.), *The Ethics of Assistance* (Cambridge University Press, 2004).

Clutterbuck, R. *Drugs, Crime and Corruption* (Macmillan, 1995).

Cohen, C. and Regan, T. *The Animal Rights Debate* (Rowman & Littlefield, 2001).

Cohen, G. A. 'Are Disadvantaged Workers who Take Hazardous Jobs Forced to Take Hazardous Jobs?' in *History, Labour, Freedom* (Oxford University Press, 1988).

Cohen, G. A. 'Incentives, Inequality, and Community', in G. Peterson (ed.), *The Tanner Lectures on Human Values*, vol. 13 (University of Utah Press, 1992).

Cohen, G. A. 'The Pareto Argument for Inequality', *Social Philosophy and Policy*, 12, 1 (1995).

Cohen, G. A. *Self-Ownership, Freedom and Equality* (Cambridge University Press, 1995).

Cohen, G. A. 'Back to Socialist Basics', in J. Franklin (ed.), *Equality* (London: Institute for Public Policy Research, 1997).

Cohen, G. A. 'Where the Action Is: On the Site of Distributive Justice', *Philosophy and Public Affairs*, 26, 1 (1997).

Cohen, G. A., 'Once More into the Breach of Self-Ownership: Reply to Narveson and Brenkert', *Journal of Ethics*, 2, 1 (1998).

Cohen, G. A. *If You're an Egalitarian, How Come You're so Rich?* (Harvard University Press, 2000).

Cohen, G. A. 'Facts and Principles', *Philosophy and Public Affairs*, 31, 3 (2003).

Cohen, G. A. 'Capitalism, Freedom, and the Proletariat', in D. Miller (ed.), *The Liberty Reader* (Edinburgh University Press, 2006).

Cohen, G. A., 'Freedom and Money', http://www.pem.cam.ac.uk/international-programmes/Cohen.pdf.

Cohen, J. 'Democratic Equality', *Ethics*, 99 (1989).

Cohen, J. 'Taking People as They Are?' *Philosophy and Public Affairs*, 30, 4 (2002).

Cohen, J. 'For a Democratic Society', in S. Freeman (ed.), *The Cambridge Companion to Rawls* (Cambridge University Press, 2003).

Cohen, J. 'Is There a Human Right to Democracy?' in C. Sypnowich (ed.), *The Egalitarian Conscience: Essays in Honour of G. A. Cohen* (Oxford University Press, 2006).

De Greiff, P. (ed.), *Drugs and the Limits of Liberalism* (Cornell University Press, 1999).

Dower, N. 'World Poverty', in P. Singer (ed.), *A Companion to Ethics* (Blackwell, 1991).

Downing Street Strategy Unit Drugs Project, *Phase 1 Report: Understanding the Issues*, available at http://www.guardian.co.uk/drugs/Story/0,,1521501,00.html

Dworkin, R. *Taking Rights Seriously* (Duckworth, 1978).

Dworkin, R. 'Rights as Trumps', in J. Waldron (ed.), *Theories of Rights* (Oxford University Press, 1984).

Dworkin, R. *A Matter of Principle* (Oxford University Press, 1986).

Dworkin, R. *Sovereign Virtue: The Theory and Practice of Equality* (Harvard University Press, 2000).

Edmundson, W. A. (ed.), *The Duty to Obey the Law: Selected Philosophical Readings* (Rowman & Littlefield, 1999).

Feinberg, J. *Social Philosophy* (Prentice Hall, 1973).

Feinberg, J. 'The Nature and Value of Rights', in *Rights, Justice, and the Bounds of Liberty* (Princeton University Press, 1980).

Feinberg, J. *Harm to Others (The Moral Limits of the Criminal Law, Volume 1)* (Oxford University Press, 1984).

Feinberg, J. *Offense to Others (The Moral Limits of the Criminal Law, Volume 2)* (Oxford University Press, 1985).

Feinberg, J. *Harm to Self (The Moral Limits of the Criminal Law, Volume 3)* (Oxford University Press, 1986).

Feinberg, J. *Harmless Wrongdoing (The Moral Limits of the Criminal Law, Volume 4)* (Oxford University Press, 1988).

Feinberg, J. 'Civil Disobedience in the Modern World', in J. Feinberg and H. Gross (eds), *Philosophy of Law*, 4th edn. (Wadsworth, 1991).

Feinberg, J. 'The Justification of Punishment: The Classic Debate', in J. Feinberg and H. Gross (eds.), *Philosophy of Law*, 4th edn. (Wadsworth, 1991).

Feinberg, J. 'In Defence of Moral Rights', *Oxford Journal of Legal Studies*, 12, 2 (1992).

Feinberg, J. *Freedom and Fulfillment: Philosophical Essays* (Princeton University Press, 1992).

Feinberg, J. 'Freedom and Liberty', *Routledge Encyclopedia of Philosophy* (Routledge, 1998).

Forst, R. 'Justice, Morality and Power in the Global Context', in A. Follesdal and T. Pogge (eds), *Real World Justice* (Springer, 2005).

Frankfurt, H. 'Equality as a Moral Ideal', in L. Pojman and R. Westmoreland (eds), *Equality: Selected Readings* (Oxford University Press, 1996).

Freeman, S. 'Utilitarianism, Deontology, and the Priority of Right', *Philosophy and Public Affairs*, 23, 4 (1994).

Freeman, S. 'Liberalism, Inalienability, and Rights of Drug Use', in P. De Greiff (ed.), *Drugs and the Limits of Liberalism* (Cornell University Press, 1999).

Freeman, S. (ed.), *The Cambridge Companion to Rawls* (Cambridge University Press, 2003).

Frey, R. G. 'Act Utilitarianism', in H. LaFollette (ed.), *The Blackwell Guide to Ethical Theory* (Blackwell, 2000).

Friedman, M. 'Prohibition and Drugs', in J. Rachels (ed.) *The Right Thing to Do*, 3rd edn. (McGraw-Hill, 2003).

Goldman, A. 'The Paradox of Punishment', in A. J. Simmons et al. (eds), *Punishment* (Princeton University Press, 1995).

Goodin, R. 'Utility and the Good', in P. Singer (ed.), *A Companion to Ethics* (Blackwell, 1991).

Goodin, R. *Utilitarianism as a Public Philosophy* (Cambridge University Press, 1995).

Greenawalt, K. 'Justifying Nonviolent Disobedience', in H. Bedau (ed.), *Civil Disobedience in Focus* (Routledge, 1991).

Hardin, G. 'Living on a Lifeboat', in S. Luper and C. Brown (eds), *The Moral Life*, 2nd edn. (Harcourt Brace, 1999).

Hare, R. 'Justice and Equality', in J. Arthur and W. Shaw (eds), *Justice and Economic Distribution* (Prentice Hall, 1978).

Hare, R. *Moral Thinking: Its Levels, Methods and Point* (Oxford University Press, 1981).

Hare, R. 'Ethical Theory and Utilitarianism', in A. Sen and B. Williams (eds), *Utilitarianism and Beyond* (Cambridge University Press, 1982).

Harman, G. 'Is There a Single True Morality?' in P. K. Moser and T. L. Carson (eds), *Moral Relativism: A Reader* (Oxford University Press, 2001).

Harsanyi, J. 'Rule Utilitarianism, Equality, and Justice', *Social Philosophy and Policy*, 2, 2 (1985).

Hart, H. L. A. *Punishment and Responsibility* (Clarendon Press, 1968).

Haslett, D. *Capitalism with Morality* (Oxford University Press, 1994).

Hayek, F. 'Freedom and Coercion', in D. Miller (ed.), *The Liberty Reader* (Edinburgh University Press, 2006).

Herman, B. *The Practice of Moral Judgement* (Harvard University Press, 1993).

Hill, T. 'Kantian Normative Ethics', in D. Copp (ed.), *The Oxford Handbook of Ethical Theory* (Oxford University Press, 2006).

Honderich, T. *Punishment: The Supposed Justifications Revisited* (Pluto Press, 2006).

Hooker, B. 'Rule Consequentialism', in H. LaFollette (ed.), *The Blackwell Guide to Ethical Theory* (Blackwell, 2000).

Hurley, S. L. *Justice, Luck, and Knowledge* (Harvard University Press, 2003).

Husak, D. *Drugs and Rights* (Cambridge University Press, 1992).

Husak, D. and de Marneffe, P. *The Legalization of Drugs: For and Against* (Cambridge University Press, 2005).

James, O. *Juvenile Violence in a Winner–Loser Culture: Socio-economic and Familial Origins of the Rise of Violence against the Person* (Free Association Books, 1995).

Jones, P. *Rights* (Macmillan, 1994).

Kant, I. *Grounding for the Metaphysics of Morals*, trans. J. W. Ellington (Hackett, 1981).

Kant, I. *Political Writings*, ed. H. Reiss, trans. H. Nisbet, 2nd edn. (Cambridge University Press, 1991).

Kant, I. *Perpetual Peace: A Philosophical Essay*, trans. M. Campbell Smith (Thoemmes Press, 1992).

Kant, I. *Critique of Practical Reason*, ed. and trans. L. W. Beck, 3rd edn. (Prentice Hall, 1993).

Kant, I. *The Metaphysics of Morals*, ed. and trans. M. Gregor (Cambridge University Press, 1996).

Kant, I. *Lectures on Ethics*, ed. P. Heath and J. B. Schneewind, trans. P. Heath (Cambridge University Press, 1997).

Kant, I. 'On a Supposed Right to Lie from Philanthropy', in S. Darwall (ed.), *Deontology*, (Blackwell, 2003).

Korsgaard, C. *Creating the Kingdom of Ends* (Cambridge University Press, 1996).

Kristol, I. 'Pornography, Obscenity, and the Case for Censorship', *The New York Times Magazine*, 28 March 1971, reprinted in G. Dworkin (ed.), *Morality, Harm, and the Law* (Westview Press, 1994).

Kropáček, L. 'Islam and Human Rights', in J. Krejčí (ed.), *Islam in Contact with Rival Civilizations* (Prague: Filosofia Publications of the Institute of Philosophy of the Academy of Sciences of the Czech Republic, 1998).

Kymlicka, W. *Contemporary Political Philosophy*, 2nd edn. (Oxford University Press, 2002).

Luper-Foy, S. and Brown, C. (eds), *Drugs, Morality, and the Law* (Garland, 1994).

Lyons, D. *Forms and Limits of Utilitarianism* (Clarendon Press, 1965).

Lyons, D. 'Utility and Rights', in *Rights, Welfare, and Mill's Moral Theory* (Oxford University Press, 1994).

Lyons, D. 'Liberty and Harm to Others', in G. Dworkin (ed.), *Mill's On Liberty: Critical Essays* (Rowman & Littlefield, 1997).

MacCallum, G. 'Negative and Positive Freedom', in D. Miller (ed.), *The Liberty Reader* (Edinburgh University Press, 2006).

MacIntyre, A. *After Virtue*, 2nd edn. (University of Notre Dame Press, 1984).

Mackie, J. 'Can There Be a Rights-Based Moral Theory?' in J. Waldron (ed.), *Theories of Rights* (Oxford University Press, 1984).

Mandle, J. *Global Justice* (Polity Press, 2006).

McPherson, C. B. *The Rise and Fall of Economic Justice* (Oxford University Press, 1985).

Mill, J. S. *On Liberty*, various editions.

Mill, J. S. *Utilitarianism*, various editions.

Miller, D. (ed.), *The Liberty Reader* (Edinburgh University Press, 2006).

Mitchell, R. et al., *Inequalities in Life and Death: What if Britain were More Equal?* (The Policy Press, 2000).

Moser, P. K. and Carson, T. L. (eds.), *Moral Relativism: A Reader* (Oxford University Press, 2001).

Nadelmann, E. 'The Case for Legalization' in J. Inciardi (ed.), *The Drug Legalization Debate* (Sage, 1991).

Nagel, T. *The View from Nowhere* (Oxford University Press, 1989).

Narveson, J. 'Feeding the Hungry', in J. Rachels (ed.), *The Right Thing to Do*, 3rd edn. (McGraw-Hill, 2003).

Nozick, R. *Anarchy, State, and Utopia* (Basic Books, 1974).

Nutt, D. et al., 'Development of a Rational Scale to Assess the Harm of Drugs of Potential Misuse', *The Lancet*, vol. 369 (2007), pp. 1047-53.

O'Neill, O. 'Kantian Approaches to Some Famine Problems', in J. Feinberg and R. Shafer-Landau (eds), *Reason and* Responsibility, 11th edn (Wadsworth, 2002).

Parfit, D. 'On Doing the Best for Our Children', in M. D. Bayles (ed.), *Ethics and Population*, (Schenkman, 1976).

Parfit, D. *Reasons and Persons*, rev. edn. (Oxford University Press, 1987).

Parfit, D. 'Equality or Priority?' in M. Clayton and A. Williams (eds), *The Ideal of Equality* (Palgrave Macmillan, 2002).

Pettit, P. 'Consequentialism', in P. Singer (ed.), *A Companion to Ethics* (Blackwell, 1991).

Plato, *Crito*, in H. Bedau (ed.), *Civil Disobedience in Focus* (Routledge, 1991).

Pogge, T. *World Poverty and Human Rights* (Polity Press, 2002).

Pogge, T. ' "Assisting" the Global Poor', in D. Chatterjee (ed.), *The Ethics of Assistance: Morality and the Distant Needy* (Cambridge University Press, 2004).

Pogge, T. 'Equal Liberty for All?' *Midwest Studies in Philosophy*, XXVIII (2004).

Pogge, T. 'The Incoherence between Rawls's Theories of Justice', *Fordham Law Review*, 72, 5 (2004).

Pogge, T. 'A Cosmopolitan Perspective on the Global Economic Order', in G. Brock and H. Brighouse (eds), *The Political Philosophy of Cosmopolitanism* (Cambridge University Press, 2005).

Pogge, T. 'The First UN Millennium Development Goal: A Cause for Celebration?' in A. Follesdal and T. Pogge (eds), *Real World Justice* (Springer, 2005).

Pogge, T. 'Real World Justice', *Journal of Ethics*, 9, 1–2 (2005).

Pogge, T. 'World Poverty and Human Rights', *Ethics and International Affairs*, 19, 1 (2005).

Quinton, A. 'On Punishment', in H. B. Acton (ed.), *The Philosophy of Punishment*, (Macmillan, 1969).

Rachels, J. 'Moral Philosophy as a Subversive Activity', in E. R. Winkler and J. R. Coombs (eds), *Applied Ethics: A Reader* (Blackwell, 1993).

Rachels, J. *The Elements of Moral Philosophy*, 5th edn. (McGraw-Hill International, 2007).

Rachels, J. *The Right Thing to Do* (McGraw-Hill, 3rd edn. 2003; 4th edn., 2007).

Rawls, J. *A Theory of Justice* (Harvard University Press, 1971).

Rawls, J. *Political Liberalism* (Columbia University Press, 1993).

Rawls, J. *The Law of Peoples* (Harvard University Press, 1999).

Rawls, J. *A Theory of Justice: Revised Edition* (Harvard University Press, 1999).

Rawls, J. *Collected Papers*, ed. S. Freeman (Harvard University Press, 1999).

Rawls, J. *Lectures on the History of Moral Philosophy*, ed. B. Herman (Harvard University Press, 2000).

Rawls, J. *Justice as Fairness: A Restatement* (Harvard University Press, 2001).

Raz, J. 'Rights-based Moralities', in J. Waldron (ed.), *Theories of Rights* (Oxford University Press, 1984).

Raz, J. *The Morality of Freedom* (Oxford University Press, 1986).

Raz, J. 'The Obligation to Obey: Revision and Tradition', in W. Edmundson (ed.), *The Duty to Obey the Law: Selected Philosophical Readings* (Rowman & Littlefield, 1999).

Regan, T. *The Case for Animal Rights* (Routledge, 1984).

Reiman, J. 'Drug Addiction, Liberal Virtue, and Moral Responsibility', in *Critical Moral Liberalism* (Rowman & Littlefield, 1997).

Richards, D. *Sex, Drugs, Death and the Law* (Rowman & Littlefield, 1982).

Riley, J. 'Mill on Justice', in D. Boucher and P. Kelly (eds), *Social Justice: from Hume to Walzer* (Routledge, 1998).

Scanlon, T. *The Difficulty of Tolerance: Essays in Political Philosophy* (Cambridge University Press, 2003).

Scanlon, T. 'The Diversity of Objections to Inequality', in *The Difficulty of Tolerance: Essays in Political Philosophy* (Cambridge University Press, 2003).

Scanlon, T. 'Human Rights as a Neutral Concern', in *The Difficulty of Tolerance: Essays in Political Philosophy* (Cambridge University Press, 2003).

Scarre, G. *Utilitarianism* (Routledge, 1996).

Scheffler, S. 'Is the Basic Structure Basic?' in C. Sypnowich (ed.), *The Egalitarian Conscience: Essays in Honour of G. A. Cohen* (Oxford University Press, 2006).

Sen, A. *Inequality Re-examined* (Oxford University Press, 1992).

Sen, A. *Development as Freedom* (Oxford University Press, 1999).

Sen, A. 'Elements of a Theory of Human Rights', *Philosophy and Public Affairs*, 32, 4 (2004).

Shaw, W. *Contemporary Ethics: Taking Account of Utilitarianism* (Blackwell, 1999).

Shaw, W. *Business Ethics*, 4th edn. (Wadsworth, 2002).

Sidgwick, H. 'Issues for Utilitarians' (excerpt from *The Methods of Ethics*, 7th edn. [Macmillan, 1907]), in P. Singer, *Ethics* (Oxford University Press, 1994).

Simmons, A. J. 'Political Obligation and Authority', in R. Simon (ed.), *The Blackwell Guide to Social and Political Philosophy* (Blackwell, 2002).

Simmons, A. J. 'The Duty to Obey and Our Natural Moral Duties', in C. Wellman and A. J. Simmons, *Is There a Duty to Obey the Law?* (Cambridge University Press, 2005).

Singer, P. *Practical Ethics*, 2nd edn. (Cambridge University Press, 1993).

Singer, P. *Animal Liberation*, 2nd edn. (Pimlico, 1995).

Singer, P. 'Famine, Affluence, and Morality', in H. LaFollette (ed.), *Ethics in Practice* (Blackwell, 1997).

Singer, P. *Unsanctifying Human Life*, ed. H. Kuhse (Blackwell, 2002).

Singer, P. *One World: The Ethics of Globalization*, 2nd edn (Yale University Press, 2004).

Singer, P. 'Outsiders: Our Obligations to those Beyond our Borders', in D. Chatterjee (ed.), *The Ethics of Assistance* (Cambridge University Press, 2004).

Singer, P. 'Ethics and Intuitions', *Journal of Ethics*, 9, 3–4 (2005).

Singer, P. 'The Singer Solution to World Poverty', in J. Rachels (ed.), *The Right Thing to Do*, 4th edn. (McGraw-Hill, 2007).

Skorupski, J. *Why Read Mill Today?* (Routledge, 2006).

Smart, J. J. C. 'An Outline of a System of Utilitarian Ethics', in J. J. C. Smart and B. Williams, *Utilitarianism: For and Against* (Cambridge University Press, 1973).

Smart, J. J. C. 'Distributive Justice and Utilitarianism', in J. Arthur and W. Shaw (eds), *Justice and Economic Distribution* (Prentice Hall, 1978).

Smilansky, S. *Ten Moral Paradoxes* (Blackwell, 2007).

Smith, M. B. E. 'Is There a Prima Facie Obligation to Obey the Law?' in W. A. Edmundson (ed.), *The Duty to Obey the Law: Selected Philosophical Readings* (Rowman & Littlefield, 1999).

Smith, P. 'Incentives and Justice: G. A. Cohen's Egalitarian Critique of Rawls', *Social Theory and Practice*, 24, 2 (1998).

Steiner, H. 'Individual Liberty' in D. Miller (ed.), *The Liberty Reader* (Edinburgh University Press, 2006).

Stevenson, R. 'Can Markets Cope with Drugs?' *The Journal of Drug Issues*, 20, 4 (1990).

Stevenson, R. *Winning the War on Drugs: To Legalise or Not?* (Institute of Economic Affairs, 1994).

Sullivan, R. *An Introduction to Kant's Ethics* (Cambridge University Press, 1994).

Sumner, L. W. 'Rights', in H. LaFollette (ed.), *The Blackwell Guide to Ethical Theory* (Blackwell, 2000).

Swift, A. *Political Philosophy* (Polity Press, 2001).

Szasz, T. *Our Right to Drugs: The Case for a Free Market* (Syracuse University Press, 1996).

Taylor, C. 'What's Wrong with Negative Liberty', in D. Miller (ed.), *The Liberty Reader* (Edinburgh University Press, 2006).

Temkin, L. 'Equality, Priority, and the Levelling down Objection', in M. Clayton and A. Williams (eds), *The Ideal of Equality* (Palgrave Macmillan, 2002).

Unger, P. *Living High and Letting Die: Our Illusion of Innocence* (Oxford University Press, 1996).

United Nations Office on Drugs and Crime, *World Drug Report 2005*, http://www.unodc.org/en/world_drug_report_2005.html

Van Parijs, P. 'Difference Principles', in S. Freeman (ed.), *The Cambridge Companion to Rawls* (Cambridge University Press, 2003).

Vlastos, G. 'Justice and Equality', in J. Waldron (ed.), *Theories of Rights* (Oxford University Press, 1984).

Waldron, J. (ed.), *Theories of Rights* (Oxford University Press, 1984).

Waldron, J. 'Introduction' to J. Waldron (ed.), *Theories of Rights* (Oxford University Press, 1984).

Waldron, J. 'Nonsense upon Stilts? – a Reply', in J. Waldron (ed.), *'Nonsense Upon Stilts': Bentham, Burke and Marx on the Rights of Man* (Methuen, 1987).

Waldron, J. *Liberal Rights* (Cambridge University Press, 1993).

Waldron, J. 'A Right to Do Wrong', in *Liberal Rights* (Cambridge University Press, 1993).

Wasserstrom, R. 'Rights, Human Rights, and Racial Discrimination' in B. Boxill (ed.), *Race and Racism* (Oxford University Press, 2001).

Wellman, A. *The Proliferation of Rights: Moral Progress or Empty Rhetoric* (Westview Press, 1999).

Wilkinson, R. *Unhealthy Societies: The Afflictions of Inequality* (Routledge, 1996).

Wilkinson, R. *The Impact of Inequality* (Routledge, 2005).

Williams, A. 'Incentives, Inequality, and Publicity', *Philosophy and Public Affairs*, 27, 3 (1998).

Wilson, J. Q. 'Against the Legalization of Drugs', in H. LaFollette (ed.) *Ethics in Practice* (Blackwell, 1997).

Wood, A. *Kant's Ethical Thought* (Cambridge University Press, 1999).

INDEX